FROM ENGLAND TO BOHEMIA

This is the first book-length study of the influential cultural and religious exchanges which took place between England and Bohemia following Richard II's marriage to Anne of Bohemia in 1382. The ensuing growth in communication between the two kingdoms initially enabled new ideas of religion to flourish in both countries but eventually led the English authorities to suppress heresy. This exciting project has been made possible by the discovery of new manuscripts after the opening up of Czech archives over the past twenty years. It is the only study to analyze the Lollard–Hussite exchange with an eye to the new opportunities for international travel and correspondence to which the Great Schism gave rise, and examines how the use of propaganda and the Council of Constance brought an end to this communication by securing the condemnation of heretics such as John Wyclif.

MICHAEL VAN DUSSEN is Assistant Professor in the Department of English, McGill University.

CAMBRIDGE STUDIES IN MEDIEVAL LITERATURE

This series of critical books seeks to cover the whole area of literature written in the major medieval languages – the main European vernaculars, and medieval Latin and Greek – during the period *c.*1100–1500. Its chief aim is to publish and stimulate fresh scholarship and criticism on medieval literature, special emphasis being placed on understanding major works of poetry, prose, and drama in relation to the contemporary culture and learning which fostered them.

FROM ENGLAND TO BOHEMIA

Heresy and Communication in the Later Middle Ages

MICHAEL VAN DUSSEN

CAMBRIDGE
UNIVERSITY PRESS

CAMBRIDGE UNIVERSITY PRESS
Cambridge, New York, Melbourne, Madrid, Cape Town,
Singapore, São Paulo, Delhi, Mexico City

Cambridge University Press
The Edinburgh Building, Cambridge CB2 8RU, UK

Published in the United States of America by Cambridge University Press, New York

www.cambridge.org
Information on this title: www.cambridge.org/9781107016798

© Michael Van Dussen 2012

First published 2012

Printed in the United Kingdom at the University Press, Cambridge

A catalog record for this publication is available from the British Library

Library of Congress Cataloging-in-Publication data
Van Dussen, Michael, 1977–
From England to Bohemia : heresy and communication in the later Middle Ages / Michael Van Dussen.
p. cm. – (Cambridge studies in medieval literature)
Includes bibliographical references and indexes.
ISBN 978-1-107-01679-8
1. Reformation – Early movements. 2. Church history – Middle Ages, 600–1500.
3. England – Church history – Middle Ages, 600–1500.
4. Bohemia (Czech Republic) – Church history – Middle Ages, 600–1500.
5. Lollards. 6. Hussites. I. Title.
BR295.V36 2012
274'.05–dc23
2011041595

ISBN 978-1-107-01679-8 Hardback

For my grandparents
John Barry Hinds
Winifred McCabe Hinds
Dean John Van Dussen
Dorothy Farley Van Dussen

Contents

vii

Acknowledgments

I offer my deepest gratitude to Richard Firth Green and Alastair Minnis, constant sources of encouragement from the very beginning of this project. I am also indebted to the generosity of my good friend and colleague Pavel Soukup, who commented on many sections of this book and facilitated my access to Czech publications at the Centrum medievistických studií (CMS) and elsewhere in the Czech Republic. David Holeton and Peter Morée were tremendously helpful in granting me access to the Bartoš Library at the Evangelická teologická fakulta of Charles University. I have also valued the ideas and suggestions from the following group of colleagues and friends as this book took shape: Daniel Collins, Frank Coulson, Greti Dinkova-Brunn, Kantik Ghosh, Phillip Haberkern, Daniel Hobbins, Anne Hudson, Christopher Jones, John King, Andrew Kraebel, Leslie Lockett, David Mengel, A. G. Rigg, Jana Zachová, and the two anonymous readers from Cambridge University Press. Thanks also to Benjamin Barootes for compiling the index. Librarians from the Národní knihovna, the Knihovna Metropolitní kapituly, the Archiv Univerzity Karlovy and the Národní muzeum in Prague, the Státní oblastní archiv in Třeboň, the National Archives in London, and the Österreichische Nationalbibliothek in Vienna graciously allowed me to access many of the manuscripts discussed in the coming chapters. The cover image and plate are reproduced by permission of the Prague Castle Archive, Metropolitan Chapter Library (MS H.15, fol. 96ʳ).

Part of Chapter 1 and Appendix A appeared as "Three Verse Eulogies of Anne of Bohemia," in *Medium Aevum* 78 (2009): 231–60. An early version of Chapter 3 was published as "Conveying Heresy: 'a certayne student' and the Lollard-Hussite Fellowship," in *Viator* 38 (2007): 217–34; and parts of Chapter 5 were published in an earlier version as "Bohemia in English Religious Controversy before the Henrician Reformation," in *The Bohemian Reformation and Religious Practice*, vol. VII, edited by Zdeněk V. David and David R. Holeton (Prague: Filosofický časopis, 2009), 42–60.

Abbreviations

EETS   Early English Text Society
ÖNB   Vienna, Österreichische Nationalbibliothek
PKMK   Prague, Knihovna Metropolitní kapituly
PNK   Prague, Národní knihovna
STC   A. W. Pollard et al., eds. *A Short-Title Catalogue of Books Printed in England, Scotland, & Ireland and of English Books Printed Abroad, 1475–1640.* 2nd edn. 3 vols. London: Bibliographical Society, 1976–91.
Wing   Donald Wing, comp. *Short-title Catalogue of Books printed in England, Scotland, Ireland, Wales, and British America, and of English Books Printed in Other Countries, 1641–1700.* New York: Index Society, 1945–51.

Introduction

Beyond reformist historiography: communication in Schism Europe

When Anne Hudson published *The Premature Reformation* (1988), little did she know how timely her call for further study of Lollard–Hussite communication would prove to be. For the very next year, the Velvet Revolution in Czechoslovakia, followed by the removal of Cold War-era boundaries, would open up new possibilities for communication between Anglophone and Slavic scholars, renewing access to archives that outsiders previously could consult only with difficulty. This book benefits from this increased contact, both through access to Czech archives, and through the generosity of Czech scholars and curators. It also tells the story of a period six centuries ago when the Great Schism in Europe (1378–1417) brought about not a narrowing of communication, but a momentous period of contact between the same regions that the Cold War later divided.

The underlying argument of this study is that Ricardian and early Lancastrian political alliances with Bohemia, the political heart of the Holy Roman Empire during much of the period in question, drew a variety of English texts into wider continental circulation, and brought English responses to domestic heresy into the orbit of international politics. England's alliance with Bohemia was negotiated in response to the eruption of schism in 1378, when rival popes were elected in Avignon and Rome, each claiming to be the rightful head of the Church hierarchy. But the partnership also ushered in a range of communication opportunities between two regions that previously had little contact. An examination of the communication networks and patterns of textual circulation that developed as a result of this alliance forms the heart of this study.

Indeed, some puzzling irregularities in patterns of textual transmission must be addressed from the start. Why, for example, did relatively few – indeed, scarcely any – texts move toward England from Bohemia during this period, as far as the archival record reveals?[1] Even when we consider the destruction and decay of texts during the intervening centuries, one would expect something more to have survived. Yet aside from some scattered diplomatic correspondence, there is little to show for the relationship in English archives in the form of textual evidence. As in England, the destruction of books in Bohemia by burning, the pillaging of libraries, warfare, and other forms of damage and decay likewise reduced the total amount of manuscripts that once existed by numbers that can never be known. Even so, significant quantities of texts remain in Central European libraries that attest to the vibrancy of Anglo-Bohemian communication. Early modern Protestant historiographers like John Foxe would attribute this unilateral transmission to the Bohemians' providential encounter with the writings of the Oxford theologian John Wyclif. Wyclif was associated in Foxe's narrative with a particularly Anglocentric brand of evangelism, and England, for Foxe, was a sort of Promised Land, as well as the place where the initial stirrings of Reformation could be discerned. Evangelical truth naturally flowed from its source to places like Bohemia and then (as other controversialists would elaborate) to Wittenberg.

My story is concerned less with textual transmission and communication as assisted by the guiding hand of Providence than with how texts and ideas were transacted through material and human interventions. What may come as some surprise is that, during the late Middle Ages, England was not an especially vibrant center for manuscript production, at least relative to Central European regions like Bohemia. Indeed, as Uwe Neddermeyer has shown in his impressive and comprehensive study of book production in late medieval and early modern Europe, the Holy Roman Empire set the pace for European book production, a trend which began during the Schism and continued through the introduction of print.[2] Bohemia largely drove this trend, though its contribution would decrease noticeably after the Council of Constance (1414–18), when Bohemia became embroiled in bitter internecine conflict, and eventually a period of war with crusading forces from the outside. Before Constance, however, Prague formed a center of international culture that attracted texts from across the continent and England. Large numbers of English texts were copied by Czechs and taken to Bohemia where they were often copied again many times over. This activity may in part account for the fact that today, despite the undoubtedly large numbers of texts that have been lost in both regions, Bohemian manuscripts containing Wyclif's writings outnumber those in England by nearly three to one.

Meanwhile, book production in England remained among the lowest in Europe. To provide one striking comparison, according to Neddermeyer's figures, between 1410 and the start of the Council of Constance, when Hussite controversy surrounding Wyclif in Prague was at its height, the Empire was producing nearly six times the number of manuscripts as

England (and climbing, with Bohemia outpacing the rest of the Empire during those years).[3] Even given differences in population, the same upward trends in manuscript production are not nearly as discernible in England. And while it is wrong to suggest that England was a cultural backwater during this period, it is equally mistaken to argue that English texts moved to Bohemia because of a provincial Bohemian interest in English cosmopolitanism. To many in Prague, England was extremely attractive and even exotic – but not exactly central.

There is, of course, more to the picture than quantitative assessments and models reveal. The cultural currency of England (or of Bohemia) did not necessarily correspond to levels of manuscript production, and this discrepancy is in part why the present study takes in evidence of other forms of communication and experience. Bohemia produced more books than England, but aspects of English culture nevertheless held an impressive appeal in places like Prague. The same was true of French culture (France was producing books at only slightly higher levels than England in the early fifteenth century). The attraction to both countries for many Bohemians was attributable in part to the established reputations of the universities of Oxford and Paris, and of course academic ties between these universities and the newly established *studium* of Prague (founded 1347) began before the Anglo-Bohemian alliance was formed.[4] Some level of cultural contact would have gone on regardless of the alliance, though certainly not on such a broad scale and on so many levels of society.

I am interested in determining how Anglo-Bohemian cultural contact took shape during the Schism, and what I have found accords very much with what W. G. Sebald's melancholic Austerlitz observed about human experience: that it "disregards linear regularity, does not progress constantly forward but moves in eddies, is marked by episodes of congestion and irruption, recurs in ever-changing form, and evolves in no one knows what direction."[5] Neddermeyer's graphs show the "shape" of the archive and of medieval European book production in sharp detail – what Franco Moretti would call "distant reading," in which texts undergo "a process of deliberate reduction and abstraction," and where there are "fewer elements, hence a sharper sense of their overall interconnection."[6] At the same time, the material circumstances that have conditioned the form of extant archives – the physical realities of decay, destruction, loss, and circulation – compel us to pay very close attention to specific acts of human intervention and textual transmission, as well as to individual texts. Too often the processes and forces to which physical objects are susceptible through time leave us with little to quantify. Medievalists rarely have the luxury of constructing abstract models from a "large mass of facts"[7] – the luxury that Moretti has had, for example, in his work on the evolution of the novel. Neddermeyer's research, of course, provides one exception. He has indeed produced enormously useful graphs from quantitative research. But as I have said, his models have their limitations. They cannot really represent the day-to-day practice of book production and circulation. They do not explain *how* texts moved, and only partially help us understand why they were produced in such quantities in particular places like Bohemia in the first place. To approach these questions, the particular or trace is often all we've got. In the face of such limitations we have to extrapolate from the particular not simply because it is exceptional in the context of the "large mass of facts" – this is not antiquarianism or curiosity-hunting, strictly speaking – but because we have little else with which to compare the scattered traces of communication using quantitative methods. We must, in other words, perform highly self-conscious acts of extrapolation from scattered trees to get a sense of a forest which no longer exists, but whose contours we may nonetheless come close to discerning. In so doing we come to a greater understanding of the fact that the production, copying, movement, and reading of texts was (and is) inseparable from the physical mediations that condition each of these activities.

The stories of textual circulation and communication which I tell in each chapter of this study examine what are often minute particulars from a position of necessity, and admittedly, I have shaped highly impressionistic narratives out of traces that may not be representative of wider trends. At the same time, I find that the communication networks that emerge do begin to form discernible patterns. My method of archival research furthermore has not been to comb manuscript archives for that which is exceptional, standing out from the sea of facts and records – if I have found something exceptional, its pursuit was not what drove me to analyze the particular. Rather, I have attended to particulars for what they tell me about the contingencies of communication and textual transmission. For there can be no doubt that while specific instances of textual transmission may be abstracted after the fact into coherent models and patterns, each instance comes about through a localized, material transaction whose participants acted in the present as they experienced it. As I have worked to locate these material acts within a wider narrative of Schism-era communication, I have been reminded consistently of something that Bourdieu observes about the vastly different perspectives and aims of analyst and actor:

Because he has every likelihood of ignoring the social and logical conditions of the change in nature that he imposes on practice and its products and therefore the nature of the logical transformations he imposes on the information that has been gathered, the analyst is liable to fall into all the errors that flow from the tendency to confuse the actor's point of view with the spectator's point of view, for example looking for answers to a spectator's questions that practice never asks because it has no need to ask them, instead of wondering if the essence of practice is not precisely that it excludes such questions.[8]

"A more rational literary history," then, has its uses, but rational models cannot explain entirely the contingencies of communication on the ground.[9]

This is the first book-length study of Lollard–Hussite communication in any language. It is also the only study to analyze this exchange with an eye to the new opportunities for international travel and communication to which the Great Schism gave rise. Historiography centering on Anglo-Bohemian cultural communication has consistently given Lollard–Hussite relations pride of place, whereas in reality heterodox contacts grew out of a wider and less controversial cultural exchange between England and Bohemia. As I say above, an Anglo-Imperial alliance was negotiated to help resolve the Great Schism, with the intention of forming a "liga . . . contra scismaticos [league against the schismatics]"[10] – that is, against the Avignonese papacy and its adherents – and opening up new commercial channels between England and all the lands of the Holy Roman Empire.[11] The level of communication between these two regions which the alliance promoted was far-reaching at least in theory. In 1381, Richard II and Václav IV agreed that Richard's subjects would have nearly unlimited access, commercial and otherwise, to the lands of the Empire including Bohemia.[12] The alliance was not immediately effective in ending the Schism. As the chapters of this study show, however, it did provide occasions for textual exchange and other forms of communication along routes that passed directly between England and Bohemia, as well as in places like Rome, where efforts to end the Schism were carried out. Part of my discussion takes in diplomatic correspondence and otherwise official modes of communication. But most of this study examines a rise in cultural contact that was almost completely unregulated. I suggest, in fact, that the very terms which established the parameters of Anglo-Imperial commerce simultaneously limited the ability of secular officials to control the lines of communication in any centralized way, even if such control were possible. The stage was set for relatively unrestricted communication on many levels. And eventually – after Anglo-Bohemian cultural communication had been established for several years – heterodox relations came to dominate the exchange.

Heterodox relations were not the only instance of widespread Anglo-Bohemian contact during this period, but they do provide a fascinating example of how transnational communication channels that were forged in response to the Schism were successfully exploited. The success of the Lollard–Hussite exchange also highlights just how difficult it was for Church and secular officials to establish any kind of centralized control over the dissemination of news and documents between these regions. Heretical groups came to dominate these channels even as Church and secular officials caught on to the fact of their correspondence. The authorities had little choice but to respond reactively to a Wycliffite communication network that transgressed jurisdictional boundaries, employed official documentary forms and developed within sanctioned spaces for preaching, disputation and textual production. Through the course of the controversy John Wyclif attained international fame, rather than infamy, for his theological and ecclesiological doctrines (as opposed to just his theories on logic, which were already widely known)[13] for the first time outside of England, and large numbers of Bohemians followed closely the activities of Wyclif's English disciples. The result was the formation of an enormously agile apparatus for disseminating Wycliffite (and other) texts, combined with a Bohemian market that lent authority to Wycliffite missives and provided an impetus for continued contact and textual production. An Anglo-Bohemian "internationale" took shape around a set of shared doctrines and sentiments[14] – what Rita Copeland has called a "confederation at the level of intellectual [and, I would add, emotional] identity."[15] In diplomatic negotiations preceding the Council of Constance – an assembly which aimed to end the Schism – English officials struggled to catch up with the Wycliffites by using Anglo-Imperial communication channels in a campaign to propagandize against Wycliffite news and documents. The Council of Constance helped bring an end to Lollard–Hussite communication by securing the condemnations of Wyclif (1415), Hus (1415) and Jerome of Prague (1416), and by circulating documents that established an official stance on Wycliffite heresy from the position of a broadly representative ecumenical gathering.

A crucial point, however, is that no previous official effort to trump Wycliffite communication with the Hussites ever did so with such decisiveness. One reason that this narrative struggle was not won by Church and secular authorities from the start, I suggest, is that Lollard–Hussite communication employed mainstream documentary forms and authenticating signs within uncentralized communication channels. Further (as Kantik Ghosh discusses in an analogous situation), the reformists brought "out of the Schools, and into the domain of the non-clerical and the vernacular, intellectual discourses of considerable complexity, sophistication and latitude, and thereby changed the always problematic ideological positioning of such discourses within contemporary culture."[16] The same process by which international communication became a "town and gown" affair similarly blurred the distinction between "official" and "heterodox" communication, and (as I discuss in Chapter 4) much of the alarm created by heterodox correspondence was precisely that it employed the tools and materials of established pastoral and academic institutions. So while it may be true, as Sophia Menache has argued (discussing communication among earlier heretical sects), that antagonism by the establishment compelled the heretics "to utilize to the maximum all the communication channels available at the time," it is difficult to state unequivocally that heretics in the fifteenth century "lack[ed] the support of the establishment."[17] Many of them, as this study shows, did indeed enjoy "establishment" support, and even when they did not, their university or aristocratic ties afforded their propaganda a great deal of credibility.

The chapters in this study, then, have wider applications for the study of communication before print. A new model for understanding late-medieval communication is essential, as medieval news and texts were transmitted along the available networks in ways that cannot be understood using print-era paradigms. I treat late-medieval communication, in Latin and in the vernacular, as a practice that lacked a single stabilizing framework.[18] Consequently, I do not see medieval attempts to propagandize as conforming to the *ancien régime* style of political maneuvering that New Historicists have applied anachronistically to the Middle Ages. On the contrary, communication channels were extremely difficult to police. The desire to exert centralized control (and to express this desire in narrative form) is very different from the ability to enact that desire in a manuscript culture. As a highly contingent, localized practice, communication was mediated and conditioned by ad hoc personal contact and unstable documentary forms. Texts were often whimsically collected, not necessarily transmitted or bound with other material as part of a reformist program. The situation was highly fluid, complex, and often confused. European religious politics during the Schism period, however, lent urgency to the need to establish authoritative dominance over communication channels. Therefore, I argue that, during the Great Councils of the fifteenth century, there was a shift toward more centralized communication and textual dissemination.

At Constance, the council that is most central to this study, thousands of representatives of Church and secular institutions gathered from across

Europe, not for a short administrative meeting, but for months and often years, far outnumbering the town's native population. Procurators and officials there also needed to maintain contact with those on whose behalf they had been sent, and so communication networks spread outward from this German town to the rest of Europe. Constance has often been characterized as a "book market," attracting texts from everywhere in Europe which were then read, copied, and disseminated to new audiences on a scale rarely if ever witnessed before that time.[19] Neddermeyer shows that the number of books produced in the Empire during these years spiked dramatically.[20] The apparatus for textual production and circulation at Constance could efficiently disseminate tracts and other missives which established authoritative positions on the Wycliffite heresy and other matters, reaching large audiences in a matter of weeks. Men like Jean Gerson, as Daniel Hobbins has recently discussed, used the opportunities for rapid dissemination at Constance to address a staggering number of pressing issues, in Latin and the French vernacular, by deftly circulating short, reproducible tracts.[21] The Constance *Acta* were copied by several notaries at once, and could be recopied quickly, establishing more or less standard or approved accounts of conciliar trials and sessions.[22] In so doing, council officials could effectively combat and overwhelm what had become a highly developed Wycliffite propaganda network. Transnational communication of the kind I discuss was made far less practicable in part because official positions were disseminated from a newly centralized platform and with an unprecedented level of efficiency. And while efforts by officials to control reformist communication domestically was less impacted – in England, certainly, repression of heretical communication grew increasingly fierce in the fifteenth century, long after Constance – transnational and inter-jurisdictional communication between reformists was dealt a serious blow.

My central narrative culminates, then, with the effect of Constance on Lollard–Hussite communication. When the range of Anglo-Bohemian communication is considered as a whole, however, we see that the rise and fall of Lollard–Hussite contact was part of a larger story in the development of European textual transmission and communication. How does this crucial adjustment of the narrative frame change the way we perceive the transmission of Wyclif's texts to Bohemia? No longer are we studying the movement of Wycliffite texts as the central narrative in a story of reformist history, but rather Wycliffite communication as an episode, however important, in a more intricate story of pan-European religious politics in the Middle Ages. As I have already suggested, the transmission of Wycliffite texts must be seen in the context of competing communication channels that often overlapped and crossed in ways that make it difficult to analyze in terms of centralized models. Only by attending to the material realities of communication can we approach a full understanding of the enormous success of Wycliffite textual transmission and the making of Wyclif as a public intellectual in Bohemia. But just as importantly, it was through rigorous competition to dominate the lines of international communication that active Lollard–Hussite exchanges came to an abrupt end. This part of the process was effected primarily through the prosecution of Wycliffism at Constance, but as I show, the targeted deployment of damaging anti-Wycliffite propaganda along the available lines of communication was set in motion during negotiations preceding the council.

My story in the first chapter begins in 1381, when Anne of Bohemia first set foot on English soil to become the queen of England. The fact that many of Wyclif's texts later ended up in Prague has led many to link Anne to heretical communication. While the connection is tenuous, it also ignores more generally the terms of the alliance, which (as I have already discussed) succeeded in establishing cultural communication on a broad scale, and with little regulation. I concentrate on Anne's funeral (1394), and use the event as a focal point for understanding Anne's position at the intersection of European religious politics and communication. I reveal three previously unexamined verse eulogies of the queen, edited in Appendix A, which were written in England and then copied and taken to Prague by a Bohemian knight. The eulogies cast Anne's legacy in terms of a religious politics that has little in common with Wycliffite tenets, and show that a number of interested parties vied to establish an authoritative version of Anne's legacy in the wake of her death. Anne of Bohemia's symbolic value was publicly available, and the Wycliffites were as much a part of that public as anyone else. I demonstrate this point by examining the transmission of the verse eulogies to Prague. In one manuscript, the poems are accompanied by an itinerary which describes how and where they were discovered, and provides valuable new information about Anglo-Bohemian communication channels that had nothing to do with heterodox exchange. Yet one of the poems also appears in a Hussite manuscript alongside other texts from England. This instance of convergent transmission highlights the range of possible cultural contact between England and Bohemia at this time, and shows that when we consider the material circumstances of textual transmission, we see a fluidity in the communication networks that defies strict ideological categories.

Extending the argument of Chapter 1, the second chapter shows that the transmission of texts between England and Bohemia reflected trends in readership and textual circulation that cannot be reduced to heterodox interests. Between the 1380s and 1413, the popular mystical writings of the English hermit Richard Rolle reached Bohemia and were frequently copied there. They survive in thirteen Bohemian manuscripts, some studied for the first time in this chapter. At least one of these texts traveled to Prague via Rome, and can be traced to churchmen in England, Prague, and at the Curia whose pious interests intertwined with the politics of establishing new liturgical feasts at the end of the fourteenth century. The transmission history of Rolle's texts becomes more complicated, however, when other copies of his writings turn up in Bohemian manuscripts alongside heterodox material. I demonstrate how Rolle's texts, which enjoyed a revival in England during Anne of Bohemia's reign, entered a devotional and reformist environment in Prague that was remarkably similar to that of contemporary England. Reformers in Prague who would later become bitter rivals were at this early stage reading the same texts and discussing a variety of reformist programs. As the lines between reformist positions became more rigid, the demand for texts like Rolle's endured. My analysis of the context of Rolle's writings in Bohemian manuscripts also helps us situate Lollard–Hussite textual circulation within a more porous model of devotion and reform in Bohemia and England.

From *c.*1406 onward, in the years preceding the Council of Constance, Anglo-Bohemian cultural exchange became dominated by heretical communication – a marked change from what had once been the case. Chapter 3 examines the materiality of heterodox communication, arguing that the most active period of Lollard–Hussite correspondence was in part provoked by official attempts in both England and Bohemia to narrow the field of acceptable reformist thinking. In Prague, efforts to defend Wyclif in the face of frequent book-burnings prompted Bohemian couriers to travel regularly to England in search of replacement copies of Wyclif's writings and for objects and news from his followers. An international Lollard–Hussite fellowship developed, extending beyond textual exchange to more personal instances of interaction. Hussite contacts with living followers of Wyclif in England, combined with spirited attempts to popularize Wyclif in Prague using visual aids (such as images of Wyclif and a piece of stone taken from his tomb) and Czech translations of Wycliffite texts, also gave Wyclif, for the first time, a posthumous fame (as opposed to infamy) as a radical reformer, and for a broad range of his teachings, among proponents outside England. Chapter 3 traces how Bohemian courier activity helped secure Wyclif's fame as a public intellectual in Prague, remarkably transforming an English theologian into a culturally relevant figure for significant numbers of Bohemians, lay and cleric.

In the fourth chapter, I argue that the English discovery of international heretical correspondence marked the beginning of the end for a Lollard–Hussite fellowship that had been formed almost completely through communication and textual mediation. A substantial lag separated the most intense period of heterodox exchange and the moment when officials became aware of its existence. The discovery came unexpectedly, when English diplomacy with the Holy Roman Emperor before the Council of Constance became linked with intensified drives by English authorities to eradicate Wycliffism at home. English embassies became vehicles for the first attempts to repair England's damaged reputation for what continental commentators saw as a botched prosecution of heresy. I show how English officials gained control over the Anglo-Bohemian communication channels that the Wycliffites had dominated for several years before the Council of Constance. One component of this campaign was an effort to promulgate news of Henry V's overwhelming defeat of the Oldcastle Rising (1414). I edit a previously unstudied account of the Rising from two Bohemian sources in Appendix B. English embarrassment about Wycliffism had dramatic consequences at Constance during the trials and executions of Jan Hus (1415) and Jerome of Prague (1416). By energetically prosecuting the Bohemian reformers as Wyclif's surrogates, the English aimed to shore up their reputation for orthodoxy. The transmission of heretical texts, then, and the attention it attracted to itself, also helped draw the prosecution of Wycliffism into an international forum.

The fifth chapter extends the discussion beyond the fifteenth century, tracing Bohemia's continued use in English religious controversy from the Council of Constance to the Henrician Reformation. A significant effect of Anglo-Bohemian cultural communication was that English consciousness of continental religious politics expanded to include Slavic regions with which England previously had only limited ties. The urgency with which English controversialists addressed the religious and political climate in Bohemia provides a measure of the enduring English fascination with Central Europe, and of the persisting relevance of medieval taxonomies of heresy in the controversies of the Reformation.

CHAPTER I

"The occasion of Queene Anne"

Also þe bischope of Caunturbiri, Thomas Arrundel þat nowe is, seide a sermon in Westminster þer as weren many hundred puple at þe biriyng of quene Anne, of wos soule God haue mercy, & in his comendynges of hir, he seide: it was more joie of hir þan of any woman þat euere he knewe ffor, not-wiþstanding þat sche was an alien borne, sche hadde on Engliche al þe foure Gospeleris wiþ þe doctoris vpon hem. And he seide sche hadde sent hem vn-to him, and he seide þei weren goode and trewe and comended hir in þat sche was so grete a lady, & also an alien, & wolde so lowliche studiee in so vertuous bokis. And he blamed in þat sermoun scharpeli þe necligence of prelatis and of oþer men, in so miche þat summe seiden he wolde on þe morowe leue vp his office of chaunceler and for-sake þe worlde & þan it hadde be þe [b]est sermoun þat euere þei herde.[1]

The commonplaces most people have in mind about Anne of Bohemia, Richard II's first queen, come on the one hand from Chaucer's *Legend of Good Women* and the Lancastrian official histories of Richard II's disposition.[2] Anne is the figure of queenly intercession, the balance to the *rex iratus*. Protestants (no less than Lancastrians) had a different story. And, as I discuss in this chapter, I offer yet another one – a story based on new evidence that sheds light on how Anne fits into Ricardian literary politics and into the development of Anglo-Bohemian cultural communication to which the marriage alliance gave rise. I want to stress from the beginning, though, that my aim in this chapter is not to recover the "historical Anne." I am interested rather in revising and modifying previous accounts of the queen by situating her symbolic availability within a local English culture and examining the implications of that availability on specific material acts of textual transmission. I will argue that the *idea* of Anne was not the exclusive property of any particular ideological camp (e.g., "Wycliffite," "orthodox"), but held currency in a promiscuous ideological environment – what Andrew Cole has aptly described as "a middle zone of openly shared ideals and typologies," and what Ralph Hanna has characterized as "a range or spectrum of literary communities"[3] – an environment that was initially represented in the eclecticism of textual transmission between England and Bohemia.

The customary narrative about Anne in the context of Anglo-Bohemian cultural exchange casually asserts that the Wycliffites came into contact with the Hussites as a result of Anne's presence in England. It is reasonable, of course, to suggest that Anne's position as queen of England had some bearing on subsequent heterodox communication. But as I argue in this study, reformist communication was neither immediate nor automatic, and would form only a part – though a very significant part – of the total range of communication between the two regions. And further, if we view Anglo-Bohemian communication with a wider lens, then we also have to situate Anne of Bohemia in a narrative that takes in far more than heterodox communication. The problem is not that the familiar narrative is wrong, but that it is limited and has tempted some (as I shall discuss), in their fits of enthusiasm, to imply that Anne actively abetted the Wycliffites.

The contingencies of narrative framing in sixteenth-century Protestant accounts are in part to blame for this limited view. Protestant historiographers appraised Anne for her value in reformist history, and Anglo-Bohemian cultural communication held their interest only insofar as it had bearing on reformist relations. Still today, Anglo-Bohemian cultural contacts fall mainly under the purview of Lollard or Hussite studies, and the way we frame our narratives has had profound implications for what we see as the contours of Anglo-Bohemian cultural contact: in discussing Anne and Anglo-Bohemian relations solely as components of reformist history, we have granted hetero-dox communication an exclusivity it never enjoyed in the wider context of the exchange. And significantly, we have consistently oversimplified the circum-stances in which heterodox communication itself developed.

Let me emphasize that the Reformation account of Anne was a product of the sixteenth century, not a received narrative. Medieval commentators had almost nothing to say about the queen, but nearly two hundred years after Anne of Bohemia died, her specter walked again in the antiquarian narratives of English Protestants. To outline the development of her Reformation reputation, I begin with the words of the martyrologist John Foxe, whose characterization of Anne in later editions of the *Actes and monuments* was enormously influential:

But howsoeuer the doings of [Richard II] are to be excused, or not, vndouted it is that Queene Anne hys wife most rightly deserueth singular commendation: who at the same time liuing with the kyng had the gospels of Christ in English, with 4. doctours vpon the same. This Anne was a Bohemian borne, and sister to Wincelaus K[ing] of Boheme before: who was maryed to king Richarde about the 5. (some say, the 6.) yeare of hys reigne, and continued with hym the space of 11. yeres. By the occasion whereof it may seeme not vnprobable, that the Bohemians comming in wyth her, or resorting into thys realme after her, perused and receiued heere the bookes of Iohn Wickleffe, which afterward they conueied into Bohemia.[4]

Then as now, little was known about this queen from Bohemia, the daughter of a Holy Roman Emperor. What was known (or believed) was that her virtue was sufficient and that she read the Gospels in English. Most importantly, though, she was ideally situated to provide a credible link between persecuted members of the "True Church" in England and Bohemia.

In sixteenth-century narratives, much depended on the not-improbability of Anne's influence on communication between the Lollards and Hussites, groups to which English Protestants frequently traced their reformist lineage. John Foxe's embroidered account of Anne in his *Actes and monuments* cleared a narrative path for less cagey claims about the queen's role as patroness of reform. Foxe, commenting on the prospect of Anne's instrumentality in promoting reformist relations ("it may seeme not vnprobable"), was likely aware of the slipperiness of his litotes; later in his *Book of martyrs* (as the *Actes and monuments* was familiarly termed), at the beginning of the expansive "entry of the story of the Bohemians," he asserts more confidently:

I Declared a little before howe by the occasion of Queene Anne, which was a Bohemian and maried to king Richard 2. the Bohemians comming therby to the knowledge of Wickliffes bookes here in England, began first to taste and sauor Christes gospell, til at length by the preaching of Iohn Husse, they increased more and more in knowledge.[5]

At this later stage of Foxe's martyrology, the "occasion of Queene Anne" – a phrase which now suggests that Anne "happened" to England – was not simply the basis for the spread of Wycliffism, but for introducing "Christes gospell" to reformers in Prague as well (Foxe's accompanying marginal note reads: "The Bohemians receiuing the Gospell").[6] Foxe presumably meant that the Bohemians in England began to adopt the Wycliffite *approach* to the Gospel, perhaps including the vernacular translation of Scripture, but his tone suggests a more apostolic brand of evangelization. And in citing Anne's devotion to an *English* Bible, questions arise as to the language in which the Bohemians received their Gospel.

Soon the causal relationship which Foxe posited between Anne's presence in England and the spread of Wycliffism encouraged details of the queen's position in reformist history to accrue around his influential core narrative. For Thomas James, the Bodleian's first librarian, Anne was one of John Wyclif's covert aristocratic abettors, assisting him against the bishops who pursued him in the later years of his life. During one of his evasions, writes James in *An apologie for Iohn Wickliffe* (1608), Wyclif was aided "by meanes of a messenger that came from the *Queene*."[7] His source for the reference is not clear. The claim comes amidst more general comments on the support Wyclif enjoyed from the English nobility, particularly from Edward III and later John of Gaunt. Perhaps James confused Anne with Joan of Kent, Richard II's mother, who ordered the suspension of proceedings against Wyclif at Lambeth in 1378, three years before Anne came to England.[8] James extended this support not only to Anne, but also to Richard, who, he says, "secretly abetted and maintained" Wyclif, and "whose Chaplaine [Wyclif] appeared to haue beene."[9]

The account that reached the most dizzying heights of fancy, however, appeared in 1656, when William Sanderson really exposed what the Protestants' business with Anne was all about. Anne, he writes, bore no heir,

yet the conversion of Boheme *from Popery may not unfitly be stiled the issue of her Mariage; for they that brought her hither, carried over* Wickliffs *Works, anno 1382. to* John [Hus] *and* Jerome [of Prague]; *So then* England *was Grandfather of Reformation,* Boheme *the Father, and* Germany *the Son.*[10]

English Protestants quickly grasped that Wyclif's appeal for the Bohemians could be used to show that the beginnings of English reform played an initiatory role in continental reformations. And following Martin Luther's claim in 1520, "sumus omnes Hussitae ignorantes [we are all Hussites without knowing it],"[11] Lutheran influences in England could be (and were) traced to their putative English origins in Wyclif, whose struggles allowed England, in Milton's words, to "blow the first *Evangelick Trumpet* to the *Nations*."[12] The Bohemian queen of England was gradually recognized in this context as an attractive link in the English Protestant narrative of salvation history.

Meanwhile, the same impulse to tell the history of dissent and reform that turned Anne into an honorary Protestant also placed so much emphasis on the story of Wyclif's influence in Bohemia that it became virtually the only connection between the two countries that was known or commented on for this period. And although the Protestant veneer has fallen away, the narrative of Anglo-Bohemian cultural communication that reduces these relations to reformist trafficking has remained more or less intact as the modern orthodoxy. Protestant nationalism leaves its traces in the way scholars today see these heretical relations as looking forward to the Reformation.

I want to show that more was happening, and to do this, I am running the thought experiment that the Reformation never happened[13] – an experiment that encourages me to attend more closely to the fact that the Anglo-Bohemian alliance, formed in response to the Great Schism of the Western Church, prompted a major realignment of European cultural communication, where (as the alliance established)

vassalli et subditi … Regis Angliae et Franciae possint libere, secure, et absque impedimento seu perturbatione quacumque, intrare, transire, morari, conversari, et mercari, tam per terram, quam per mare, in omnibus terris Imperii, et in quibuscumque terris regnis et dominiis ipsius Romanorum et Bohemiae Regis.[14]

[the vassals and subjects of the King of England and France may freely, safely, and without impediment or disturbance whatsoever enter, cross, stay, abide, and trade, both by land and by sea, in all the lands of the Empire, and in any lands in the kingdoms and dominions of the King of the Romans and Bohemia whatsoever.]

Heretical communication was an unexpected consequence of the cultural interchange which that agreement promoted. I want to tell a story of Anglo-Bohemian communication that situates heretical relations within a far more variegated landscape of cultural contact – a landscape that takes in secular literature, mainstream devotion, tourism, and other forms of material exchange *in addition to* heterodox correspondence. I will proceed by examining the production of commemorative texts in England in the wake of Anne's death, looking not only at how these texts shaped the queen's legacy, but also at how their circulation represents the possibilities for textual transmission between England and Bohemia that existed during this period.

A BOHEMIAN QUEEN, HER DEATH, AND ENGLISH RELIGIOUS POLITICS

Anne of Bohemia's special position as a nexus of political and pious symbolism was revealed in greatest detail after her reign had come to an end, when some of the fullest narratives of her perceived significance in England began to surface. One particular narrative which appeared in the wake of Anne's death was also, I suggest, the main source for later Protestant claims about her role as a Wycliffite sympathizer. Let us backtrack from the Protestant narrative to its source in order to put that source text in conversation with other narratives that circulated at about the same time, all of them jostling to represent the official version of Anne's legacy.

To understand why John Foxe implicated Anne of Bohemia in the transmission of Wycliffite texts to Prague, I shall concentrate on the queen's funeral (or at least what was said about it) as a moment when opinion about Anne crystallized and began to take shape in the making of her legacy. Many of Foxe's sources for his lengthy account of the Bohemians – particularly Thomas Netter, Aeneas Silvius and Silvius' admirer and imitator Johannes Cochlaeus – show some interest not only in the fact of Wycliffite influence on the Hussites, but also in the circumstances of Lollard–Hussite textual transmission which facilitated the relationship. Yet none of Foxe's sources discusses Anne of Bohemia in this context: each attributes the trafficking of texts instead to couriers passing between England and Bohemia in the fifteenth century – that is, long after Wyclif's death in 1384, as well as Anne's a decade later.

Anne's role in reformist textual transmission was not initially part of the Foxean narrative either. In the 1563 edition of *Actes and monuments*, Foxe had already begun to situate the inception of Lollard correspondence with the Bohemians during the time when Wyclif was still openly lecturing at Oxford, but he fails to indicate the reason for his assumption.[15] He does not self-consciously acknowledge the narrative value of another text he included in the same edition, which Foxe calls *A compendious olde treatise, shewing how that we ought to haue the scripture in Englishe*.[16] Embedded in the tract is a now familiar anecdote, printed in the epigraph to this chapter, in which Thomas Arundel, then Archbishop of York, praises Anne of Bohemia during her funeral for reading the glossed Gospels in English. Foxe transcribed the tract from a 1530 edition by Hans Luft, which circulated widely in England.[17] Anne Hudson has shown in detail the complicated history of the text, which is a late version of a fifteenth-century Latin tract in favor of vernacular translation. The original tract was written by the orthodox Richard Ullerston (whose text does not contain the anecdote about Anne), probably around the time of the 1401 Oxford debate on translation.[18] It was subsequently translated and interpolated by an unknown Lollard who added the funeral anecdote, and then it was revised again in the fifteenth century before appearing in Luft's edition. By the 1583 edition of *Actes and monuments*, Foxe no longer prints the full tract, but he does quote the funeral anecdote in isolation, and places it immediately after his first reference to Anne in connection with Wycliffite textual trafficking.[19]

The funeral anecdote presumably contributed to Foxe's notion that the Bohemians received the Gospel along with Wyclif's texts (or at least that the transmission of Wyclif's texts was an evangelizing act), while cementing the position of Anne, an alleged reader of Scripture, as an agent of reformist textual exchange.[20] Foxe does not seem to have been aware, however, of two fourteenth-century references to Czech Bibles from English sources (one of them in connection with Anne), the first in Wyclif's *De triplici vinculo amoris*, and the other in the so-called "General Prologue" to the Lollard Bible. Admittedly, even if he knew of the references, he would have had little incentive to mention them, as drawing attention to a vernacular Czech Bible as forerunner to the English Wycliffite Bible would diminish the Anglocentric force of his narrative.[21] This narrative suggested that, through Anne, Wyclif's evangelization could be achieved not by his own active preaching in Bohemia (though this was at least insinuated in contemporary accounts),[22] but providentially, by the coming of the Bohemians to drink from England's deep well of evangelical truth.

Early modern polemical accounts of Anne of Bohemia take us a long way from the immediate aftermath of the queen's death, where we find a different kind of legacy-making, suited to a political environment which had its own pressing narrative demands. Anne of Bohemia died on June 7, 1394, after a short struggle with what may have been the plague. Her funeral on August 3, nearly two months after she died, was an occasion to focus on her deeds and character, to reflect on the past and on how her reign had impacted England. Yet the crowd that gathered at Westminster Abbey that day did not check its politics at the door. The Earl of Arundel, for one, was not in a particularly reflective mood; arriving late to the funeral (and asking to leave early on pressing business), his audacity provoked Richard to physical violence, which caused a delay in the proceedings until Arundel's blood could be cleared away and the church re-consecrated.[23]

As Anne and Richard had been childless, her death also brought to the fore a looming crisis of succession, and this just added to the widespread anxiety over whether or not Richard was fit to rule. Richard was under enormous pressure, then, to turn the occasion of Anne's funeral to his own political advantage. It was to be an affair of state which would command a degree of obligatory cooperation and, as Richard made clear to Arundel, the "unity" of all factions, however coerced.[24] Any commemoration that might have been offered for Anne thus presented its narrative of the past under the duress of tremendous political tensions.

What else was said of Anne during or after her funeral? Is there any evidence that her legacy was shaped to address Ricardian political woes? Up to now, with the exception of a scattering of brief eulogizing generalities in the chronicles and a specious anecdote about a funeral sermon by Archbishop

Thomas Arundel (which I have just discussed),[25] what scholars have known about Anne's legacy has had more to do with her contemporaries' commemoration through indirection. Most notable are Chaucer's efforts to edit out what many have read as references to Anne between the F and G Prologues to the *Legend of Good Women*. Anne's absence has also been credited for much of Richard II's subsequent tyrannical bent, no longer moderated by a queen who was celebrated for her meek supplications.[26] John Bowers has argued that the Middle English *Pearl* may eulogize Anne, but if he is right, then the poet does so (as Bowers admits) by carefully avoiding direct association with any particular mourner, or any specific deceased maiden.[27] Other eulogizers latched on to Anne's more trivial contributions, like her alleged introduction of decadent shoes with long beaks, or "pykys."[28] It seems, in light of such commemoration, that Anne of Bohemia left the world quietly, relegated to near total obscurity, the medieval legacy of her twelve-year reign reduced to stock characterizations of piety, veiled literary allusions, and indignant remarks about modish footwear.

Recently, however, new evidence has surfaced in Prague which serves to fill out what we know both of Anne's position in English religious politics and of the scope and nature of Anglo-Bohemian cultural and textual communication. Our story continues not at Anne's funeral, however, but with a Bohemian traveler whose adventures intersected with the traces of his deceased countrywoman. Many Bohemian visitors traveled to England before and after Anne's death, but one in particular left an invaluable and previously unexamined record of his journey. What appears to be his small, private notebook forms the final quire of Prague, Knihovna Metropolitní kapituly (PKMK) MS H.15. The gathering is markedly more soiled than those that precede it and some of the folios have suffered water damage, suggesting that it was carried on its own before being bound in its present form. The manuscript seems to have been the book of a pious but secular owner who was literate in the traditional sense, probably the person indicated by the colophon "Liber Wenceslai militis" which is written on the unassuming vellum cover. The primary text of the manuscript is a copy of the *Liber Kalilae et Dimnae* of Raymond de Béziers (fols. 1^r–89^r), a collection of exemplary beast fables, which, according to the explicit, came originally from Paris.[29] Other items include prayers, penitential material, and a text on the planets. The owner was especially devoted to St. Christopher, the giant and mythic patron of travelers, as is suggested by a cluster of three prayers to the saint (fols. 95^v–96^r).[30] There is also evidence that he subscribed to one of the most popular beliefs of his day: that St. Christopher offered protective power against sudden death, and that looking upon his image – an image in which Christopher raises the Christ Child above his head like a priest raising the host during consecration – would guard against unexpected tragedies. "Tu, Ihesus, es testis," records the traveler, "ubi Christophorus memoratur, vix fames aut pestis, mala mors dominatur [You, Jesus, are witness, that where Christopher is remembered, scarcely does hunger, or pestilence, or evil death hold sway]."³¹ And here in his notebook he includes a private, talismanic image of the saint to gaze upon for protection any time he wished (96ʳ, Figure 1).³²

The image and devotional material are scattered throughout a longer itinerary that reveals the wonder the traveler experienced as Prague receded into the distance. I imagine him carrying this notebook as he made his way

Figure 1 Sketch of St. Christopher carrying the Christ Child across the torrent, from Prague Castle Archive, Metropolitan Chapter Library (Knihovna Metropolitní kapituly) MS H. 15, fol. 96ʳ. Reproduced by permission of the Metropolitan Chapter Library.

from Prague to Regensburg, on to Frankfurt, Cologne, and then to Brussels – all places he mentions. From Brussels his notes become much more descriptive, and there is a sense that he was moving into less and less familiar territory. As he moves southwest into France, he begins to visit shrines and to measure structures.[33] He tells of a treacherous bridge in Paris where French kings always dismount before crossing for fear of the fall. At Saint Denis he sees the hand of Thomas, still bearing the flesh that touched the side of Christ.

From Paris he traveled northwest, skirting the coast as he made his way to Calais. As he crossed to England from Calais, his descriptions become even more detailed, providing an extremely rare glimpse of the way England looked and seemed to an outsider during this period, and of what interested him about English culture. The narrative itself seems modeled after the much-imitated *Book of John Mandeville*, a text that was extremely popular in Bohemia where it had been translated into Czech.[34] At Dover he admired the town and its castle before departing for Canterbury. There he visited the shrine of Thomas Becket, filled with gold and silver images, as well as the cathedral, commenting in particular on the beautiful tombs of past bishops.

From Canterbury it was on to London. His description of the city is one of the most detailed accounts of London's monuments and architecture to appear before Stow published his *Survey of London* at the turn of the sixteenth century, and a rare description of the city by any medieval observer. The traveler was impressed, for example, by London Bridge (which, contrary to Stow's assumption, was lined with houses),[35] but most of all by Westminster Abbey. Among his observations in the abbey, the visitor made the following remarkable discovery:

ibi est sepulcrum pulcrum aureum Beati Edwardi et alia multa sepulcra regium et reginarum, et specialiter sepulcrum Regine Anne, que fuit filia Inperatoris Karoli IIIIti et Boemie Regis; et ibi sunt epitaphia multa, que superius sunt scripta.

[there is the beautiful golden tomb of Blessed Edward, together with many other tombs of kings and queens, and especially the tomb of Queen Anne, who was the daughter of Charles IV, Emperor and King of Bohemia; and there are many epitaphs, which have been written just above.]

The epitaphs which he says "superius sunt scripta" are indeed three verse eulogies of Anne of Bohemia which he transcribes immediately before this itinerary in MS H.15.[36] They are furthermore the only poems known to survive (apart from the epitaph engraved on her tomb) which treat Anne unambiguously as their primary material.

The poems' textual history and material context reveal one of the most important means by which texts moved between England and Bohemia during this period – not only by the transfer of so-called bespoke manuscripts and texts whose couriers were motivated to seek them out in advance, but often through ad hoc encounter and the contingencies or whims of personal interest and experience. As Ralph Hanna reminds us, texts are the products of a number of often localizable material mediations,[37] and as I discuss here, specific acts of textual transmission similarly arise from personal contact, through a confluence of utterly material and often serendipitous human interventions. As we have already begun to see, in the case of Anne's eulogies, we are fortunate to be able to establish the locality of their production and of the traveler's happenstance encounter with them in remarkable detail.

Though they survive nowhere in England today, the English origin of the eulogies is clear: "Anglica regina" remarks that "Germany and all Bohemia will grieve [Anne] at heart," but that "more will England, and with it Wales, weep for her death [Hinc Almania, tota Boemia corde dolebunt: / Sed magis Anglia iunctaque Valia pro nece flebunt]" (ll. 11–12). The third and longest of the poems, "Nobis natura florem," refers to Bohemia as the land of Anne's upbringing, but frames the reference in terms of reported speech (l. 3). Later in the same poem we hear that "our king made Anne his queen [rex noster reginam fecerat Annam]" (l. 41), and that "death snatched Anne away from our prince [Annam mors rapuit . . . ab principe nostro]" (l. 45).

But the most surprising evidence of the poems' English origin likewise serves to fill out the backstory to the construction of her funeral monument which still survives in Westminster Abbey. In addition to the unremarkable fact that the tomb epitaph and the first two of the eulogies (though not the third) are written in leonines, several lines scattered throughout these two eulogies bear a striking resemblance to her tomb inscription, which reads:

> Sub petra lata, nunc Anna jacet tumulata.
> Dum vixit mundo, Ricardo nupta Secundo.
> Christo devota, fuit hec factis bene nota:
> Pauperibus prona semper sua reddere dona;
> Jurgia sedavit et pregnantes relevavit.
> Corpore formosa, vultu mitis speciosa,
> Prebens solamen viduis, egris medicamen:
> Anno milleno, ter C, quarto nonageno,
> Junii septeno mensis migravit ameno.[38]

> [Under this wide stone, now Anne lies entombed.
> While she lived in the world, married to Richard II.

Devoted to Christ, she was well known for her deeds:
She was always eager to give her gifts to the poor;
She settled quarrels and relieved pregnant women.
Beautiful in form, meek with a pleasant face,
Offering solace to widows, medicine to the sick:
In the year one-thousand, thrice C, four and ninety,
On the pleasant seventh of June, she departed.]

The eulogies in the Prague Castle Archive reveal that Anne's Westminster epitaph seems to be the end result of a lot of fuss over what it should say, and there are details which suggest that they were used as poems-in-process en route to the engraved verses. The poet of "Femina famosa," for example, writes that "Pure, she was married to the pure Richard II [Munda fuit mundo Riccardo nupta Secundo]" (l. 5; cf. epitaph l. 2); "Anglica regina" claims that Anne "was always eager to give gifts to the poor [Pauperibus prona semper fuit add<e>re dona]" (l. 9; cf. epitaph l. 4), and also alludes to the aid she reputedly gave to pregnant women (ll. 13–14: "Pregnantes pena mulieres vissit amena, / Et per eam plena quevis relevatur egena"; cf. epitaph l. 5).

The eulogies' relationship to the Westminster epitaph requires an explanation, not least because a space of more than three years separated Anne's funeral and the tomb's completion. Internal evidence indicates that the eulogies were composed either for or very soon after her funeral in August 1394. For example, "Anglica regina" uses the future tense to describe the grief that Germany, Bohemia, England, and Wales will suffer, a usage that would be strange if much time had passed since Anne died. And "Nobis natura florem" is filled with topical references, purporting to recount, for instance, the funeral ceremony itself, listing and numbering the attendees (ll. 55–70).

Whatever monument there was at the time of the poems' composition must have been a temporary structure. Richard II commissioned Henry Yevele and Stephen Lote to build a tomb of Purbeck marble, designed to enclose both himself and Anne, on April 1, 1395. Two weeks later, on April 25, he likewise commissioned Nicholas Broker and Godfrey Prest to design the gilt copper effigies and other metalwork for the tomb. The entire monument was to be completed by Michaelmas two years later.[39] Most relevant to the present discussion, however, is the engraved epitaph, the text of which was to be provided to the coppersmiths ("Escriptures d'estre gravez entour la dite Toumbe, tiels come as ditz Nicholas & Godfrey serront delivres, resonablement pur ycell Toumbe").[40] Richard likely commissioned the epitaph along with the rest of the tomb.[41] If this is the case, then the commission was carried out, I suggest, by incorporating elements from eulogies that were composed at an earlier date, making the epitaph on her tomb in part a composite of multiple verse eulogies – a fascinating development from a relatively ephemeral set of documents to a much more permanent commemorative text. The process of incorporation may also suggest if not Richard's patronage of the earlier eulogies, then at least his approval of their verses; in which case, this is arguably the most solid evidence to date that Richard II had much to do with poetry during a period that has become known to us perhaps more than anything else for its flowering of literature.

The practice of displaying verse epitaphs on tombs is well documented in England, particularly in the fifteenth century. An epitaph was apparently placed on the tomb of Humfrey, Duke of Gloucester (†1447), as is suggested by the poem's refrain, "Have mercy on hym buryed in this sepulture."[42] A similar text was displayed on the tomb of Richard, Duke of York (†1460),[43] and as Caxton reports, Chaucer's tomb (set up well after his death in 1400) had next to it "wreton on a table honging on a pylere his Epitaphye maad by a poete laureate." Long after Henry VII had died, too, John Skelton's verses adorned the former king's tomb.[44] And Shakespeare refers to the practice in *Much Ado about Nothing*, in Act V scene 1, Leonato, addressing Claudio (who mourns for Hero), tells him: "if your love / Can labor aught in sad invention, / Hang her an epitaph upon her tomb" (ll. 282–4).[45] Anne of Bohemia's eulogies, I suspect, were originally attached or placed near her ornate hearse at Westminster, which was illuminated by a costly display of candles, and included a wooden effigy of the queen.[46] They may even have comprised an obit roll, much like those which once circulated among religious communities for the purpose of collecting prayers or verses eulogizing a famous person.[47] Supporting this possibility is the fact that the H.15 scribe separates the second and third eulogies with "sequitur," which may suggest that the poems' exemplars were somehow joined together, rather than placed separately on or around the tomb.

It is difficult to say exactly when the Bohemian traveler who recorded the eulogies actually encountered them in London, but his itinerary offers some clues. First, however, as the eulogies are also political poems, I shall say a few words about the political landscape in England during the period when the traveler's trip could reasonably have occurred. Diplomatic correspondence between England and the Holy Roman Empire (including Bohemia) continued long after Anne's death, and the initial Anglo-Bohemian alliance which was formalized by the marriage of Anne and Richard in 1382 was renewed several times under Henry IV and Henry V.[48] Friendly relations continued, that is, long into the fifteenth century under the Lancastrians, meaning that the date when the Bohemian traveler discovered the poems does not necessarily fall within the reign of Richard II. Admittedly, the possible survival of eulogies commemorating Richard II's first queen could have alarmed Henry IV in particular, who, having usurped the throne in 1399, feared widespread rumors that Richard was still alive and that his supporters planned to depose his usurper. Yet Henry's anxiety seems never to have included Anne; nor does the possible survival of the poems at Westminster automatically suggest that interest in Anne endured (other than by occasional Bohemian visitors who understandably took interest in one of their own), and may only indicate that no one had bothered to remove them from her tomb. In other words, Henry's nervousness about Richard's supporters cannot be cited on its own as evidence that the H.15 itinerary fell before 1399.

More specific dating of the traveler's trip, however, rests on relative chronology, which must proceed cautiously. In addition to Westminster Abbey, he took great interest in St. Paul's Cathedral, making special note of "the very fine tomb of the Duke of Lancaster [sepultura valde pulcra Ducis Langastrie]." This could only have been the large canopied tomb of John of Gaunt, the first Duke of Lancaster, which Gaunt commissioned Henry Yevele to build, and which (as Stow later attests) was indeed set up in St. Paul's.[49] Gaunt died on February 3, 1399, but this does not necessarily mean, of course, that the Bohemian visitor saw the tomb after Gaunt's death: Gaunt commissioned his tomb in 1375, to be completed in 1378.[50]

For other reasons it seems likely that Gaunt may very well have been in his tomb by the time our Bohemian traveler toured London. At one point in his diary he describes the stunning timber construction of Westminster Hall ("preparacio pallacii de lignis pulcra qua umquam est visa talis"). Though the hall was built during the reign of William II, its reconstruction – including most notably its fine timber ceiling – was commissioned by Richard II in 1394 (Yevele was here, too, involved), and was completed in 1402 after the king's death (†1399).[51] Perhaps the traveler was permitted to view the hall midway through reconstruction, but enough progress must have been made for him to record measurements of the hall ("longitudo lx vi gladiorum et latitudo xviii gladiorum") and to get a sense of its impressive craftsmanship. It is relatively safe, then, to assign the traveler's visit a date of c.1402 as a *terminus a quo*.

It is interesting, too, that in his description of Anne's tomb the visitor fails to mention Richard, even though it was a joint tomb. This could just mean that his visit fell between Anne's funeral and the completion of the tomb in 1397, during which time a less permanent monument was on display. Then again, it is important to point out that Richard II was not actually placed in the tomb until Henry V ceremoniously translated Richard's body from King's Langley to Westminster Abbey in 1413, and laid it (as was originally intended) next to that of Anne. The traveler's description of the tomb as belonging to Queen Anne (and not Richard) may only mean that he knew Richard's body was not in fact in it.[52] Ultimately, the details presented in the itinerary leave many uncertainties. I suggest a probable dating of the traveler's visit as between *c.*1402 and *c.*1413, although an earlier date is certainly possible.

PIETY AND THE POLITICS OF LEGACY-MAKING

Our new knowledge of the eulogies' existence, together with evidence that they were publicly displayed, suggests that there was less squeamishness about discussing Anne after she died than has sometimes been supposed.[53] Yet it is also clear that whoever wrote the eulogies was fully invested in the Ricardian cause. The most detailed expression of political allegiance – and the fullest evidence of authorship – is found in the third and longest of the eulogies, "Nobis natura florem." The two shorter poems, "Anglica regina" and "Femina famosa," seem initially to be unremarkable expositions of Anne's nobility and acts of mercy – similar in many ways to her tomb epitaph and to the chroniclers' estimations of her piety.[54] While these two eulogies are valuable for their apparent hagiographical references (to which I shall return) and their parallels with the Westminster epitaph, they offer little help with determining authorship. These ordinary eulogistic leonines, though not without interest, must for now remain anonymous.[55]

The situation is very different with the third poem, "Nobis natura florem," whose author I suspect was the Carmelite friar Richard Maidstone. That possibility is immensely significant because, as I shall discuss, it suggests that Maidstone was on his way to becoming a go-to poet in a campaign of Ricardian poetic propaganda just before and after Anne's death. Two notable English poets were writing occasional poetry in unrhymed elegiac couplets during Richard's reign: John Gower, whose *Vox clamantis* treats the 1381 Peasants' Revolt (particularly in the *Visio*); and Maidstone, who commemorated Richard II's 1392 reconciliation with the city of London in his 548-line *Concordia*, written in 1393.[56] And although Gower had dedicated his *Confessio amantis* to Richard in 1390, by the time of Anne's death in 1394 he had revised and rededicated it to Prince Henry, the future King Henry IV. Admittedly, in Book VIII of the *Confessio* Gower (even after the rededication) intimates what I take to be a nostalgic fondness for Anne,[57] but even so we would not expect such a royalist composition as "Nobis natura florem" to come from Gower's pen in the mid-1390s.

Maidstone's overtly royalist *Concordia*, however, written just a year before Anne's death, is in keeping with attempts in "Nobis natura florem" to achieve Ricardian unity and to buttress the notion of Richard's legitimacy. The eulogy's treatment of the problem of Plantagenet succession is disarmingly direct. It casts Richard's discernment in selecting a queen as a way of safeguarding the royal line (Richard is "Edwardi Principis heres," l. 33), and to do so a suitable virgin is sought for the king's embraces ("Optatur virgo regis complexibus apta," l. 35). Dignitaries traverse many lands seeking a bride for Richard, and their search turns up several which would make excellent matches for kings. Of all these, Richard chooses Anne.[58] In the preceding verses Anne has already been described in terms of the Bride of Lebanon from the Canticum canticorum ("Flos campi," l. 4); this prepares us to think of Richard as another Solomon, a parallel which Maidstone – who according to Bale wrote a commentary on the Song of Songs[59] – also draws in *Concordia* lines 37–8 ("Talis adolescens toto non restat in orbe, / Qui sciat ut Salomon regna tenere sua").

For those who criticized the wisdom of the alliance in the first place (and there had been many), or who might adduce the fruitless marriage as a sign of Richard's illegitimate kingship, the epithalamic first half of this eulogy shifts the terms of the discussion away from politics to a hagiographic mode. The poet may even have singled out men like Thomas Walsingham who had several years earlier interpreted natural events as portents of a troubled marriage to come. In telling of Anne's arrival in 1381, Walsingham mentions a "disturbance of the sea" which destroyed the Bohemians' ships immediately after Anne disembarked, describing the event as "a dark, perplexing omen of doubtful meaning."[60] It may be with this kind of report in mind that the "Nobis natura" poet similarly tells of an eclipse that occurred at the time of Anne's death (l. 52: "Eclipsim patitur Anglia tota simul"). I am aware of no other report of such an event at this time, but the reference could be an allusion to what was thought to be an eclipse during Christ's crucifixion, based on accounts in the Synoptic Gospels (Matthew 27.45, 51–4; Mark 15.33; and Luke 23.44–5). The sense is that any doubt there may be about this omen (whether or not it actually appeared)[61] has more to do with uncertainty in an England *without* Anne, not *because* of her.

The poem's floral references furthermore prepare us to think of Anne in terms of the Virgin Mary, whom the Bride of the Song of Songs, the "flos campi," was traditionally said to prefigure.[62] But the allusions also suggest that the poet was familiar with contemporary poetic representations of the queen. Chaucer had evoked similar comparisons in the F Prologue to the *Legend of Good Women*, where Alceste, widely thought to represent Anne, is dressed like a daisy, but also the sun, "the 'ye of day', / The emperice and flour of floures alle" (F. 184–5).[63] Like the sun (and Anne), this exotic queen comes from the east (her crown is made "o perle fyn, oriental," F. 221), recalling established Marian imagery in tandem with the Canticum canticorum. Chaucer's overdetermined symbolism was part of a long tradition of similar exegesis, but it also had contemporary parallels with the language of the many Marian cults which proliferated at the end of the fourteenth century. One of his contemporaries, for example, Philippe de Mézières, spent much of his energy in his later years promoting the Feast of Mary's Presentation. In his *Sermo de presentatione Marie in templo*, interpreting Matthew 24.27 ("Sicut enim fulgur exit ab oriente et paret usque in occidente," etc.), Mézières argues (citing Isidore of Seville, the Song of Songs and the Apocalypse) that

Hec lux Virgo Maria exit ab Oriente, quia in Oriente per respectum ad nos . . . exijt primo in mundum in sua natiuitate, quando scilicet "Iudeis noua lux oriri visa est" primo et consequenter "gaudium et honor et tripudium apud omnes populos, urbes atque prouintias" et per consequens ad prouintias Occidentis scribitur Hester 8°.[64]

[This light [i.e., the light from the lightning], the Virgin Mary, comes forth from the East, for in the East, out of consideration for us . . . she first came into the world through her birth, when indeed first "a new light was seen by the Jews to rise," and as a result "[there was] gladness and honor and celebration among all the peoples, cities and provinces," and, as a consequence, to the provinces of the West, as it is written in Hester 8.]

Like Chaucer, the poet of "Nobis natura florem" relies on established traditions of similar Marian interpretation to cast Anne of Bohemia in a salvific role within a highly charged English political context – and in doing so, the author situates himself as a court poet who, though certainly less skilled than Chaucer, nevertheless participates in a shared poetic discourse that addresses the queen's significance for the English. But uniquely in this case, the "Orient" – the Lebanon – from which this "flos campi" comes is also Bohemia, the eastern source of graciousness that dignifies England.

The "Nobis natura" poet is not concerned with strict typologies, however, and admits associations not only between Anne and Mary, but between the queen and Mary's mother, St. Anne, as well. Here again, *Concordia* and "Nobis natura" are remarkably similar in their common allusions to the queen as another St. Anne. Throughout *Concordia*, hope (*spes*) anticipates mercy (*gracia*), and the instrument by which the Londoners hope to attain mercy from Richard is Queen Anne – whose name, "Anna" (Hebrew "Hannah"), was widely reported by the *vitae* of St. Anne to mean "grace."[65] In *Concordia*, Maidstone draws on this etymology in his rendering of the episode in which a warden presents the queen with a golden tablet depicting her patron saint,[66] addressing Anne with these words:

> Inclita Cesareo soboles propagata parente,
>   Quam decor et forma nobilitant nimium,
> Matris christifere nomen sortita Marie,
>   Quod titulis, Anna, "gracia" sonat idem.
> Non decet hunc titulum vacuum fore, nam gerit illum
>   Gracia que populis nunc valet esse suis.   (ll. 431–6)

> [Famed offspring of a father born from Caesar's line,
>   Ennobled greatly by your beauty and your grace,
> Who bears the name of Mary's mother, Mary who
>   Bore Christ – the name of Anna means the same as "grace."
> This name should not be meaningless, for it is hers
>   Who now for all her people can display her grace.][67]

The hope that Anne will fulfill the promise of her name refers back to an earlier passage, "Anna sibi nomen; re sit et Anna, precor [Her name is Anne; I pray she may be Anne in deed]" (ll. 121), and corresponds (as I have said) to the alignment of "spes" and the queen throughout the poem.

The poet of "Nobis natura florem" had even further cause to bolster Anne's association with St. Anne following the queen's death. The Evesham Chronicler, writing his own eulogy for the queen, mentions Anne's instrumentality in having the Feast of St. Anne "more solemnly celebrated" in England – an act which would have been especially praiseworthy for a monk at Evesham, where the feast had been celebrated since at least the thirteenth century.[68] It is not clear whether Anne of Bohemia really was responsible for this more solemn celebration. A bull issued by Pope Urban VI in 1381, before Anne arrived in England, suggests either that St. Anne was already popular there without the queen's help, or that measures were being taken to facilitate the soon-to-be queen's transition with the English people. Urban intended to extend that devotion to make the feast a day of obligation, perhaps in order to facilitate Anne's smooth transition to England, where the marriage was not initially thought to be of much use to the English.[69] By the time Anne died, however, she had become firmly associated with the feast. Anne's funeral was held within the octave of St. Anne's

Day, but the chronicler's remark that Anne "Sepulta est . . . cum maxima solennitate in ecclesia de Westmonasterio, in die Sancte Anne sequente [was buried . . . with the highest solemnity in the church of Westminster, on St. Anne's day following (i.e., following her death in June)]" may indicate that she was entombed on July 26, the day of the feast itself, and not on August 3 when her funeral was held.[70]

Mindful of the queen's special devotion to St. Anne and of Richard's no doubt deliberate choice to schedule the queen's obsequies within the octave of St. Anne's feast, "Nobis natura florem" draws on the etymology of Anne's name, and – in a passage which recalls Maidstone's alignment of the queen and hope – likewise aligns "spes" with "gratia":

> Nam de se gignunt Annam, que nomine tanto
>   Digna vocari sit, "gratia" quod resonat.
> Cogeris asserere quod gratia fulsit in Anna,
>   In qua fulserunt spes, pietas et amor:
> Spes pecata fugat, pietas succurrit egeno,
>   Regna mererique celica fecit amor.   (ll. 23–8)

[For from themselves they brought forth Anna, worthy to be called
    By such a name, which resounds "grace."
You will have to admit that grace shone forth in Anne,
    In whom shone hope, piety and love:
Hope drives away sins, piety runs to the aid of the destitute,
    And love caused [her] to win heavenly kingdoms.]

Finally, while both poems remark on Anne's illustrious lineage, "Nobis natura florem" goes further not only in the number of lines devoted to the subject, but in linking her noble birth to that of St. Anne by drawing on the offices for St. Anne's feast. In the *sequentia* for the office in the Sarum Missal, for example, St. Anne is said to have come from a royal line ("de stirpe regia"),[71] much as the queen from Bohemia "grew bright in a noble line [claruit . . . in stirpe . . . generosa]" (l. 29). The wording of the sequence in the Hereford Missal ("Anna stirpe generosa") presents an even more direct parallel.[72]

In conflating queen and saint, the St. Anne link in "Nobis natura" had a clear and timely political application. Notably, the oblique and direct references to the Feast of St. Anne in the poem help to explain references to Queen Anne as a helper to pregnant women in "Anglica regina" as well as in her Westminster epitaph. As I mentioned above, in "Anglica regina," "Cheerful" Anne "visited pregnant women in their suffering [Pregnantes pena mulieres vissit amena]" (l. 13) – a line which closely parallels the verse on her tomb which says she relieved pregnant women ("pregnantes relevavit").

It is difficult not to read these references in terms of Anne and Richard's conspicuous lack of a successor. The reference to Anne's aid to pregnant women on her tomb epitaph has been interpreted as an indication of the queen's "ambivalent heritage – good deeds but no heir."[73] In light of the verse eulogies, however, which cast Anne in liturgical and hagiographical terms, endowing the queen with attributes of her patron saint, I think this characterization calls for reassessment. St. Anne, significantly, was the patron of pregnant women. The association was a development of the tradition that Anne had been barren into old age (recounted in the hagiography, in the *sequentiae* to the offices for her feast, and elsewhere), but through prayerful petitioning had been granted a child, the Virgin Mary. Her ability to petition God specifically with regard to pregnancy – and with such tremendous success! – made her an obvious candidate to be an intercessory figure in her own right for women who had similar concerns.[74]

The eulogies, then, aimed to explain away the problem of succession by creating a royalist version of Anne's devotion that would justify her childlessness in terms of familiar paradigms for piety, particularly the piety of queens and holy mothers.[75] There is a sense, too, in which these claims about her religious practice rely comfortably upon a wider public perception of the queen's exceptional devotion. This possibility is confirmed by the statements of men like Thomas Walsingham, who, although consistently unimpressed by Anne throughout his chronicle, nevertheless praised the queen's "unbelievable devotion to God," calling her "a lover of almsgiving, supporter of the poor and of the church, a devotee of the true faith and of justice, who carried out her penance in secret."[76]

To revisit the Lollard anecdote of Anne's funeral with which we began, then, we must reconsider it in the context of this good will surrounding Anne's death, much of it intended to shape the queen's legacy for political deployment through the help of liturgical and devotional intertexts. There is little to recommend the story about Thomas Arundel's eulogy of Anne as an authentic account,[77] but, as we have seen, there is much to recommend such glowing assertions of her devotion as the order of the day. Physical reminders of the commemoration of Anne in the form of verse eulogies also remained around her tomb for years to come. Whoever inserted the anecdote of the funeral sermon into Richard Ullerston's tract on vernacular translation may have acted not so much with positive evidence of Anne of Bohemia's devotion to vernacular Scriptures in mind as with an opportunistic alertness to the general consent regarding the queen's devotional probity.

This last point bears reiteration. Anne's piety was publicly available and attested, and the Lollards were as much a part of that public as anyone else – not relegated, in other words, to a closed system of radical reformist texts and ideologies. Indeed, the circumstances in which Anne's piety was co-opted to such divergent ends are analogous to the many contemporary instances of textual circulation in which Wycliffites read and adapted mainstream devotional texts, just as those who were not suspected of unorthodoxy, or who were even overtly anti-Wycliffite, knowingly read and circulated Wycliffite texts. Several of Richard Rolle's writings, for instance, which I shall discuss in greater detail in the next chapter, circulated in exactly this kind of fluid environment. And further, just as Anne of Bohemia's position at the center of English culture was readily adaptable to the political, reformist, or other aims of particular interest groups, the communication lines to which the Anglo-Bohemian marriage alliance gave rise were also utilized by a number of parties, forming varied and flexible networks of textual transmission.

What, then, of Foxe's claim – connected, though not entirely dependent on the Lollard funeral anecdote – that "the Bohemians comming in wyth [Anne], or resorting into thys realme after her, perused and receiued heere the bookes of Iohn Wickleffe, which afterward they conueied into Bohemia"?[78] Anne's direct involvement with heterodox textual exchange has not been demonstrated. Although the increased traffic which passed between England and the Holy Roman Empire as a result of the marriage alliance likely had some bearing on the initial movement of Wyclif's texts to Bohemia, the context of the eulogies in the traveler's notebook in PKMK H.15 reminds us that cultural communication between England and Bohemia encompassed more than the transmission of Wycliffite texts. Here is an instance where a secular knight, subscribing to an entirely conventional brand of piety, enthusiastically recorded his observations of England. While his purpose for coming to England in the first place is unknown, his activities there included a substantial amount of travel to satisfy what may be styled a tourist's curiosity about England's history, relics, and monuments.

There is one previously unexamined instance of convergent transmission, however, in which Anne of Bohemia is implicated in what on the surface seems to be heterodox textual exchange, and which further confirms my previous characterization of Anglo-Bohemian cultural communication. This instance also illustrates Anne's public availability, and attests to the possibilities for diversified textual transmission during this period of cultural contact. A second copy of the eulogy "Anglica regina" also survives in PKMK MS D.12. The manuscript is a Hussite compilation, consisting primarily of texts by Jan Hus, together with a sermon by Jakoubek of Stříbro, and a polemical tract by Štěpán Páleč written in response to an earlier position (not included) by Hus. Colophons in the explicits of two of these items indicate that they were copied in 1414: the copy of Hus' commentary on the *Sentences*, the main text of the collection (fols. 1^r–108^v), was finished "a. d. 1414 quinta die mensis Junii hora quintadecima." A later item, Páleč's 1413 tract against Hus (fols. 157^r–167^v), was completed "a. d. 1414 in die S. Castuli [26 March] hora completorii [compline]." On the final pastedown also appears the intriguing colophon "pro Magistro Jacobo de Strziebro [for Master Jakoubek of Stříbro]," who, as I shall discuss in Chapter 3, was likely the "Jacobellus" known to the English Lollard Richard Wyche.[79]

From this wider collection of Hussite texts, several of which contain references to Wyclif,[80] we come to the manuscript's later contents, which mark a shift but not a break with the earlier material. In its immediate context in MS D.12, the poem "Anglica regina" is situated between two unrelated poems, and distinguished from the first by only a paraph. The preceding ten-line antifraternal poem (fol. 217^r) is as follows:

> Per decies quinos rapiat Sathanas Jacobinos;
> propter et errores, Ihesu, confunde Minores.
> Augustinenses, Pater Inclite, sperne[81] per enses,
> Ac Carmelitas tamquam falsos heremitas.
> Sunt confessores dominorum tum dominarum,
> Et seductores ipsorum sunt animarum.
> Ipsis destructis et abhinc cum demone ductis,
> Fraus, dolus exibunt pax et bona vita redibunt.
> Hii non scribantur cum iustis sed deleantur
> De libro vite quibus Deus dicat "Ite."[82]

> [May Satan snatch the Jacobins fifty at a time;
> On account of their errors, Jesus, confound the Minorites.
> The Augustinians, Glorious Father, scatter by swords,
> And also the Carmelites, as false hermits.
> They are confessors to lords and ladies both,
> And seducers of their souls.
> When they are destroyed and led hence by the demon,
> Fraud and treachery will leave, peace and good life will return.
> May they to whom God says "Go" not be written with the just,
> But blotted out from the book of life.]

The poem that follows "Anglica regina" is the well-known "Heu quanta desolatio Angliae praestatur," the refrain of which ("Wyt a O and a I"), as well as occasional words throughout,[83] make it the only known text in a Bohemian manuscript to contain examples of the Middle English language. "Heu quanta," extant in five manuscripts, is likewise an antifraternal poem, written in the aftermath of the Blackfriars Council of 1382 which condemned twenty-four conclusions derived from Wyclif's writings, although the poem does not name Wyclif specifically.[84]

The transmission history of the copy of "Anglica regina" in PKMK D.12 is more difficult to explain than that of the eulogies in PKMK H.15. Was it copied from H.15? Or was it conveyed independently, perhaps sent from England by one of Hus' Lollard correspondents? One complication for the possibility that it was copied from H.15 is that only one of the eulogies appears in D.12, as opposed to three in H.15. The eulogy in D.12 is also accompanied by other unrelated poems, one of which is, if not a Lollard composition, at least sympathetic with Wycliffite positions; this perhaps indicates that several poems were sent at one time by an English Wycliffite or collected by a Bohemian courier. On textual evidence, the copy of "Anglica regina" in D.12 is less corrupt than its counterpart in H.15. This does not necessarily disqualify H.15 as the exemplar for D.12; a good Latinist could have recognized the corruptions and offered reasonable emendations in his own copy without having recourse to another exemplar. At the same time, we have seen from the H.15 account of the eulogies' placement in Westminster that the poems were accessible to the public and may have remained on display as late as the most active period of correspondence between Lollards and Hussites *c*.1406–14. Considering the frequent communication between Lollards and Hussites in the years preceding the Council of Constance, there is a reasonable chance that the copy of "Anglica regina" in D.12 was brought to Bohemia independently, perhaps copied from the exemplar on display at Westminster. Further, I have already mentioned that the second and third eulogies ("Femina famosa" and "Nobis natura florem") may have been joined together (they are separated by the word "sequitur" in H.15). If the copy of "Anglica regina" in D.12 was copied separately, and at a later time, it is entirely possible that the other two poems had already been removed or lost, no longer available for copying.

It should be stressed that the question of agency in this particular instance of textual transmission is entirely unclear. Was the D.12 eulogy sent or carried to Bohemia, perhaps along with the other poems, by an English Wycliffite? Or did this material come to the attention of some Bohemian courier while he was in England? Perhaps one such courier, making his rounds of England, came across "Anglica regina" in much the same way as did the traveler who transcribed the three eulogies in H.15, quite understandably taking interest in another Bohemian in England – the deceased Queen Anne. I see no reason to think of the presence of the eulogy in D.12 as *ipso facto* evidence of reformist identification with the queen – that is, of reformist association with Anne *as* a supporter of Wycliffism. Equally likely, in fact, this instance of textual transmission arguably demonstrates the ad hoc manner in which many texts that made their way to Bohemia were collected, and suggests that reformist parties had a palette for reading and circulating a wider range of English texts than only those which advocated an exclusively Wycliffite program. As further evidence of this practice, the poem "Per decies quinos," mentioned above, is broadly antimendicant, not specifically Wycliffite.

The suggestion that Bohemian interest in English texts and culture was perhaps broader than previously thought is made all the more compelling by the presence of another text which was also included in D.12. In addition to the eulogy of Anne of Bohemia and two other poems, at least one of which came from England, there is a hitherto unstudied copy of Richard Rolle's *Super threnos Jeremiae* (fols. 193^r–202^r). Rolle's commentary is unascribed in the manuscript, listed in the table of contents located on the initial paste-down only as "Quoddam pulchrum et breve super [librum] Trenorum de Anglia allatum." The text survives in three other manuscripts, two in England and a third in Dublin, but until now no one has commented on its continental circulation.[85] Lollards are known to have used and adapted other Rolle material (though not this text), particularly his *English Psalter Commentary* and *Form of Living*. The issue of the transmission of Rolle's texts to Bohemia is the subject of the next chapter; for now it is enough to emphasize that the presence of *Super threnos* in D.12 suggests that the interest Bohemian reformers had in English texts took in far more than just Wycliffite writings.[86]

I have asserted repeatedly in this chapter that the circumstances of textual transmission on the ground between England and Bohemia were far more complex and uncentralized during this period than previous narratives have shown. The "occasion of Queene Anne,"[87] to borrow Foxe's phrase, may very well have facilitated the transmission of Wycliffite texts to Bohemia. But if so, the queen's presence did not lead to heterodox communication alone. Anne's own direct agency, furthermore, is doubtful. As I shall continue to explore in the next chapter, there was plenty of common ground between the kind of conventional piety that Anne was made to represent and the devotional interests of Lollards (or Lollard sympathizers) who were associated with the Ricardian court. In any case, whoever was responsible for conveying texts between England and Bohemia, the texts they chose to circulate reflected the variegated devotional and reformist landscape of the society which produced them.

Anne of Bohemia lived at the center of a court in which fashionable strands of piety often flirted with heterodox or otherwise controversial ideas. As we have begun to see, the dissemination of texts from England to Bohemia reflected that same cultural environment. In fact, it is not inappropriate to regard the public placement of the eulogies around Anne's tomb, and their convergent transmission to Bohemia, as symbolic or representative of Anne's public availability, and of the opportunities for diversified textual transmission during the Schism period. We may never come closer to knowing Anne's views on Wycliffism. We can say, however, that posthumous attempts to shape her legacy go a long way in describing the devotional concerns of the court which surrounded her, and the possibilities for textual exchange that were available in the complicated arena of English religious politics.

CHAPTER 2

Common ground: Richard Rolle at the edges of orthodoxy in England and Bohemia

Et alii episcopi habent suum cor ad suam propriam devocionem privatam exquirendam, eo minus cor suum ad suos filios, id est curatos.[1]

[And other bishops see to their own private devotion, and less to their children, that is, their ecclesiastical charges.]

Ypocrites ne heretikes feele not this mekenesse, neither in good wille, ne in affeccioun; but wel drie and wel cold aren here hertis and here reynes fro the softe feelynge of this vertu; and so mykil thei aren the ferther fro it, that they wenen for to have it. Thei gnawen upoun the drie bark withoutyn, but the swete kirnel of it and the inli savoure may he not come to. Thei schewen outward mekenesse, in habite, in hooli speche, in loweli berynge, and, as it semeth, in many grete bodili and goostli vertues. But netheleees in the wille and the affeccioun of here herte, where mekenesse schulde principali be, it is but feyned.[2]

The information supplied by the Bohemian traveler's itinerary in PKMK MS H.15, discussed in the previous chapter, clears the way for an expanded discussion of Anglo-Bohemian cultural exchange in the late fourteenth and early fifteenth centuries that takes in much more than heterodox communication. The traveler's diary suggests that among Bohemians there was a level of interest in aspects of English culture other than Wycliffism, and there are signs that the Bohemian knight's experience is representative of more widespread attitudes and patterns of textual acquisition. In the present chapter I want to continue to examine Anglo-Bohemian cultural communication in terms of a broad exchange and, in the process, argue that a wider scope of inquiry can help us contextualize and redefine what would later come to be the dominant channel of communication between these two regions – the Lollard–Hussite transmission network.

Wycliffite writings were not the only English texts to form large concentrations in Bohemia during the Schism period. Many years ago, H. E. Allen, in her landmark study of Richard Rolle, the eccentric hermit of Hampole in

South Yorkshire (*c.*1300–49),[3] noted a sizeable group of Bohemian manu-scripts containing Rolle material. She identified two copies of the *Incendium amoris*, six of Rolle's *Latin Psalter* (with an additional two copies linked to the Bohemian region), and a single copy of the *Emendatio vitae*. Attached to both copies of the *Incendium*, furthermore, is the *Oleum effusum*, also known as the *Encomium nominis Jesu* (an extract from Part IV of Rolle's *Super Canticum canticorum*, together with extracts from the *Incendium*), combined with a compilation of passages concerning devotion to the Holy Name of Jesus drawn from other sources.[4] I have also identified an addi-tional copy of the *Incendium*, as well as a copy of Rolle's Lamentations commentary, which I shall discuss below in greater detail.

In accounting for the presence of Rolle's texts in Bohemia, Allen noted two possible transmission routes. The explicit found in both Bohemian copies of the *Incendium* with which Allen was familiar indicates that the Cardinal of Bologna (the future Pope Innocent VII) approved a copy of the text for a certain "Cardinal John" (called "Archbishop of Prague" in a later gloss to one copy) at some point when the two men were in Rome. Cosmato de' Migliorati, the Bolognese cardinal in question, had been papal collector in England earlier in his career, and it is likely, suggests Allen, that he brought Rolle's text back with him from there.[5] Allen is more speculative in account-ing for the many Bohemian copies of Rolle's *Latin Psalter*. Noting that four of them are dated 1412–13, she suggests: "It would appear that at that period (just before the condemnation of Huss, when Hussite influence must have been at its height) the work of Richard Rolle was energetically propagated in Bohemia."[6] In a later study of Carthusian agency in the circulation of Rolle's works between England and the continent, A. I. Doyle (rightly dis-missing any connection between the Carthusians and the Bohemian Rolle manuscripts) similarly expresses the view that Rolle's *Psalter* may have reached Bohemia through a combination of Wycliffite and non-Wycliffite channels.[7] To my knowledge, no other scholar has ventured to discuss the transmission of Rolle's texts to Bohemia other than to repeat similar assumptions about Lollard or Hussite involvement.[8]

I will discuss the possible Wycliffite ties to some of these texts in due course, but heterodox associations with Rolle should not distract us from what must certainly come first – an examination of the pre-Hussite and non-Wycliffite movement of Rolle material to Bohemia via Rome. The history of this transmission presents many gaps, which may at times be filled with careful speculation, but what can be recovered opens up a fascinating view of the role of devotional literature in the early Bohemian reform – the reformist movement before Hus – while situating this devotionalism within a broad network of European textual transmission that included England. The first part of this chapter traces the contours of the earliest transmission of Rolle's texts from England to Bohemia, demonstrating that the Rome connection was instrumental in facilitating cultural communication between these regions on administrative and devotional levels. I intentionally keep discussion of heterodox communication at a distance for two reasons: first, because I follow (as far as possible) the chronology of transmission for Rolle's texts, and heterodox groups do not appear to have been the initiators; and second, in an effort to correct the notion that Anglo-Bohemian textual transmission during this period was somehow synonymous with Lollard–Hussite communication.

A complete examination of the circulation of Rolle's texts in Bohemian manuscripts quickly reveals, however, that as in England, Rolle's readership in Bohemia was surprisingly diverse, and that not all of the hermit's writings which ended up in Prague came through Rome. The second part of this chapter accounts for the circumstances in which disparate groups of readers coalesced around Rolle's writings in Bohemia. It appears (again, in Prague as in England) that there was more common ground than we often recognize between otherwise antagonistic groups when it came to certain elements of devotion. In fact, the factional groupings scholars typically use to discuss reformists and their opponents during this period tend to blur when we consider the circulation of Rolle's texts. This readership is reflective of what Kantik Ghosh has described as

a religio-intellectual *mentalité* which deliberately rendered problematic and porous both the real and the imagined boundaries between "heretical" and "orthodox," lay and clergy, English [and, I would add, Czech] and Latin, academic speculation and religious politics, scholastic philosophical rationalities and the necessary affectivities – what Matthew Arnold would have called the "poetry" – of organised religious practice.[9]

Religious controversy was indeed a practice or fluid temporal process, and this realization, I suggest, helps to explain the circumstances of reformist textual exchange between England and Bohemia in its early stages. Although the transmission of Rolleana to Bohemia never reached anything near the volume of the Wycliffite material, Rolle's texts were sufficiently popular in Prague to give Bohemians an idea of the range of religiosity that could be found in contemporary England, a diversity which complemented their own.

A ROLLEAN COTERIE AT THE CURIA

If the Bohemian group of Rolle's texts does not owe its presence in Prague to the highly efficient Carthusian apparatus of copying and dissemination (which did not really mobilize, in the case of Rolle, until about 1415),[10] and if the early transmission of these texts cannot be traced to Lollard agency, then how did they circulate? One of them at least was transmitted in what seems to have been an ad hoc manner, by a coterie whose members were drawn together through the otherwise unrelated affairs between Rome and its outlying regions, linked through the administration and liturgical politics of the Church. The copy of Rolle's *Incendium amoris* in Vienna, Österreichische Nationalbibliothek (ÖNB) MS 4483, a manuscript of Bohemian origin, provides some important details about the text's movement to Bohemia through Rome. The colophon, as I mention above, claims that the *Incendium* was approved ("concessa fuit") by Cosmato de' Migliorati, Cardinal of Bologna, for "Johanne cardinali" at the Roman Curia. From a later gloss to the colophon we learn that this "cardinal John" was also an archbishop of Prague. Considering other details which I shall elaborate, the "John" in question was most likely Jan of Jenštejn, Archbishop of Prague from 1378 until his retirement in 1396. One complication for this interpretation, however, is that Jenštejn was never a cardinal. The Vienna manuscript is not unique in calling John (whoever he was) by this title: the shorter colophon which accompanies Rolle's *Incendium* in Prague, Národní knihovna (PNK) MS V.A.23 also indicates that the text was approved "pro Johanne cardinali," as does the slightly different colophon in a third and completely unexamined copy in the Metropolitan Chapter Library in Prague (PKMK), MS D.125.[11] However, all three copies likely derive from a common exemplar (either directly or indirectly), making the repetition of the colophon unhelpful as corroborative evidence.

The only Prague archbishop in the medieval period to become a cardinal, however, was Jenštejn's immediate predecessor in the archbishopric, Jan Očko of Vlašim (elected cardinal 1378; †1380).[12] Less likely, but nevertheless possible, is that the colophon refers to Jan Kardinál of Rejnštejn, who was often (confusingly) called in Latin "Johannes Cardinalis." Kardinál was not a prelate, but rather a reformist (and later Hussite) master associated with the Carolinum from about 1394.[13] The confusion which arises from trying to identify the Cardinal John mentioned in the Bohemian copies of Rolle's *Incendium amoris* makes it somewhat tricky to use the other reference to "Cardinal" Cosmato de' Migliorati for dating or other purposes, but nevertheless it should be noted that Cosmato actually did become a cardinal in

1389. It is doubtful, however, that he was in a position to approve books like Rolle's *Incendium* (an episcopal duty) until around the time he finished his term in England as papal collector, which roughly coincided with his preferment to Archbishop of Ravenna and, shortly thereafter, Cardinal of Bologna.[14] This means that the reference to Cardinal John in the Bohemian copies of Rolle's *Incendium* probably does not indicate Cardinal Jan Očko of Vlašim, who died several years before Cosmato became an archbishop. It furthermore seems unlikely, though not impossible, that the reformist master Jan Kardinál was terribly interested in having books approved in Rome by any cardinal. Of course, the cardinal in question need not to have been Bohemian; however, I have found no other cardinal who was named John, loyal to the Roman papacy, and alive after Cosmato became cardinal in 1389. The reference to "Cardinal" John in the colophon, then, is probably a mistake, referring, I suggest, to Jan of Jenštejn. In the discussion which follows, then, I shall assume that Jenštejn was associated with Rolle's *Incendium*, though it should be borne in mind that his identification with the text is not absolutely certain.

Fortunately, we do not need to rely solely on the colophon in the Vienna manuscript to determine the likelihood that Jenštejn knew the Cardinal of Bologna. In fact, Jenštejn had several opportunities when he could have met with Cosmato de' Migliorati throughout his career, and, when put together, the evidence forms a picture of a fairly developed relationship. Jenštejn's *peregrinatio academica* had taken him to Bologna, where he knew the jurist John of Legnano, Cosmato's teacher.[15] Jenštejn also made several trips to Rome, usually in connection with his longstanding dispute with the Bohemian king, Václav IV, and is known on at least one of these occasions to have had direct and extensive dealings with Cosmato. Shortly after the death of Urban VI (†1389), a rare supporter of the embattled Prague archbishop, Jenštejn traveled to Rome in 1390 to ascertain how likely it was that Boniface IX would continue to back him in his controversies at home.[16] Again in 1393 he set out for the Curia to gain papal support in his struggles with Václav. Yet the most likely occasion for his discussion of Rolle's *Incendium* with the cardinal from Bologna was, I suggest, in 1395–6, when, in a moment of crisis during his protracted conflict with Václav, Jenštejn was forced to give up his archbishopric and, with his estates occupied in 1395, he left Prague for Rome to resign his office into the hands of the pope. It was to none other than Cosmato de' Migliorati that Boniface committed Jenštejn's case, and the bull releasing Jenštejn from office was issued early the next year. The colophon which is appended to the Bohemian copies of the *Incendium* suggests, however, that Jenštejn's

interactions with Cosmato went beyond official business. Nor indeed was
their probable discussion of Rolle's *Incendium* the only instance of textual
circulation between them: the single extant copy of Jenštejn's *Libellus de
justitia et divina iustitie observantia*, now in the Vatican Library, is also
dedicated to Cosmato.[17]

In addition to the evidence of a known meeting between Jenštejn and the
Cardinal of Bologna, the possibility that Jenštejn came to know of the
Incendium (or at least that he paid more attention to it) at this late stage in
his career is strengthened by signs of his increased devotion to the Holy Name
of Jesus during the final years of his life. By the end of the fourteenth century
the cult of the Holy Name, inspired to a large extent by the Christocentric
mysticism of Bernard of Clairvaux, was widespread in Europe, and devotion
to the Name of Jesus would continue to flourish into the fifteenth century,
spurred on by the controversial efforts of John of Capistrano and Bernardino
of Siena. Earlier, the writings of Heinrich Suso, the major fourteenth-century
German proponent of the cult, spread widely throughout Europe, including
England, while in England (and gradually spreading to the continent, as
I discuss in this chapter), the texts of Richard Rolle, the most active insular
advocate of the cult of the Holy Name, experienced an enthusiastic revival in
the later years of the fourteenth century.[18]

Rolle's devotion to the Holy Name infuses many of his writings. His
discussion of the ascent of the spirit, most famously delineated in the
Incendium amoris, associates the contemplation of Jesus with *dulcor* (a sensa-
tion of sweetness) in particular,[19] which, together with *fervor* and *canor*, was
one of the experiences that characterized his mystical system. The so-called
"short text"[20] of the *Incendium* – an abridgment for which Rolle himself was
probably not responsible – frequently circulated with one of three compilations of extracts drawn from Rolle's and others' writings on the Holy Name,
and the widespread dissemination of these compilations suggests that many of
Rolle's readers considered his comments on the Name of Jesus to be one of
the most compelling features of his contemplative program. The Vienna and
Prague copies of the *Incendium* – all of them representing the short text – are
accompanied by the following unique compilation, not previously identified
in full, and found nowhere else as a group:[21]

1 [**Auctor incertus**], the compilation *Quandoque tribularis memento*.[22]
   [PNK V.A.23, fol. 16^v; PKMK D.125, fols. 52^{r-v}; ÖNB 4483, fols. 133^v–134^r]
   Incip.: "Quandocumque temptaris vel tribularis . . ." Explic.: ". . . et
   subtrahit graciam suam consolamen et solacium a nobis." Compilation
   includes Latin translations of two excerpts from the Middle English
   Ancrene Riwle.

2 **Richard Rolle,** *Oleum effusum.*[23] [PNK V.A.23, fols. 16^v–18^r; PKMK D.125, fols. 52^v–57^v; ÖNB 4483, fols. 134^r–135^v] Heading: *Richardus heremita de nomine Ihesu.* Incip.: "Oleum effusum nomen tuum ideo adolescentule dilexivit te nimis . . ." Explic.: "Ergo benedictum sit nomen Jhesu in secula seculorum amen."

3 **John of Tynemouth?,** continuation of *Historia aurea,* from *Vita Sancti Machuti.*[24] [PNK V.A.23, fol. 18^r; PKMK D.125, fols. 57^v–58^r; ÖNB 4483, fol. 135^v] Heading: *De virtute nominis Ihesu.* Incip.: "Legitur in vita Sancti Machuti Allectis civitatis episcopi quod dyabolus trahebat unum de discipulis . . ." Explic.: ". . . cuius nomen sit benedictum in secula."

4 **Odo (2nd Abbot) of Cluny,** adapted from *Collationum libri tres.*[25] [PNK V.A.23, fol. 18^r; PKMK D.125, fol. 58^r; ÖNB 4483, fols. 135^v–136^r] Heading: *Item in vita Sancti Anthonii de nomine Jhesu.* Incip.: "Beatus Anthonius cum a malignis spiritibus ita affectus . . ." Explic.: ". . . et a certa fide universi demones fugabuntur."

5 **Heinrich Suso,** from *Horologium sapientiae,* lib. II.[26] [PNK V.A.23, fol. 18^{r-v}; PKMK D.125, fols. 58^r–59^r; ÖNB 4483, fol. 136^r] Heading: *Item de eodem nomine in quodam libro vocato Orologium Sapientie.* Incip.: "Erat quidam iuvenis fervidus amator . . ." Explic.: ". . . totiens contingeret pristinam amicitiam rememorando quasi recenter in corde suo renovari."

6 **Bernard of Clairvaux,** from *Sermo in Cantica XVI.*[27] [PNK V.A.23, fol. 18^v; PKMK D.125, fol. 59^{r-v}; ÖNB 4483, fol. 136^{r-v}] Heading: *Item Bernhardus super Cantica sermone XVI° in fine de hoc nomine Ihesus.* Incip.: "Oleum plane quod dum supernat . . ." Explic.: ". . . in tantum usquequaque infusum est."

7 **Bernard of Clairvaux,** *Sermo in Cantica XV.*[28] [PNK V.A.23, fols. 18^v–19^r; PKMK D.125, fols. 59^v–60^v; ÖNB 4483, fol. 136^v] Heading: *Item de nomine Jesu.* Incip.: "Non tantum lux est nomen Ihesu sed et cibus." Explic.: ". . . itemque unde tuos sensus aut serves ne corrumpantur autsi corrumpantur sanes."

Colophon. [PNK V.A.23, fol. 19^r; PKMK D.125, fol. 60^v; ÖNB 4483, fol. 136^v] "Explicit pulcher libellus qui Incendium amoris nuncupatur, per quemdam nobilem et sanctum virum Anglicum heremitam compositus revelacione divina in spiritu, qui multa valet pro viris contemplativis, cuius copia concessa fuit per Reverendissimum in Christo patrem dominum Cosmatem Cardinalem dignissimum Bononiensem pro Johanne Cardinali in Curia Romana."[29]

In Bohemia, the cult of the Holy Name seems not to have achieved quite the level of popularity that it attracted in some other parts of Europe. The Feast of the Holy Name appears nowhere in medieval Bohemian liturgical calendars, and there is no mention of it in the *Litoměřice Gradual* of 1517, which indicates that, if it had been used, the feast was not adopted into the surprisingly conservative Utraquist calendar.[30] Jenštejn was known for championing devotional projects that did not enjoy mainstream support, and yet there is select evidence that the Holy Name had its devotees in Bohemia, however small in number. Jenštejn's interest in the cult, for example, seems to have coincided with the introduction of Suso's *Horologium sapientiae* to Prague, or at least with its revival there. A copy of that text was made in Prague in 1393, along with the continuation *Cursus de aeterna sapientia* which likewise accompanies the *Horologium* in several subsequent Bohemian manuscripts.[31] (And as I mention above, an excerpt from Suso's *Horologium* also follows Rolle's *Incendium amoris* in the Bohemian copies.)

Jenštejn's devotion to the Holy Name was pronounced in his own writings as well. Sometime just before he died, he dedicated his *Libelli de laude nominis Jesu Christi et Marie* to his successor Olbram of Škvorec.[32] In the dedication Jenštejn refers to himself as Patriarch of Alexandria, the honorary title which he received from Boniface IX sometime *c.*1399.[33] Jenštejn's *De laude nominis* survives in three copies, one of them in PNK v.a.23, the same manuscript which includes (as I have said) a copy of Rolle's *Incendium amoris* and the compilation of passages on the Name of Jesus, together with an unascribed sermon on the Holy Name.[34] Probably just after he wrote the *De laude nominis*, Jenštejn also wrote the related tract *De divinis nominibus*, which elaborates on some of the contemplative methods that were introduced in the earlier tract.

Unfortunately, there is no direct evidence to suggest that Jenštejn borrowed from Rolle's *Incendium* or *Oleum effusum* when composing either tract. There could be many reasons for this, but Jenštejn's painstakingly methodological approach to contemplation on the Holy Name in his own writings may in part have determined his use or exclusion of sources. The mystical system that Rolle delineates in the *Incendium* never really explains how meditation on the Name of Jesus, which Rolle emphasizes much more in some of his other writings like the *Oleum effusum*, is incorporated into that system methodologically speaking. Those of Rolle's texts which do treat the Holy Name – for example, the ones which were available in Bohemia – do so rather in an evocative or inspirational sense.

Jenštejn's focus, on the other hand, was much narrower, and, particularly in his earlier tract, his approach was defined less by an aim to inspire his addressee than by his narrative purpose of instruction in a very specific mode of contemplation. His attention to the Holy Name in the tract addressed to Olbram is far more systematic (and far less affective) than Rolle's. He concentrates relatively little attention on evoking the Holy Name in the course of the text itself – in contrast to Rolle's writings on the Holy Name, his tract is less an act *of* contemplation as it is a manual *for* contemplation, its methods to be adopted (it was hoped) in the contemplative life of Jenštejn's successor. Jenštejn's *De divinis nominibus*, which is not addressed to Olbram, takes up aspects of the contemplative system as delineated in *De laude nominis*, and extenuates in particular a linguistic consideration of the individual letters of the names for the Divine as an expedient to meditation, a path to understanding the Person and Passion of Christ.[35]

If there is little else to say about the ways in which Rolle's *Incendium* or *Oleum effusum* were read in Bohemia, there is something more to add about the circumstances of the compilation's transmission, and about the fascinating devotional environment in Rome in which it participated. H. E. Allen speculated that Cosmato may first have brought the *Incendium amoris* to Rome, citing the fact that at one time he had been papal collector in England.[36] It should be stressed, however, that the colophons in the three Bohemian copies of the *Incendium* do not rule out the possibility that someone else carried the text from England; we know only that Cosmato *approved* the text for someone called John, who was probably Jenštejn. Little is known of Cosmato's term as papal collector, let alone of his literary or devotional interests. He appears with some regularity in English records beginning in 1379, when he swore fealty to Richard II, until the end of 1388, when he is referred to as "late the pope's collector in England."[37] That this ten-year span is probably accurate is also suggested by an entry in the *Gesta pontificum Romanorum*, which says that Cosmato "was made collector in England for ten years [factus [est] in Anglia collector annis X]" under Urban VI.[38] Cosmato appears to have been popular at the Ricardian court; on several occasions Richard II refers to him as "dilecto suo," and (later) "amico nostro precarissimo."[39] As papal collector, furthermore, Cosmato exported many things from England, though I have found no reference to his transmission of books.[40] We can be fairly certain that he or his surrogates at least read the *Incendium* at some point during his probable interactions with Jenštejn, and there is a strong possibility that he already knew of the text's popularity in England. Beyond that, the tracks grow faint for Cosmato in connection with Rolle's text.[41]

Fortunately, the investigation is not yet at an impasse. Several details in the notes which accompany the copy of the *Incendium* in ÖNB MS 4483 indicate that it circulated among members of a larger group of churchmen in Rome than the colophon alone would seem to suggest. These notes provide unique details about Rolle's biography, together with some additional clues pertaining to the transmission history and readership of the *Incendium* in Rome.[42] The Vienna colophon is followed by a note which indicates that "a certain English monk, bachelor of sacred theology" reported some of the information regarding Rolle to the annotator ("Ita retulit mihi quidam monachus Anglicus, baccalarius sacre theologie").[43] Elsewhere we learn that an unspecified English doctor ("doctor quidam de Anglia") told the original annotator ("mihi") that William Stopes was responsible for appending Rolle's *Oleum effusum* (called *De nomine Ihesu*) to the *Incendium amoris*.

The group of churchmen surrounding Rolle's text, then, seems to have formed a coterie of readers from three separate regions – Jenštejn, Cosmato, and the Englishmen – who discussed not only the text of the *Incendium*, but also its history and the biography of its author in Rome.[44] Once the text reached Bohemia, furthermore, its author continued to attract interest. The notes in MS 4483 are transcriptions from a lost exemplar, as is suggested by the frequency with which abridgements are marked by "etc.," as well as by hints that the copyist experienced some difficulty in deciphering the original notes ("videtur hic," he comments at one point).[45] In fact, the scribe who later copied the notes concerning Rolle seems to have gone beyond the original to update some of the information. He notes, for example, that "Both the said cardinal [i.e., Jenštejn] and Richard [of Hampole] are now standing near merciful God [Tam cardinal dictus quam Rychardus nunc adhuc deo propicio superstites sunt [i.e., they are dead]]," and further adds that "now indeed Lord Cosmato, in the year of the Lord 1405, has been chosen for pope as Innocent VII [Dominus vero cosmatus nunc anno Domini m.cccc.v in papam assumptus Innocencius vij^us]." The evidence that the scribe was concerned to alter and comment on the annotations suggests that the text of the *Incendium* and the details of Rolle's biography were still considered to be worth the bother of transcribing (despite the seeming difficulty which the copyist faced in deciphering them) at least until 1405, when the Vienna copy was apparently made.

Beyond the references in MS 4483 to "doctor quidam de Anglia" and "quidam monachus Anglicus, baccalarius sacre theologie," further identification of these Englishmen remains tantalizingly beyond reach. The English expatriate community in Rome during the late fourteenth century was fairly large, and Cosmato kept many of its members in his service even after his term as collector in England had come to an end.[46] Cosmato could also be relied on to lend support to English petitions in Rome after his elevation to cardinal.[47] When he briefly became pope (1404–6), he furthermore received the English chronicler Adam Usk into his service as papal chaplain and auditor of the apostolic palace.[48] In other words, Jenštejn's earlier conversations with the Cardinal of Bologna could easily have brought him into contact with Englishmen like the ones mentioned in the notes to Rolle's *Incendium* in the Vienna manuscript, though of course there is no reason why he could not have met Englishmen independently of Cosmato.

In fact, we know that he did. The discussion of Rolle's *Incendium* in Rome seems to have been part of a much wider devotional discourse which likewise included some identifiable Englishmen and Jenštejn. The only thing which surpassed the archbishop's veneration of the Holy Name was his devotion to the Virgin Mary (to whose name, as I have said, he was also devoted). In 1386, Jenštejn began a campaign to institute the Feast of the Visitation of the Blessed Virgin, first in his own archdiocese, and later throughout the entire Church.[49] Jenštejn was convinced that the institution of the new feast would help put an end to the Schism that plagued Christendom, as he had been assured in a vision. Urban VI evidently recognized the political benefit of pursuing Jenštejn's proposal: at some point between 1386 and 1388 an investigation into the proposed feast was begun in Rome, and in 1389 Urban announced his intention to institute the Feast of the Visitation. Urban died before he could issue the requisite bull, but the cause maintained enough momentum to receive Boniface's immediate attention; a bull was finally issued on November 9, 1389.[50]

Earlier, however, while the cause of the proposed feast was still pending, Urban charged a number of theologians then in Rome with examining the feast's theology and liturgy (whose initial texts were Jenštejn's compositions), including the English Benedictines Adam Easton and Edmund Bramfield.[51] When in 1389 Bramfield preached in favor of the new feast and Urban accepted his recommendation, there was yet another delay in completing the process of its institution and promulgation because the feast still did not have a universally accepted date and office. Jenštejn traveled once again to Rome in 1390 to petition Boniface to finish the process, at which time the pope commissioned four theologians – one of them being Easton – to examine the proposed offices. By this point no fewer than eight offices (including Jenštejn's) had been submitted, but it was Easton's own text, *Accedunt laudes*, which was ultimately adopted most widely.[52]

Easton and Jenštejn probably became known to each other during the examination process, but there is little evidence to suggest that their interactions concerning devotional matters went beyond that.[53] The clearest consequence of Easton's interactions with Jenštejn in Rome seems to have been indirect, manifested in the subsequent diffusion of devotional interest in the Visitation in England, Central Europe, and elsewhere. Easton's office, which was not the only one to circulate, can be found, for example, in a fine Franciscan antiphonal in Moravia, now Olomouc, Vědecká knihovna MS M. IV.6. In England, Boniface IX licensed Thomas Mowbray, Earl of Nottingham, to found the Carthusian Charterhouse of the Visitation of the Blessed Virgin Mary on the Isle of Axholme (Lincolnshire) in 1396. In the charter which the earl issued shortly afterward, Mowbray cites the "special devotion which he has for the Feast of the Visitation of the Blessed Virgin Mary, newly instituted by the pope."[54] Back in Rome, although Easton and Jenštejn crossed paths with regard to liturgical and devotional matters, speculation as to whether the two might also have discussed Rolle's *Incendium* together (was Easton the "doctor quidam de Anglia" mentioned in ÖNB 4483?) is unlikely to be profitable. Easton's vast library – sent after his death to Norwich in six barrels – would seem to be a good place to look for evidence, and yet our knowledge of its contents is very limited.[55] To date, only a fraction of his books have been identified and, though they present an incomplete picture, none of them confirms specifically that Easton was interested in Rolle. The fragments of interaction which I have outlined, however, form the impression of a vibrant exchange in Rome concerning devotional matters, an exchange which likely brought Jenštejn into contact with English and other churchmen on a number of occasions. I can only add that Easton's involvement in the politics of devotion while in Rome was not limited to investigating the Feast of the Visitation; he was also (and simultaneously) one of the most vocal advocates for the canonization of Bridget of Sweden.[56]

CONVERGENT TRANSMISSION: CROSS-PURPOSES, OR CONTINUITY?

The foregoing discussion accounts for just a fraction of the total number of Richard Rolle's texts which are now found in Bohemian manuscripts. The England–Rome–Prague transmission route was clearly instrumental in facilitating the initial Bohemian circulation of Rolle's *Incendium*, but it remains to be seen whether Rolle's continued popularity in Bohemia can be attributed to native circulation and transcription (perhaps emanating from Jenštejn's circle); fresh and unrelated exchanges between England and Bohemia; or, as I shall argue, a combination of the two. From this point forward, the manuscripts seldom offer help by way of colophons or marginalia, and so we encounter the thorny problem of attempting to determine readership and circulation by examining the complicated manuscript contexts of Rolle's writings in Bohemia, several of which appear in miscellanies or compilations. In considering each of these manuscripts as a whole, however, patterns emerge in the circulation and readership of Rolle's texts in Prague which resemble (and intersect with) similar networks in contemporary England. Manuscript compilations often attest to the practice of controversy through time – that is, to the ways in which controversialists adapted and responded as events unfolded – and, when these manuscripts are considered in their entirety, they can be valuable tools for understanding textual circulation and religious polemic as fluid temporal processes.

ÖNB MS 4483, discussed extensively in the previous section, is an instructive case in point. I have said that the notes which accompany the *Incendium* in the Vienna manuscript point to an earlier exemplar which is not known to survive. Yet equally important are the clues which the manuscript as a whole provides about the subsequent circulation of the *Incendium amoris* in Bohemia. But circulation by whom? The transmission history of MS 4483 to its present location in Vienna sheds some light on how it was later read at least in the sixteenth century. This was one of a large number of manuscripts brought from Prague to Vienna by Kaspar von Niedbruck, a diplomat and librarian under Archduke (and later Emperor) Maximilian II.[57] Von Niedbruck was interested in reformist history, and became involved in the large antiquarian projects of men like Matthias Flacius Illyricus, who encouraged von Niedbruck to use his Bohemian connections to access and copy sources on reformist forebears like Hus and Wyclif. On a visit to Prague in 1556, von Niedbruck convinced officials at Charles University to lend him nearly fifty manuscripts, including the compilation that is now ÖNB 4483, with at least the stated intent of returning them safely. However, von Niedbruck died the following year, before he could follow through on his promise; his property was subsequently forfeit to the emperor, and the manuscripts have remained in Vienna ever since.

The fact that MS 4483 caught von Niedbruck's attention suggests that the manuscript was thought to contain useful documents for compiling a history of the Bohemian reform, and indeed some of the polemical texts in this manuscript survive nowhere else.[58] This is not to say that the manuscript is necessarily a Hussite compilation. Of the texts which pertain to controversy involving the Hussites, the manuscript represents two main disputes: the longstanding debate on universals, and related polemic surrounding the metaphysics of the Eucharist. Concerning the former, the manuscript contains (in whole or in extract) Stanislav of Znojmo's *Tractatus de universalibus realibus* (48^r–52^r), Štěpán Páleč's *Quaestio utrum universale sit aliquid extra* (61^v–67^r), Jerome of Prague's *De universalibus* (71^r–78^v), and a disputation of John of Münsterberg (Ziębice) on universals (57^v–61^v). The

Eucharistic controversy is represented by a sermon of Wyclif on the body and blood of Christ (67^r–69^r),[59] Stanislav of Znojmo's *Tractatus de corpore Christi* (144^r–168^v), and Hus' tract on the same subject (169^r–174^v). The manuscript also includes a list of articles which were drawn up against Hus in 1408, along with his replies to them (176^v–179^r); a *questio* of James of Nouvion on ecclesiastical temporalities (169^r–282^r), referring to "nostri adversarii ... Wyclifiste heretici"; and a previously unknown copy of an Oxford letter attesting to Wyclif's virtue.[60] None of these texts post-dates 1409, though of course some of them may have been copied later.

The sections of the manuscript which are concerned with Hussite controversy furthermore represent opposing positions in the debates. On the problem of universals, for example, Jerome of Prague advocated a distinctly realist metaphysics, while John of Münsterberg was one of the nominalists who left Prague in 1409 to establish the new university at Leipzig, where he became the first rector.[61] The situation is also complicated for the texts on the Eucharist. Stanislav of Znojmo's *Tractatus de corpore Christi*, for example, promotes a moderate remanentist doctrine (approaching consubstantiation), much less extreme than Wyclif's teachings on remanence. However, the marginal notes to Znojmo's text indicate that at least one reader's subscription to an entirely conservative doctrine of transubstantiation caused him to object to much of the tract.[62]

ÖNB 4483 also defies straightforward classification as a manuscript attesting strictly to Hussite debates. Aside from the texts I have just mentioned, which were produced during the controversies of the early fifteenth century and often centered on Wyclif's doctrines, there are signs that someone involved in the manuscript's production was equally familiar with strands of reformist and devotional thinking that were current in Bohemia during the last quarter of the fourteenth century. I have already discussed the notes to the *Incendium*. In addition, we find the tract *De devolucionibus non recipiendis*, written in opposition to the theologian Vojtěch Raňkův of Ježov (Adalbertus Ranconis de Ericinio) by Kuneš of Třebovle, a canon of the Prague cathedral under Jenštejn. A copy of this text in another manuscript indicates that Kuneš dedicated the tract to Jenštejn himself.[63] As a further link between ÖNB 4483 and the disputes of the early Bohemian reform, a note to the Vienna copy of Kuneš's tract states that he had at one time written in support of the Feast of the Visitation – the institution of which, it should be mentioned, Vojtěch Raňkův energetically opposed.[64] Elsewhere the manuscript includes Richard FitzRalph's extremely popular *Defensio curatorum*. FitzRalph's writings remained influential in Bohemia well into the fifteenth century, but they first gained prominence there among a group of Prague scholars from the early Bohemian reform who had spent time at Paris, including Jenštejn and Raňkův.[65] Also included in the manuscript are texts on the Virgin Mary, a short text on the contemplative life, and the *Revelaciones* of Bridget of Sweden, whose canonization process, I have said, coincided with the mutual affairs of Jenštejn and Adam Easton in Rome surrounding the Feast of the Visitation.

Taken as a unified whole, then, MS 4483 appears to represent a transitional stage in the Bohemian reform. Devotional texts of the kind that interested Jenštejn, and which informed his own special brand of reformism in the late fourteenth century, give way to texts that participated in the highly polarizing disputes in Prague concerning Wyclif's doctrines before the exodus of German masters from Prague to Leipzig in 1409. As I say above, manuscript compilations are seldom static monuments to isolated moments of history, but are typically the results of temporal processes – in this case, forming a record of reformist controversy as factional lines are drawn – participating in and developing with the events to which they attest. Compilations like ÖNB 4483 may be regarded, in other words, as artifacts witnessing to the practice of controversy as it developed and adapted through time, not necessarily representative of unified or static controversial positions. Just as importantly, MS 4483 also provides insight into how the native Bohemian reform maintained a level of continuity through the ongoing circulation of texts which were associated with earlier moments in its history. The observation is one that holds particular importance for the examination of pre-print textual circulation, where manuscripts, unlike the majority of printed texts, were typically (as Ralph Hanna reminds us) "neither planned nor executed as (or from) whole volumes," but rather "fluid, developing entities."[66]

The presence of Rolle's other texts in Bohemia is more difficult to explain than the transmission of the *Incendium-Oleum effusum* compilation. The most frequent text, Rolle's *Latin Psalter*, survives in eight copies (one in fragment) and appears in manuscripts of impeccable orthodoxy. There are some faint but ultimately unsatisfying suggestions that the *Psalter* may have been associated with Jenštejn. A colophon to the copy now in Schlägl, Stiftsbibliothek MS Plagensis 105 indicates that its scribe was "Symon the hermit," who copied it in 1438.[67] Another text in that collection was copied the same year by "Wolfgang," who was a chaplain in the south Bohemian town of České Budějovice. The reference to Wolfgang links the manuscript to Bohemia, but the scribe of the Schlägl Psalter commentary seems to turn up elsewhere in a manuscript with at least indirect ties to Jenštejn.

A manuscript in Gdańsk contains a colophon which likewise mentions "Symon heremita reclusus," and the compilation includes a text pertaining to controversies in Prague during Jenštejn's archiepiscopacy, in which Jenštejn himself is implicated.[68] Pursuing leads of this sort runs the danger of giving way to fanciful textual relationships, but I should add that the Schlägl copy of Rolle's *Psalter* also contains an excerpt from Book VIII of Bridget of Sweden's *Revelaciones*, again suggesting a possible link to the interactions of Jenštejn and Easton in Rome.

The initial pastedown in another manuscript which contains Rolle's *Latin Psalter*, PNK IV.E.I, could also indicate that the text was associated with the archiepiscopal court under Jenštejn. The material used for the pastedown is a public document linked to a certain Nicholas, called "bishop and auditor," from 1398. This may refer to Mikuláš Puchník, Jenštejn's close friend who held a number of offices under the archbishop, and had at one time served as legate of the Apostolic See.[69] The copy of Rolle's text in PNK IV.E.I is, however, a fragment and, if the dating of an earlier document in the manuscript is any indication, was copied sometime after Jenštejn and Puchník died. In other words, it is difficult to say for certain whether Rolle's *Latin Psalter* was in Bohemia when Jenštejn was still alive. There furthermore seems to have been a flurry of interest in the text from 1412–13, when four of the surviving copies of the *Psalter* were transcribed.[70] Of course, these dates do not confirm when the text arrived in Bohemia and may only suggest a revival in the popularity of Rolle's *Psalter* during the second decade of the fifteenth century. One thing we can take away even from this uncertain evidence, however, is that Hussite interest in Rolle cannot be taken for granted.

Slightly more helpful for determining the transmission of Rolleana to Bohemia is a manuscript in the Metropolitan Chapter Library in Prague, whose contents show possible signs of Hussite contacts with English Lollards. PKMK D.12, introduced briefly in the previous chapter, contains an almost completely overlooked copy of Rolle's *Super threnos Jeremiae*, bound with at least two other poems from England (one of them is the eulogy "Anglica regina," edited in Appendix A), and a number of Hussite polemical texts.[71] Before I elaborate on the possibility of Lollard participation in trafficking Rolleana to Prague, however, I shall say a few words by way of summarizing Wycliffite interest in Rolle – an author whose writings do not initially seem to share much with a Wycliffite program – in order to reveal the pitfalls of attributing even the transmission of these texts to Lollard agency. Richard Rolle's eremitical way of life and emphasis on the *vita contemplativa* (though he never completely dismissed the active life) would seem to have made him an unlikely candidate for winning Lollard favor. The kind of seclusion which hermits and anchorites required bore resemblances to the life of monks, whose withdrawal from the world (their "priuat religion")[72] ignored what many Wycliffites considered to be scriptural injunctions to preach and administer to Christ's flock.[73] (The objection is similar, in fact, to the early Bohemian reformer Matěj of Janov's contention, cited in the epigraph, that some bishops – and here he likely alludes to his friend Jan of Jenštejn – "see to their own private devotion, and less to their children, that is, their ecclesiastical charges.")[74]

In any case, probably because Rolle's writings combined eremitic contemplation with an emphasis on pastoral care and scathing critique of pastoral neglect, Wyclif did read Rolle and, as Fiona Somerset has recently discussed, even adapted elements of Rolle's vernacular *The Form of Living*, a text which Rolle dedicated to the anchoress Margaret Kirkby, for new purposes.[75] The five questions on love which Rolle posed and answered in his text clearly resemble the same set of questions in Wyclif's *De amore*.[76] From here the questions resurface in the Lollard vernacular adaptation of *De amore*, the *Five Questions on Love*. Of Rolle's texts, however, the *English Psalter* received the bulk of Lollard attention.[77] According to Dorothy Everett's widely accepted assessment, the Wycliffite versions of Rolle's commentary can be separated into three revisions – two of them reproducing the full text with relatively minor alterations (R[evised] V[ersion] 1 and RV 2), and a third, longer version surviving in a single copy, with commentary only on Psalms 84.6–118 (RV 3).[78] And indeed the prologue to a copy of RV 2 in Oxford, Bodleian Library MS Laud Misc. 286 indicates that the circulation of Lollard versions of the commentary was not limited to an exclusively Lollard readership. The author of the prologue evidently caught word that Lollards had "ymped [interpolated]" their pestiferous heresy with certain copies of Rolle's holy book, but he was quite certain that the text in front of him was innocent of any such tampering.[79]

The prologue writer's attempt to stabilize the uncomfortable admixture of orthodoxy and heresy that were rumored to exist in copies of Rolle's *English Psalter* suggests that this kind of mingling of Lollard texts with other less contentious (or more mainstream) forms of devotional material was either fairly widespread, or thought to be so; that texts of various doctrinal stripes could be found in the same libraries, or circulating among the same coteries. In fact, as I show here, the doctrinal positions of those who read, copied, and circulated these texts were not absolute, but fluid and variable in their emphases. I have already discussed some Lollard adaptations of Rolle's writings, but heterodox interest in anchoritic devotion and contemplation was not limited to Rolle. We have only to look to the *Ancrene Riwle*, an anonymous guide for anchoresses which was (like Rolle's *English Psalter*) subject to Lollard revision, for further confirmation of this counterintuitive circulation of texts. The Lollard reviser of the *Riwle* seems to have left his work unfinished, but the fact that the text was even considered as a suitable vehicle for Wycliffite doctrine suggests a degree of Lollard affinity not necessarily with anchoresses per se, but with readers who circulated texts affiliated with anchoritic devotion.[80]

The affinity worked in the other direction, too, in cases where apparently orthodox readers of devotional texts had ready access to Wycliffite material. M. T. Brady's valuable work on the Middle English compilation *Pore Caitif* has revealed that its compiler borrowed from the Wycliffite *Glossed Gospels*, though not, in her estimate, in such a way as to render the compilation heretical. In several instances the text also borrows from Rolle's *Emendatio vitae*, his *Form of Living* (which, as I have already mentioned, was also used by Wycliffites) and his *Commentary on the Canticles*.[81] In terms of its evidently innocent incorporation of a text produced by Wycliffites (not necessarily to be confused with a heretical text) in proximity to Rolle material, *Pore Caitif* bears some resemblance to Oxford, Bodleian Library MS Laud Misc. 524, a priest's book which also excerpts *The Form of Living* and *Emendatio vitae*, together with an extract from Wyclif's *De mandatis divinis*.[82] Rachel Pyper has demonstrated the unlikelihood that the scribe knew he was copying Wycliffite material into the manuscript, noting that the existence of this compilation indicates that "interest in Wyclif's works was not confined to circles which were obviously unorthodox."[83] In other cases, though, compilers who combined Rolle material with heterodox texts clearly knew what they were dealing with. A copy of *The Form of Living* is included among several explicitly Wycliffite texts in Cambridge, Trinity College MS B.14.38, and another copy of the *Form* is bound with Wycliffite texts (together with texts of less obvious Wycliffite affiliation) in Oxford, Bodleian Library MS Bodley 938. There is furthermore reason to believe that similar patterns of readership and textual circulation were widespread in England, even after the promulgation of Arundel's *Constitutions* of 1407/9.[84]

To understand the apparent contradictions in the attraction Rolle held for the Lollards or pro-Wycliffites, as well as the appeal of some Lollard texts (recognized as such or not) for pious, orthodox readers, we must first understand that the environment in which such coupling took place seems to have exploded such polar distinctions as "orthodoxy" and "heterodoxy," or at least the use of such terms in any unequivocal sense. Walter Hilton's comments on heresy in his *Scale of Perfection* demonstrate how difficult it could be to tell the difference between a so-called heretic and what Hilton considered to be a true contemplative. Hilton composed the vernacular *Scale* for an anchoress (a certain "Goostli suster in Jhesu Crist"),[85] intending to furnish her with a detailed guide to the contemplative life. Yet Hilton betrays anxiety about his text getting into the wrong hands – or at least that corrupt forms of contemplation exist – in his efforts to distinguish the true contemplative from the false. On several occasions Hilton vents his frustration with "heretikes" – whether they are Lollards or not is unclear – whose characteristic trait of hypocrisy (they are the "whited sepulchers" of Matthew's Gospel) makes them hard to distinguish from the wretch, or "caytif," whose meekness, though expressed in private devotion, is genuine.[86] His perceived need to clarify the line between heretic and anchoress is an admission that Hilton's heretics have at least enough in common with the anchoritic life to prompt him to further define his audience. They (the heretics) are not true contemplatives (though they look like they are).

Indeed, it may have been with men like John Clanvowe in mind – a so-called "Lollard knight" – that Hilton scorned these hypocritical "contemplatives." A passage from Clanvowe's tract *The Two Ways* offers an instructive comparison by way of representing the complaint of someone on the receiving end of criticism like Hilton's:

swiche folke þat wolden fayne lyven meekeliche in þis world and ben out offe . . . riot, noise, and stryf, and lyuen symplely, and vsen to eten and drynken in mesure, and to clooþen hem meekely, and suffren paciently wroonges þat ooþere folke doon and seyn to hem, and hoolden hem apayed with lytel good of þis world, and desiren noo greet naame of þis world, ne no pris ther of, swiche folke þe world scoorneth and hooldeþ hem lolleris and loselis, foolis and schameful wrecches.[87]

No matter what critics like Hilton thought about it, then, the blurred line between contemplative and Lollard in late-medieval England – a line that was likely imposed or imagined rather than representative of contemporary groupings and patterns in textual circulation – facilitated the movement of mystical texts among Lollards (or Lollard sympathizers) and those who participated in other contemporary and coexisting forms of devotion. In fact, tracing the circulation of Clanvowe's tract *The Two Ways* reveals precisely the kind of coterie which read both kinds of text – anchoritic and pro-Lollard – and which included other possible Lollard knights. Clanvowe's *Two Ways* is not obviously a Lollard tract, even if it was written by someone who was suspected of being a Lollard knight.[88] The text has often been characterized as Lollard, though more for what it does not say than for what it does. It side-steps the staples of Wycliffite controversy – critiques of pilgrimage, ecclesiastical endowment, and so on – offering only to show how to avoid the broad way to hell and enter the narrow way to heaven. Clanvowe spends much of his time advocating the denial or moderation of worldly pleasure, and thus his text resonates with many of the wills of the period whose pronounced austerity was so fashionable among the Lollard knights, but also among men like the decidedly anti-Wycliffite Archbishop Thomas Arundel.[89] One wonders, in fact, whether those who suspected men like Clanvowe of Lollardy were really noticing that these figures lived what Walter Hilton himself called the "mixed life"[90] – an ambiguous category occupied by those who were attracted to eremitic contemplation, but who nevertheless chose to live in the world.

Notably, both extant copies of Clanvowe's tract are bound with Rolle material. Rolle's *Ego dormio*, *Commandment* and *Form of Living* appear with *The Two Ways* in the Simeon manuscript (London, British Library MS Add. 22283), and Oxford, University College MS 97 contains another copy of Rolle's *Form* together with Clanvowe's tract. The contents of this second manuscript overlap extensively with that of the Simeon and Vernon manuscripts and may derive from a common exemplar.[91] Oxford, University College MS 97 has also been traced to William Counter, a clerk of Sir William Beauchamp, and, as Jeremy Catto has suggested, it may have been in Beauchamp's library where Counter obtained some of the texts for his compilation, including perhaps Clanvowe's *Two Ways*.[92] Although the manuscript cannot be linked directly to Beauchamp (it appears to have been intended for Counter's private use), Beauchamp was a friend of Clanvowe's, and thus provides the clearest connection between the two men. Sir William was also – and more clearly than Clanvowe – a Lollard sympathizer, as is demonstrated by his probable patronage of the Lollard preacher Robert Lychlade. But he was also a devotee of the Name of Jesus: a missal which belonged to him, now Oxford, Trinity College MS 8, contains the first known copy of the Office of the Holy Name in English, composed during the revival of enthusiasm for Richard Rolle in the late fourteenth century.[93]

Richard Rolle's writings and devotional emphases appealed, then, to readers who found Wycliffite tenets compelling (as well as to many other completely orthodox readers), but who may have had flexible notions about what interest in Wyclif could mean. Rolle's widespread popularity in Lollard and affiliated circles (one commentator has called Rolle "the favourite reading of the Lollards")[94] means that Wycliffite transmission of this kind of material to Bohemia would be absolutely consistent with Lollard textual activity in England. It could also indicate, however, that diehard

Wycliffites were not exclusively responsible for transmitting this material to Prague. Just as scholars like Kathryn Kerby-Fulton have shown compellingly that Wycliffism never existed in a vacuum in England, unexposed to other contemporary devotional and reformist currents both at home and streaming from the continent,[95] so would it be reasonable to notice that English textual exchange with Bohemia was not the sole province of the Wycliffites and that Lollards themselves, an intricately varied group, transmitted non-Wycliffite texts.

To whose agency, then, do we attribute the transmission of the copy of Rolle's Lamentations commentary in PKMK D.12? In its manuscript context, the text may represent an additional instance of Wycliffite (or at least pro-Wycliffite) interest in Rolle – a significant discovery, which, if it can be demonstrated, would mark the first time the Lollards have been linked to Rolle's Latin (as opposed to his English) writings. Yet a Lollard connection is not absolutely granted. Although MS D.12 lists *Super threnos* in its table of contents as "Quoddam pulchrum et breve super [librum] Trenorum de Anglia allatum," the reference to its transmission does not rule out the possibility that the text was conveyed (for example) from England to Bohemia via Rome, perhaps in connection with Jenštejn. I have already shown that at least one of Rolle's texts, the *Incendium amoris*, circulated among early reformists in Bohemia and those who disputed Wyclif's doctrines as the native movement headed into the first decade of the fifteenth century. There is moreover nothing to suggest that Lollards or anyone else tampered with Rolle's Lamentations commentary as they did, for example, with his *English Psalter*: none of the variant readings in the D.12 copy of *Super threnos* is suspicious, and all of Rolle's discussions of the mystical experience and eremitic life have been retained.

While there is no direct evidence that Lollards were responsible for sending Rolle's *Super threnos* to Bohemia, the commentary is in character with the pervasive language of biblical lament found in complaint literature in England, which Lollards and their opponents in the fraternal orders (mainly the friars) increasingly adapted for use in their fierce controversies from *c.*1382 onward. The friars had long quoted or alluded to texts like Jeremiah 9.1 in the face of antimendicant attacks. "Quis dabit capiti," a poem which was probably written in response to Richard FitzRalph's earlier attacks on the friars in the mid-fourteenth century, opens with this verse, and the Franciscan John Pecham had earlier used it in his *Tractatus pauperis contra insipientem.* Similarly the poem "Sedens super flumina" – an "O and I" poem like "Quis dabit," and perhaps a companion to that poem – refers to the weeping by the waters of Babylon of Psalm 136.1.[96] If poems like "Quis dabit" and "Sedens" were composed during FitzRalph's disputes with the friars, they nevertheless maintained their relevance into the 1380s. Wyclif knew of "Sedens," once quoting from it in a sermon,[97] and new poems with the "O and I" refrain were produced at this time. The pro-Wycliffite author of "Heu quanta desolatio Angliae praestatur," a poem which Wendy Scase has situated among Wycliffite attempts to discredit the mendicants at Oxford in 1382,[98] similarly recalls Jeremiah weeping over Jerusalem (Jer. 12.11). The poet laments the destruction of England, where the religious (especially friars and monks) have grown corrupt and Christ is unknown. The sense is that the entire flock falters as a result of pastoral abuses:

> Clerici, qui speculum forent laycorum,
> In fastum cum libidine multi laxant lorum.
> Rectores iam rapiunt bona subditorum;
> Scitis quod hec omnia signa sunt dolorum.
>   Wyt a O and a I, hinc est mundus versus,
>   Qui luceret aliis, tenebris est mersus.[99]

[Many clergy, who should be the lay folks' mirror,
In disdain slacken the reins with wantonness.
Now rectors snatch the goods of their subordinates;
You know that all these things are signs of treachery.
   With an O and an I, hence the world is changed,
   That which should shine forth to others is sunken in shadows.]

A final example brings us to the verses on which Rolle specifically comments in *Super threnos*. The so-called *Lament of the pauperculi sacerdotes* (a text that also made it to Bohemia), beginning "Heu nobis peccatoribus," contains a protracted and previously unremarked passage taken directly from Lamentations 1.1–5, ascribed to Jeremiah, and it should be read, I suggest, as part of the lament tradition which I have just outlined.[100] The *Lament* decries the cruelty of the "lupi rapaces" who have imprisoned Christ's priests and have left England, the "civitas" of Lamentations 1.1, to suffer desolation in the absence of pastoral care. A lengthy accusation follows which exposes pastoral abuses, and the libel ends with the well-known militant claim about the large number of Lollards living in England who are prepared to advance the Wycliffite cause.

    Although none of the laments I have cited borrows directly from Rolle, *Super threnos* is, as I say above, at least consonant with the antimendicant and more broadly anticlerical polemic of Lollard and other complaints. Rolle's text comments on all five chapters of Lamentations, applying Jeremiah's lament to contemporary clerical abuses. The Church (and the soul) cries out for Christ, who has abandoned it as punishment for clerical corruption: "PRINCES, that is, pastors and rectors, HAVE BECOME LIKE RAMS THAT FIND NO PASTURE, for, wandering in the love of the world, they find no spiritual fodder in the Holy Scriptures [FACTI SUNT PRINCIPES ..., id est pastores et rectores, VELUD ARIETES NON INVENIENTES PASCUA, quia errantes in amore seculi, pabulum spirituale non inveniunt in scripturis sanctis]."[101] Rolle's criticism is directed not (as was Wyclif's) toward undermining the foundations of any particular mode of religious life (e.g., mendicant, monastic, etc.); he comments, rather, on the dissonance between scriptural injunctions and the abuses of those religious who have become too involved with worldly things, dragging the Church down with them in the process. "HOW DIM THE GOLD HAS BECOME," writes Rolle in Chapter four, "that is, the life of priests, once glorious in virtues, now made dim through worldly business [QUOMODO OBSCURATUM EST AURUM, id est, vita sacerdorum, quondam virtutibus gloriosa, nunc per negocia seculi obscurata]."[102]

A link between Rolle's text and other Lollard lament literature is uncertain, as both tap into wider complaint motifs. The most that can be claimed is that the resemblances between the two suggested themselves to the compiler of PKMK D.12, who made a similar association. *Super threnos* and "Heu quanta" were both copied into this manuscript, as were other texts which were used in the controversy against the mendicants in England.[103] I have discussed the ten-line antimendicant poem "Per decies quinos rapiat Sathanas Jacobinos" in the previous chapter. The English origin of that poem, while not certain, is suggested by its inclusion with "Heu quanta" and "Anglica regina" (one of the eulogies of Anne of Bohemia) – poems which both clearly came from England. The manuscript also contains an excerpt from the prophecies of Hildegard of Bingen. Significantly, Hildegard's prophecies had a long pedigree in antimendicant polemic, and in England Wyclif and his followers eventually picked up on her usefulness in their controversy with the friars.[104] Hildegard was of course already known in Bohemia, so it is not clear that this particular text was brought from England with the others.[105]

However, the D.12 compilation may reflect less the interests of any Lollard or other Englishman who dispatched polemical texts to Bohemia than the tastes of a Bohemian who could easily have found some of them on his own in England. "Heu quanta" seems initially to have circulated as a single vellum sheet, as attested by the only surviving copy of the poem to be found in England. A sheet containing the poem has been sewn sideways into Oxford, Bodleian Library MS Digby 98.[106] As I discuss in the previous chapter, the eulogy "Anglica regina" (which has no connection to mendicant controversy) was openly displayed on or near the tomb of Anne of Bohemia at Westminster Abbey, and was easily accessed by anyone who wished to copy it. The circulation history of "Per decies quinos" is unknown, but that poem, too, could have circulated in a more ephemeral form than the codex. The texts could then have been arranged according to the interests of the Bohemian compiler, not sent as a coherent group by some Lollard correspondent.

On the weight of evidence, it is nevertheless probable that *Super threnos* was transmitted to Bohemia not through Rome, or in connection with Jenštejn, but more directly from England by someone who was interested in Wycliffism and other aspects of English religiosity. This person (or at least a later reader) was likely a friend of the prominent reformer Jakoubek of Stříbro, to whom, according to the colophon on the final pastedown, the manuscript was given.[107] Jakoubek was probably known to at least one Lollard, Richard Wyche, who seems to mention him in a letter to Jan Hus in 1410, discussed in the next chapter.

No precise link can be made between copies of Rolle's texts and known instances of Lollard–Hussite textual transmission, but some additional details are worth noting. First, Rolle's Lamentations commentary is not the only one of his writings to appear among heterodox texts in Bohemian manuscripts. I have already mentioned the copy of the *Incendium* in ÖNB 4483, but the presence of that text in Bohemia is of course attributable to Jenštejn at the end of the fourteenth century. Additionally, however, Rolle's *Emendatio vitae* appears in PKMK MS B.6.3, a manuscript which also includes several of Wyclif's texts. The *Emendatio* is another one of Rolle's writings to display a fervent devotion to the Holy Name. It intricately parallels Rolle's extremely popular *Form of Living*, both of which texts were known to circulate with Lollard material in England.[108]

These associations between readership and variable shades of piety and reformism, while only suggestive, point to a circle of readers resembling that of Sir William Beauchamp, who, as I have mentioned, read Rolle's texts and was deeply devoted to the Holy Name. He was also an associate of John Clanvowe, a fellow Lollard knight (at least by reputation) whose *Two Ways* circulated with Rolle's *Form of Living* and other writings of the English hermit. As patron of Kemerton, furthermore, Beauchamp was probably instrumental in securing a living there for the Lollard preacher Robert Lychlade in 1401. His associations with other suspect Lollards are borne out elsewhere. In 1402 he was an executor for the will of Anne Latimer, widow of a Lollard knight from Braybrook, Sir Thomas Latimer. Other executors included yet another Lollard knight, Sir Lewis Clifford, along with the Braybrook parson and notorious Lollard Robert Hoke, as well as Philip Repingdon, who had abjured his Lollardy in 1382.

It seems to be more than a coincidence, then, that in 1406–7, two Bohemian students, Mikuláš Faulfiš and Jiří of Kněhnice, in an effort to obtain authoritative copies of a number of Wyclif's texts in England, made several stops in places which were associated with many of the figures I have just mentioned. One of their stops was at Braybrook, the home of Robert Hoke, where they copied Wyclif's *De dominio divino*. They moved from there to Kemerton, where they may have met the Lollard preacher Robert Lychlade.[109] In Kemerton they copied Wyclif's *De ecclesia*; earlier they had also copied *De veritate sacre scripture* at Oxford, where Hoke and Lychlade still maintained contacts.[110]

The temptation, of course, is to attribute any text that made its way to Bohemia to the efforts of Faulfiš and Kněhnice. Their activities, as I discuss in Chapter 3, are known to modern scholars in greater detail than those of anyone else involved in the transmission of texts to Prague, but surely there must have been many other couriers or colporteurs passing between the two regions during this period. What I mean to suggest is not that these two Bohemian students were necessarily responsible for carrying some of Rolle's texts to Bohemia, but that their contacts in England may at least be attributable to networks similar to those I have outlined – networks which included fervent Lollards, but also moderates like Beauchamp, who also nourished an ardent devotion to the Holy Name. In other words, the possible acquaintance between the Bohemian students and the others I have mentioned (Lollard knights, Wycliffite preachers, devotees of the Holy Name and so on) may be *symptomatic* of similar associations in cases for which we have less evidence. It is perhaps significant that some of the later correspondents of the knight and Lollard John Oldcastle – a less circumspect man than Beauchamp or Clanvowe – were men who might be regarded as a pair of "Hussite knights." These men (discussed in the next chapter) surface in defenses of Wyclif in the years before the Council of Constance, as well as in a protest against the Council's treatment and execution of Jan Hus. The origin of Oldcastle's acquaintance with these knights is unknown, but perhaps he knew of them from earlier ties between the Bohemian and English courts.

The context of some of Richard Rolle's texts in Bohemian manuscripts, then, brings us a step closer to understanding the nature of the Lollard–Hussite exchange by situating that relationship within a more nuanced and fluid model of devotion and reform in Bohemia and England. As I have suggested in this chapter, we should be cautious not to characterize each of the participants in this network of correspondents as men or women who

necessarily subscribed to the most extreme tenets of Wyclif's doctrine. Some
may not have been Lollard sympathizers at all.

What might the implications of this last point be, then, for our consideration of the possibility, as stated by John Foxe, "that the Bohemians
comming in wyth [Anne of Bohemia], or resorting into thys realme after
her, perused and receiued heere the bookes of Iohn Wickleffe, which
afterward they conueied into Bohemia"?[111] Perhaps a detail from another
text by John Clanvowe can offer some help. Clanvowe, like Chaucer, wrote
a poem which likely alludes to Queen Anne of Bohemia.[112] In the *Boke of
Cupide*, a work which shares much in common with Chaucer's *Parliament
of Fowls* and with the F Prologue to the *Legend of Good Women*, Clanvowe
tells of a quarreling group of birds which agrees to resolve its dispute in the
queen's presence:

> And this shal be, withouten any nay,
> The morowe of Seynt Valentynes day,
> Vnder the maple that is feire and grene,
> Before the chambre wyndow of the Quene
> At Wodestok, vpon the grene lay.[113]

Allusions of this kind are not automatically to be read as sure signs of
patronage by Queen Anne, or even as evidence that the queen knew
Clanvowe or his work. Yet Clanvowe and several of the Lollard knights,
like the small group of Bohemians in Anne's entourage, remained close to
the Ricardian court. It would be surprising if some interaction did not take
place between them. The allusion to the queen in Clanvowe's poem – and the
possibility of their acquaintance which it insinuates – adds to the growing
number of suggestions, outlined above, that some of the texts which made
their way from England to Prague may have done so in connection with
figures whose piety resembled that of the Lollard knights, many of whom, like
Anne, also fostered or represented fashionable currents of devotion. Whoever
was responsible for conveying these texts, certainly several Bohemian compilations of Rollean and Wycliffite material would have been quite at home in
the libraries of some high-profile courtiers in England.

CHAPTER 3

Conveying heresy: texts, tidings, and the formation of a Lollard–Hussite fellowship

Salutat Christi ecclesia de Boemia ecclesiam Christi in Anglia, optans esse particeps confessionis sancte fidei in gracia domini Ihesu Christi.[1]

[The church of Christ from Bohemia salutes the church of Christ in England, desiring to be a sharer of the profession of the holy faith in the grace of the Lord Jesus Christ.]

On June 16, 1410, churchmen who had gathered at the archiepiscopal court in Prague sang a *Te Deum* with a great din and, in what must have seemed a mockery to many in the city, rang the bells solemnly as was customary for a funeral.[2] This odd liturgical combination marked the burning of John Wyclif's books. Cast as a joyful death, the occasion which would (it was hoped) put an end to the proliferation of Wycliffism in the region was at the same time a dangerous provocation to proponents of the Englishman's teachings in Bohemia.

The tension must have been palpable during those few minutes when the sombre sound of bells rang out over Prague. Immediately following the book-burning, many of Wyclif's most vocal proponents in the city began to mobilize for what would be the first major disputation of Wyclif at the university. Jan Hus initiated the proceedings on July 27 with a defense of Wyclif's *De Trinitate*; the next day Jakoubek of Stříbro defended the *Decalogus* (or *De mandatis divinis*), followed on July 29 by Šimon of Tišnov, who defended Wyclif's *De probatione propositionum*. On the following day, Jan of Jičín defended *De materia et forma*; Prokop of Plzeň defended *De ideis* on July 31; and Zdislav of Zvířetice made his defense of *De universalibus* on August 6.[3] Clearly many of Wyclif's texts had escaped the flames earlier that summer.

Yet those who might presume that the protest was the rarefied business of theologians would be mistaken. Even the prospect of the book-burning aroused fears of what such measures might provoke. The day before the conflagration, masters and doctors of the university in Prague had convened to protest Archbishop Zbyněk's impending action, urging the king to restrain the metropolitan "ne exinde confusio toti Regno, Domino Regi et universitati inferatur [lest confusion be inflicted on the whole kingdom, the Lord King, and the university]."[4] Václav IV seems to have taken the warning seriously, initially convincing Zbyněk to hold off with his sentence until Jošt, the Margrave of Moravia, could arrive. For whatever reason, the archbishop did not wait for the margrave, but peremptorily ordered the books to be burned.[5]

Later chroniclers' reports affirm just how prescient the warning of the previous day had been. According to the *Old Czech Chronicle*:

> There was a great riot and dispute about [the burning of Wyclif's books]. Some said that many other books were burned besides Wyclif's, and for that reason the people rioted in these times; and most of the king's courtiers, and with them all the commoners in Prague, [fought] against the canons and the priests; but some adhered to the canons, and others to Master Hus, so that among themselves they composed disparaging songs about each other. And from that time a great loathing arose among the people.[6]

Some of these "disparaging songs," like the following verses, have managed to survive:

> Sbyněk biskup abeceda
> spálil kniehy, a nevěda,
> co je v nich napsáno.[7]

> [Zbyněk, "bishop ABCD,"
> burned the books, and didn't know
> what was written in them.]

The Old Czech Chronicler was at a loss to explain the popular reaction; his best guess was to suggest that other books must have been ignited along with Wyclif's: why else would so many people care about the books of an English theologian?

The chronicler was at least correct, I think, to suggest that the popular and violent protest was not about Wyclif's books per se. For one thing, the debate over Wycliffite doctrine had become associated with the longstanding rivalry between Czech- and German-speaking Bohemians, a rivalry which bled into economic and political discrepancies in Prague, and was the source of frequent conflict.[8] That said, at this stage of the controversy there was scarcely any attempt to understand the proliferation of, and enthusiasm for, Wyclif's doctrines in Bohemia as stemming in part from an ongoing trade in Wycliffite texts from England, a trafficking that by 1410 had become increasingly regular and efficient. Ondřej of Brod, for example, had warned Zbyněk just a few years earlier that Wyclif's texts were multi-plying in his jurisdiction, but he discussed the problem as a purely arch-diocesan issue.[9] The books were in Bohemia: that was all that mattered.

Moreover, as this chapter shows, the texts themselves – and the material circumstances of their transmission to Bohemia – were only part of the story: through the efforts of Jan Hus and his associates, Wycliffite objects from England had become linked to the *idea* of Wyclif, the *Doctor Evangelicus*, fueling enthusiasm for the Hussites' continued correspondence with active proponents of Wyclif's doctrines in England. Shaped and communicated in ways that maximized accessibility – through sermons, anecdotes, translations, and physical objects – the Bohemian fellowship with English Wycliffites took on a life of its own, spilling out of the halls of the Carolinum, and into the streets. As I argue, the popularization of Wyclif in Prague went hand-in-hand with continued Bohemian communication with English Lollards. And as a result, Wyclif gained a broad, though posthumous, base of support for the first time outside of England. This chapter explains the paradox of Wyclif's popular appeal in Bohemia by examining the materiality of Lollard–Hussite communication and the ways in which a wider significance was attached to this material exchange in Prague.

THE NETWORK EXPANDS

Tidings from Prague traveled fast. At some point during the 1410 contro-versy surrounding Wyclif's books, Hussite messengers departed for England, and within a very short time some of Wyclif's English followers were briefed on the situation in Bohemia. Richard Wyche and John Oldcastle both dispatched letters back to Prague on September 8, 1410, sent from London and Cooling Castle (Kent), respectively.[10] Wyche's letter is addressed to Jan Hus, and Oldcastle's to Voksa of Valdštejn (or alter-natively to Zdislav of Zvířetice). The letters are largely hortatory, expressing solidarity with the Bohemians and encouraging them to persevere in their struggles for reform. There has been some debate about which Bohemian events the authors had in mind,[11] because their apocalyptic and generalizing language tends to couch topical references in terms of spiritual warfare.[12] It is nevertheless likely that the authors had a general familiarity with the increasing pressures that the Archbishop of Prague was exerting on Hus and the other reformers in the period leading up to and through the summer of 1410.[13]

Oldcastle and Wyche both describe the messengers (plural) who brought news of the events in Prague to them. Wyche writes, "Gavisus sum valde

venientibus dilectissimis mihi fratribus et testimonium perhibentibus ver-
itati vestre, quomodo et vos in veritate ambulatis [I greatly rejoiced when
dearest brothers came to me and bore witness of your truth, how you are
also walking in the truth]."[14] Oldcastle similarly writes, "Gracias ago domino meo, qui, ut audivi per quosdam veritatis amatores, cor vestrum
animavit ad zelandum et certandum pro iusticia legis dei [I thank my
Lord, who, as I have heard from certain lovers of truth, has inspired your
heart to pursue and struggle on behalf of the righteousness of God's law]."[15]
The language they use to describe the messengers (particularly Oldcastle's
"lovers of truth") approaches what has been characterized as a Lollard "sect
vocabulary," which consisted of commonplace terms like "trewe men" or
"trewe prest" that appear so often in Lollard texts.[16] Elsewhere, in a letter
from Oldcastle to Václav IV, Oldcastle similarly refers to "veros Christi
sacerdotes."[17] Not enough examples of Lollard–Hussite correspondence
survive to determine whether this kind of vocabulary forms a consistent
pattern, but it is interesting to imagine that correspondents from both
countries were using a common terminology, unique to them.

The messengers must have informed Wyche that Hus was central to the
reformist movement in Prague, if indeed Wyche was not already aware of
the fact. They also gave him the impression that "Jacobellus," undoubtedly
Jakoubek of Stříbro, was central to the movement there.[18] Both of
Oldcastle's addressees were members of the Bohemian nobility, and thus
of equal status with Sir John. They can also be traced to reformist activities
on a number of occasions. Zdislav's connection with Hus, and with the
Bohemian reform movement, is well established in the sources. Hus con-
ferred the degree of Bachelor of Arts on Zdislav in 1405.[19] Zdislav appears
often in connection with Hus during the summer of 1410, for instance in the
defense of Wyclif in July and August of that year, when both Hus and
Zdislav delivered defenses of Wyclif's texts. Just after Archbishop Zbyněk
burned the books, the so-called *Chronicon Universitatis Pragensis* also
reports that "Magister Johannes Hus et dominus Sdislaus de Zwierzeticz
cum sibi adherentibus appellaverunt [Master John Hus and Lord Zdislav of
Zvířetice appealed with their adherents]" in protest of the archbishop's
actions, and on July 18 Zbyněk excommunicated this same group of
appellants.[20]

Hus and Zdislav, then, were clearly associates. But what of Zdislav and
Voksa? Later documents suggest that they were at least acquaintances. Their
names appear next to each other in a letter signed by the nobles of Bohemia and
Moravia on September 2, 1415 in protest of Jan Hus' death at the Council
of Constance. Three days later, their names again appear in sequence on a

pact to protect free preaching of the Gospel and condemning unjust excommunications.[21] The connection of either of these men to John Oldcastle, however, is not possible to confirm independently of Oldcastle's letter, and Oldcastle may only have heard of them through the Bohemian messengers that visited him in 1410.

The network that linked Wyche and Oldcastle to the Bohemian reformers appears to have been expansive, as is suggested by the transmission of four letters written by the Scottish preacher Quentin Folkhyrde, which also reached Bohemia after they were written in 1410.[22] Folkhyrde's letters demonstrate that he held Wycliffite views, and they attracted enough interest in Bohemia to be translated into Czech, a point to which I shall return below. Adding another party to our growing group of correspondents proffers no new information about who might have delivered these letters (or about whether all of them were carried by the same messengers), but this detail at least suggests that the network of relations among heretics was not restricted to England and Bohemia. This possibility was certainly the concern of Dietrich von Niem, who writes in his *Avisamenta* (1414) of the

multi clerici et laici a vera via deviantes quorundam hereticorum, scilicet quondam Johannis Wiclevi precipue, errorem et hereses secuntur, prout palam est in regno Boemie, Moravia, Anglia et Scocia necnon diversis aliis provinciis et regnis.[23]

[many clerics and laymen deviating from the true path, following the errors and heresies of certain heretics, especially of course of the late John Wyclif, as is plainly the case in the kingdom of Bohemia, in Moravia, in England, and in Scotland, as well as in various other provinces and kingdoms.]

The same year, Jean Gerson similarly complained that heretics had caused tremendous damage in England and Prague, and had even infiltrated Scotland.[24]

A later connection between Scotland and Bohemia is also attested when the Bohemian doctor Pavel Kravař visited Scotland in 1433, only to be put to death at St. Andrews "on being found an obstinate heretic."[25] I am not aware of any evidence that Kravař journeyed to England or Scotland prior to this fateful visit, and thus that he ever conveyed texts by English or Scottish hands into Bohemia. However, his name appears in 1415 in the *Liber procuratorum* of the "English Nation" at the University of Paris.[26] This detail alone tells us little about his associations with students from Scotland or England there (students from Central Europe were commonly included under the *nacio Anglicana*, together with students from Scotland and Ireland), though it is suggestive of a more substantial connection. Several years earlier, in fact, prominent Czech scholars of the pre-Hussite reform – men like Vojtěch Raňkův, Matěj of Janov, and Jan of Jenštejn – had also been members of the English Nation at Paris.[27] Raňkův's controversial enthusiasm for the writings of Richard FitzRalph, Archbishop of Armagh, had earned him a reputation in Paris as another "Armachanus."[28] At one point he seems to have taught at Oxford, and made provisions to fund Czech students attending the English university after establishing a scholarship for Bohemian students from Czech-speaking families to study either at Oxford or Paris.[29] It seems safe to say, therefore, that at Paris, scholars from Central Europe were not just grouped with peers from England and its vicinity for the sake of tidy record-keeping: they interacted in more meaningful ways than that. In light of this precedent, there is good reason to believe that Kravař's trip to Scotland several years later was prompted by at least the suspicion that he would find men of like sympathies there.

On the subject of identifying couriers who moved between England and Bohemia in particular, it has long been known that two Bohemian students who studied at Oxford from 1406–7, Mikuláš Faulfiš and Jiří of Kněhnice, personally brought their own transcriptions of at least three of Wyclif's works to Bohemia in 1407, his *De veritate sacre scripture, De dominio divino* and *De ecclesia*.[30] Aeneas Silvius (later Pius II), writing about fifty years after the event, knew something of this trafficking and mentioned it in his *Historia Bohemica* (1458).[31] Aeneas is partially correct when he attributes certain transcriptions of Wyclif's writings to Faulfiš, but he clearly under-estimated the extent to which Wyclif's writings had already made significant inroads in Bohemia by the time Faulfiš became involved.

Many of Wyclif's teachings were already known in Bohemia by 1407, despite their initial chilly reception there. The earliest evidence of the reception of Wyclif's doctrines in Prague comes from when Wyclif was still alive. Mikuláš Biceps, a Bohemian Dominican, attacked Wyclif's Eucharistic doctrine not long before 1380, though this could only mean that Biceps was aware of the teaching, not that he had actually seen any of Wyclif's works.[32] In 1385, Jan of Jenštejn wrote of "that most wicked heresiarch Wyclif" in his tract *De consideratione*, which he dedicated to Urban VI.[33] The reference comes in the context of a defense of ecclesiastical temporalities, and Jenštejn perhaps had Wyclif's *De civili dominio* (but certainly his doctrine of dominion) in mind. As with Biceps, Jenštejn may only have heard about Wyclif's doctrines indirectly, rather than actually having read any of them. Jenštejn, as I say above, had studied at Paris, where some of Wyclif's texts were eventually known. And yet Jenštejn was only at Paris in 1373, several years before Wyclif's *De civili dominio* seems to have become known there *c.*1381 (not to mention, before Wyclif even wrote it).

Another possibility, I suggest, is that Jenštejn discussed Wyclif's writings on dominion with the English Benedictine Adam Easton while the two men were in Rome. Easton, whose associations with Jenštejn I have outlined in Chapter 2, was involved in compiling the list of Wyclif's articles which Gregory XI condemned in 1377 – almost all nineteen of them taken from *De civili dominio*.[34] Meanwhile, Easton was busy working on his vast *Defensorium ecclesiastice potestatis*, which he completed sometime between 1378 and 1381, and dedicated to Urban VI. The *Defensorium*, a sweeping study of the history of *dominium*, is set up as a dialogue between *Rex* (a secular representative) and *Episcopus* (the voice of orthodoxy), and includes lengthy citations from Wyclif's *De civili dominio*.[35] Just a few years after Easton completed the treatise, he and Jenštejn both became involved in composing texts for the Feast of the Visitation of the Blessed Virgin. Their conversations in Rome (if indeed they met) could conceivably have ranged over other topics like Wyclif's controversial doctrine of dominion, a topic in which they shared a common interest.

Wyclif's doctrines began to receive a warmer reception in Prague during the 1390s, when Jan Hus and others first encountered Wyclif's metaphysical texts.[36] Not long afterward, Jerome of Prague was at Oxford (*c*.1399–1401) and later claimed to have returned to Prague with Wyclif's *Dialogus, Trialogus* and two other texts on the Eucharist which he does not specify.[37] Considering the sheer volume of Wyclif's texts in Bohemian manuscripts, however, there must have been additional couriers or ad hoc conveyors who left no trace of their identities. Frequent travel between England and Bohemia was possible at least in principle. I have mentioned other instances of travel in the preceding chapters. During the Anglo-Bohemian marriage negotiations of 1381, furthermore, Richard II and Václav IV agreed to permit widespread cultural interaction between England and the lands of the Holy Roman Empire, and with little attempt at regulation.[38] Though most of the exchanges discussed in the present chapter took place long after the marriage alliance was formed, travel between the two regions would likely have had a great deal of precedent by the early fifteenth century, with trade routes and mercantile ships acting perhaps as conduits for other types of exchange.

The last known instance that must have resulted in the transmission of Wycliffite texts to Bohemia was *c*.1414, when Peter Payne fled England for Prague. It comes as some surprise, however, that during his long career in Bohemian religious politics (he died in Prague *c*.1455) Payne left no trace of continued contact with the English Lollards.[39] During the time when he was arguably the face of Wyclif in Bohemia after 1414,[40] moreover, the place of Wycliffite doctrine in the Bohemian reform became a point of serious internal contention as the movement increasingly fell into bitter factional disputes and came under the influence of a burgeoning sense of Bohemian national self-consciousness. The Lollard–Hussite exchange seems not to have continued with any regularity after Payne's arrival, and Hus' roughly contemporaneous execution at Constance in 1415 ended the life of one of the Lollards' most active contacts. As a result of these circumstances, Payne's career in Bohemia remains largely outside the present study mainly because his arrival and the events at Constance marked a clear turning point in the role and perception of Wyclif in Bohemia, and in the centrality of Lollard–Hussite relations.[41]

"A CERTAYNE STUDENT" AND THE LOLLARD–HUSSITE FELLOWSHIP

From the foregoing survey of the networks involved in Lollard–Hussite correspondence, one figure stands out, not because his contributions were necessarily more influential or even more extensive than others, but because we have more information about him than anyone else. The activities of the Bohemian student Mikuláš Faulfiš (sometimes discussed in medieval sources with Jiří of Knĕhnice) provide a valuable lens into the extent and character of the Lollard–Hussite alliance because he appears with more frequency and in greater detail than other couriers in documents which attest to the exchange. His interactions also provide a model that might have been followed by others who likewise traveled and conveyed texts between the two countries.

The role of Faulfiš in spreading Wyclif's doctrines assumed a prominent position in later Catholic and Protestant historiography from England and the continent. John Foxe, drawing on Aeneas Silvius' *Historia Bohemica*,[42] wrote of "a certayne student of the country of Bohemia" who carried Wyclif's works from Oxford to Prague, though there is no indication that Foxe knew the student's name (or that he was aware of his partner, Jiří of Knĕhnice).[43] This is no surprise, since Foxe's source refers to Faulfiš only as "vir quidam genere nobilis ex domo, quam Putridi Piscis vocant [a certain man of noble birth of the house called 'Rotten Fish']." Foxe, a capable Latinist, probably considered this to be an instance of base punning at the student's expense (a not entirely inaccurate assumption!); unaware that "Putridi Piscis" was a calque on the student's actual name (Faulfiš, pronounced "foul fish"),[44] Foxe sanitized the account for his own purposes by removing the derogatory reference. Like Aeneas, Foxe seems to attribute much of Hus' knowledge of Wycliffite doctrine to the efforts of this

Bohemian student. Hus, "hauing familiaritie with this yong man," writes Foxe, came to peruse the Wycliffite texts that the student brought from England. He then "tooke such pleasure and fruit in reading therof, that not onely he began to defend this author openly in the schooles, but also in his sermons."[45] For later commentators – and in contrast to the intelligence in Prague *c*.1410, mentioned earlier – the role of the courier at this stage of the relationship was as central as that of Wyclif's more prominent popularizer, Jan Hus.

Even if Faulfiš was not the first to introduce Wyclif's works to Bohemia as Aeneas and Foxe believed, his contribution to the Bohemian reform movement was clearly significant. Hus himself mentions Faulfiš twice, the first time in a Czech vernacular *postilla* for the first Sunday in Lent[46] and the second, according to Peter of Mladoňovice, during his trial at the Council of Constance in 1415 (Hus does not seem to have known Kněhnice very well, if at all).[47] To my knowledge, in fact, Hus never mentions Faulfiš except in the context of his interactions with the English.

In addition to conveying transcriptions of Wyclif's *De veritate sacre scripture, De dominio divino* and *De ecclesia* in 1407, Faulfiš and Kněhnice are credited with transmitting other items to Prague as well. An anonymous group of Wyclif's supporters at Oxford, one of whom may have been Peter Payne, gave the students a testimonial letter of Wyclif to bring back with them. The testimonial, affixed with the chancellor's seal, claimed that Wyclif was upstanding, that he was a most accomplished scholar and teacher of Scripture and that he had never been condemned or posthumously burned as a heretic.[48] This was the same document which Jerome of Prague would exhibit repeatedly in Prague, and for which he and Hus would be interrogated in the following years. Jerome may have alluded to Faulfiš or Kněhnice during his trial at Constance when he explained how he came to possess a copy of the testimony in the first place. It seems to have come into his hands during Matěj of Knín's quodlibetal disputation of 1409 when, as we learn from the record of Jerome's trial in Vienna the next year, Jerome rounded off his *recommendatio* of Wyclif's books to the young students by displaying the Oxford letter.[49] According to the *Acta* of Jerome's trial at Constance in 1416, a student (possibly Faulfiš or Kněhnice) had handed the document to Jerome during the 1409 disputation.[50]

The testimonial letter was used repeatedly in Prague as a kind of visual aid, and the polemicists who displayed it often drew attention to its appended seal in order to corroborate what they wanted to say about Wyclif with an authenticating sign. As I discuss more fully in the next chapter, the text was initially effective in countering charges of Wyclif's heresy: if he was the heresiarch he was said to be, then why were his bones still buried, not cremated, as was the practice for heretics? In addition to the testimonial letter – and as if to punctuate its message – Faulfiš and Knĕhnice are likewise said to have brought back another piece of tangible testimony to the "real" Wyclif, namely, a piece of his tomb "quam postea Pragae pro reliquiis venerabantur et habebant [which afterwards the Praguers venerated and regarded as relics]."[51] As I shall discuss, the students' involvement in conveying texts and "relics" to Prague represents only a small part of their level of engagement with English Wycliffism, though an involvement which indicates that Wyclif had attained a degree of celebrity in Bohemia. But did all of this interaction really take place on a single trip, between 1406 and 1407? Could either student have had a hand in other instances of exchange, for example, in conveying the letters sent by Wyche, Oldcastle and perhaps Folkhyrde to Bohemia in 1410?

In order to determine who was traveling between England and Bohemia *c.*1410, I will clarify (to the extent that it is possible) some details surrounding the materials they carried, beginning with evidence from a reply that Jan Hus sent to Richard Wyche in 1411, and then drawing on other instances of correspondence.[52] The process of reconstructing the itineraries of Hussite couriers, however, is more than an exercise in matching texts with dates, names, and specific locations; it is also about telling a story of human inter-action among people from disparate regions who have come to hold common convictions, and about the dramatic repercussions of their communication.

There are some interesting details in one of the two surviving manu-scripts containing Hus' reply to Richard Wyche, details that, in addition to an ambiguous reference to transcripts allegedly sent by Wyche, also include a reference to two other men, a "Symon" and a "Nicolaus." There is substantial variation between the closing lines of the two copies of Hus' letter.[53] The letter from PNK XI.E.3, fols. 112[v]–113[r], reads:

Valde gavisus sum et omnes, qui diligimus evangelium, quod Tua Caritas se benigne nobis exhibuit, nos salubriter informando. Dominus rex noster, tota curia sua, regina, barones et communis populus sunt pro verbo Jesu Christi. Salutat ecclesia Christi de Bohemia ecclesiam Christi in Anglia, optans esse particeps confessionis sanctae fidei in gratia domini Jesu Christi. Deus gloriosus sit merces vestra, quod tantis laboribus exempla nobis egentibus ministrasti. Pax vobis, quae superat omnem sensum. Amen.[54]

[I greatly rejoiced, together with all who love the Gospel, that your love kindly showed itself to us, guiding us profitably. Our lord the king, all his court, the queen, barons and the common people are in favor of the Word of Jesus Christ. The church of Christ from Bohemia salutes the church of Christ in England, desiring to be a sharer of the profession of the holy faith in the grace of the Lord Jesus Christ. May Glorious God be your reward, that through such great labors, you have supplied examples to us who need them. Peace to you, which passes all understanding. Amen.]

However, even in this version of the letter, a slightly different translation is allowable. The sentence "Deus gloriosus sit merces vestra, quod tantis laboribus exempla nobis egentibus ministrasti" can also be translated: "May Glorious God be your reward, that through such great labors, *you have supplied the transcripts to us who need them.*"[55] Certainly "exempla" would not have been the most obvious choice for designating "transcripts" (though it was a possible definition);[56] however, my alternative reading is supported by the strikingly different version of Hus' letter, from PNK Cim D.79 (formerly Stará Boleslav C.132), fols. 155ʳ–156ᵛ, which contains some notable details (italicized below) that are not attested in PNK XI.E.3:

Valde gavisus sum et omnes, qui diligimus ewangelium, quod tua caritas se benignum nobis exhibuit, nos salubriter informando. *De aliis Nicolaus, cui scribunt, faciet mencionem. Litere portate sunt nobis primo in 2 dominica ieiunii, quia Symon fuit in Vngaria cum eis.* Dominus rex noster totaque curia sua, regina, barones et communis populus sunt pro verbo Ihesu Christi. Salutat Christi ecclesia de Boemia ecclesiam Christi in Anglia, optans esse particeps confessionis sancte fidei in gracia domini Ihesu Christi. Deus graciosus sit merces vestra, quod tantis laboribus *exemplaria* nobis egentibus ministrastis. Pax vobis, que exsuperat omnem sensum. Amen.[57]

[I greatly rejoiced, together with all who love the gospel, that your love kindly showed itself to us, guiding us profitably. *Nicholas, to whom they are writing, shall make mention about other things. The letter was first brought to us on the second Sunday of Lent, because Simon was in Hungary with it.* Our lord the king and all his court, the queen, barons, and the common people are in favor of the Word of Jesus Christ. The church of Christ from Bohemia salutes the church of Christ in England, desiring to be a sharer of the profession of the holy faith in the grace of the Lord Jesus Christ. May Gracious God be your reward, that through such great labors, you have supplied the *transcripts* to us who need them. Peace to you, which passes all understanding. Amen.]

As Anne Hudson has argued, the additional details found in this second manuscript seem purposely cryptic, revealing only as much as the parties privy to the exchanges would need to know, while allowing them to understand its references by filling in the gaps with their mutual knowledge.[58] Examined individually, we need not attribute the variants to anything more than scribal oversight. In fact, the simplest explanation could be that the scribe for the less detailed version saw the topical references in PNK

Cim D.79 as hindrances to the potential longevity of the letter, references which later readers would find irrelevant. But Ockham's razor need not be our only guiding principle here, and the harder explanations are worth considering.

The omission of the only two sentences that contain specific references to people and correspondence (other than Hus and Wyche, whose identities are clear throughout) and the alteration of "exemplaria" to "exempla" (though, again, not surprising when taken on its own), are suspicious when seen in the aggregate. When these details are absent, Hus' epistle is innocuous, implicating only Hus and Wyche (though with nothing more than the fact that they are in contact), while the other implicates several parties who are specifically integral to textual transmission, thereby justifying the exclusion of some potentially damaging details. No matter which explanation is correct, the fuller version of Hus' letter in PNK Cim D.79 must be closer to the exemplar, while the version in PNK XI.E.3 is perhaps a later copy with significant abridgments. It furthermore seems clear that Wyche sent more than just a letter to Jan Hus. The possible valences of *exemplarium* are significantly narrower than those of *exemplum*, with *exemplarium* designating primarily a copy or transcript, not a moral example.[59]

Less clear is whether the statement "May Gracious God be your reward, that through such great labors, you have supplied the transcripts [exemplaria] to us who need them" implies that Hus requested the transcripts,[60] or indeed that Wyche volunteered them. No record of any previous correspondence between the two men survives, though if there had been such a request, it need not have been conveyed in writing. The reference to "nobis egentibus" in Hus' letter may also suggest, if not a request, at least the perception of a previous lack on Hus' part. After all, we do know of an earlier attempt to attain more accurate copies of Wyclif's works – as opposed to texts yet unknown in Prague – when Faulfiš and Kněhnice made their rounds of England in 1406–7.[61] In any case, it is entirely reasonable to think that after Archbishop Zbyněk's book-burning in the summer of 1410, "exemplaria" (of Wyclif's writings that were already known in Bohemia, for example) would have been sought from the English Wycliffites.

It would be rash speculation to suggest that Hus was referring to the letters sent by Quentin Folkhyrde, since we have no idea whether Wyche or Hus had anything to do with Folkhyrde, and it also seems unlikely that letters would be called "exemplaria."[62] However, Wyche did write an earlier letter from prison, which was brought somehow to Prague and now survives in the same manuscript as a sermon by William Taylor from 1406, as well as several works attributed to Wyclif.[63] Professor Hudson has suggested two possibilities that could account for the delivery of these documents to Prague: they may have been brought by Faulfiš and Kněhnice after their stay at Oxford from 1406–7, or Peter Payne could have brought them in person when he fled England around 1414.[64] Another possibility, however, is that these documents were sent with the letters by Wyche, Oldcastle, and perhaps Folkhyrde in 1410.

In fact, the more one digs, the larger the number of texts that were likely conveyed to Bohemia *c.*1410–11 seems to become. Elsewhere Hus again indicates that he has received documents from England and that they arrived with Wyche's letter. Our source for the reference is Štěpán Páleč, who, in an attack on Hus' *De ecclesia*, quotes directly from one of Hus' letters (now regrettably lost). Hus, writing to one of his friends, remarks:

Habeo literas de Anglia et presertim unam bonam epistolam, quam fidelibus Christi et specialiter michi scripsit Richardus Witz, presbyter Magistri Johannis Wicleff, confortando nos, ut sine advertencia censure fulminacionum predicemus efficaciter verbum dei.[65]

[I have letters from England and especially one good letter, which Richard Wyche, a priest of Master John Wyclif, wrote to Christ's faithful, and especially to me, comforting us, [saying] that without attending to the lightning of ecclesiastical censure, we zealously proclaim the word of God.]

It is tempting to speculate that these other letters – which may have been "open" letters, rather than having been addressed to anyone in particular – included those written by Folkhyrde or even Wyche's earlier letter from prison. Folkhyrde's letters are not all addressed to specific people, and even when particular addressees are singled out, Folkhyrde makes it clear that he intends his message to have a wider application.[66] In any case, Hus does not use the term *exemplaria* (or *exempla*) here, but "literas." It seems to me that he is referring to separate documents from those he mentions in his reply to Richard Wyche (where again, Hus mentions "exemplaria").

Notable, too, is the fact that Wyche's and Folkhyrde's letters were translated into Czech.[67] We do not know what prompted the translation of Folkhyrde's letters, but Hus discusses how he came to translate Wyche's letter in his reply to Wyche in 1411. He claims to have commended the letter in a public sermon ("in sermone publico") to a crowd of around ten thousand people ("prope decem milia hominum") – an enthusiastic expression paralleling what Páleč would later accuse him of doing in writing to a friend about "literas de Anglia."[68] The letter so enflamed the crowd, "quod rogaverunt me, ut ipsam transponerem in lingwarium nostre gentis [that they asked me to translate it into the language of our people]."[69] The fact that Folkhyrde's letters were also translated into Czech could indicate that they were transmitted along with Wyche's letter, and that they formed part of the packet of "literas" that were all at one time in Hus' hands while (according to Páleč's account) he wrote to his friend.

The instances of Czech translation I have mentioned call for further comment, as they are not isolated occurrences. For some reason, whether in reaction to Archbishop Zbyněk's anti-Wycliffite campaign of 1410 or something else, there was a flurry of Czech translation of Wycliffite texts *c.*1410–11. I have discussed Wyche's letter, translated in response to intense lay demand, as well as Folkhyrde's letters, which may also have been translated shortly after they were taken to Bohemia in 1410. Additionally, a translation of Wyclif's *Dialogus*, which its editor has attributed to Jakoubek of Stříbro, was written *c.*1410–11.[70] Others have posited the existence of additional Czech translations of the *Trialogus* and *De civili dominio*, though no copies have been discovered.[71] Further, Jan Hus also translated passages from a number of Wyclif's texts in his *Výklad víry* (*Exposition of Faith*),[72] contributing to a period of translation activity which starts to look more programmatic than casual.

The impression which emerges from this translation activity is that the Hussite *literati*, which likely included many of Hus' closest associates and prominent defenders of Wyclif, made every attempt to encourage popular, extramural participation and enthusiasm not only for Wyclif's teachings, but also for the man himself and for a shared experience with his living English followers. Lay participation in communication with the Lollards was about more than just fondling souvenirs from Wyclif's tomb, extending also to more sophisticated forms of involvement and indoctrination. The *Dialogus* was a particularly appropriate choice for translating into Czech. As one of Wyclif's more accessible texts, it offered a digest of the main points of his doctrine by means of a relatively unambiguous dialogue between Truth (*Veritas*) and Falsehood (*Mendacium*). The Czech translator furthermore worked to make his version even more accessible than the Latin original by reducing overly learned references, expanding passages that he considered to be too brief in the original, and removing topical references.[73]

The widespread appeal of Wyche's and Folkhyrde's letters is also easy to imagine. Wyche, whom Hus advertises as "a priest of Master John Wyclif,"[74] refers to a common struggle, linking the experiences of Hus and his friends with that of the English Lollards. Folkhyrde likewise seems to have intended his reformist message to reach a large audience (though there is no indication that he knew anything about the Bohemians). The initial description of his letters in the extant manuscripts (Latin and Czech versions) indicates that Folkhyrde rode on horseback "per patrias," distributing them widely "per cartulas et cedulas" and placing them into the hands of anyone who reached out for them. He was, in other words, portrayed as deliberately attempting to put his letters into the widest possible circulation. The letters were furthermore originally written in the vernacular, meaning that the Czech versions represent a development in a fascinating chain of translation, with Latin acting as a vehicle between separate publics and vernaculars.[75] It is not clear who was responsible for the description of Folkhyrde which introduces his letters in the surviving manuscripts, but the Czech translator (embellishing his Latin source) wanted to ensure that none of Folkhyrde's potential as a folk hero was lost on his Bohemian audience: "There was once a knight of rank," he translates, "(and perhaps there still is), first name Quentin, surname Folkhyrde, which is translated 'shepherd of the people'."[76] Not only the texts from England and Scotland, then, but also the identities and personalities of some of their authors – Wyche, a "presbyter Magistri Johannis Wicleff"; and Folkhyrde, "pastýř lida" – were conveyed to a larger Bohemian audience.

Returning to Hus' 1411 reply to Richard Wyche, we can at least be sure that Wyche sent multiple texts to Hus – or that multiple texts were sent from England with Wyche's letter – and that Hus credited Wyche for sending them. We can also be certain that the journey by Faulfiš and Knĕhnice after their stay at Oxford in 1406–7 and the journey made by unknown parties *c.*1410 are *two separate journeys*: there is no evidence that either student remained in England continuously from 1406 until 1410, bringing all of the documents in question to Bohemia at that time. Indeed, there is evidence to the contrary: Knĕhnice attained the degree of bachelor at the University of Prague in 1408, and Faulfiš was in Bohemia to receive a loan in 1409.[77]

So who were the couriers in 1410–11? The first place to look for an answer is again in Hus' reply to Wyche, where he mentions two men named "Symon" and "Nicolaus." The name "Nicolaus" immediately suggests (as others have proposed)[78] Mikuláš (Nicholas) Faulfiš, with whom, as has already been said, Hus was undeniably familiar. Hus does not indicate that Nicholas personally carried Wyche's letter to Prague, though he does mention that "Symon" (perhaps Šimon of Tišnov) was at least its immediate bearer to Hus. The references to "dearest brothers" and "certain lovers of truth" mentioned by Wyche and Oldcastle in their 1410 letters suggest that we are looking for more than one person. Whether the two men mentioned in Hus' reply to Wyche were those messengers is difficult to say, but nevertheless worth exploring.

The possibility that Hus was referring to Šimon of Tišnov is intriguing. Šimon, as we have seen, participated in the defense of Wyclif in July and August 1410. After Šimon gave his defense of Wyclif's *De probatione propositionum* on July 29, it is difficult to place him again until the end of April 1411, when he was certainly in Prague.[79] From then on, he appears often in the sources. He was rector of Prague University at least by July 3, 1411.[80] In this official role he would appear later that same year in a controversy involving John Stokes, an English ambassador who passed through Prague on his way back from official negotiations with Sigismund in Hungary.

Šimon's associations with Faulfiš are well established. He may at one time have had in his possession the copies of Wyclif's works that were brought to Bohemia by Faulfiš and Kněhnice *c.*1407. In their present arrangement in ÖNB 1294, the three texts which the students copied in England are surrounded by a foundation document for a church in Moravia for which Šimon of Tišnov was the benefactor. Šimon would also later excerpt and defend parts of Wyclif's *De ecclesia*, one of the three texts in the same manuscript, during his disputation with Pavel of Prague.[81] In 1409 he loaned Faulfiš money, and again he appears in a dispute over Faulfiš's inheritance after the student died. These fiscal affairs will resurface later in the discussion, but for purposes of linking Tišnov to England and the Lollards it is interesting to note another name that appears along with Šimon's and Mikuláš's in the documents surrounding Faulfiš's finances: Matěj of Hnátnice, also called "Matthias Engliš," a *pronunciatus* who was later responsible for dictating Wycliffite texts like the *Rosarium* and *Opus arduum* to groups of Bohemian scribes.[82] The origin of Hnátnice's *alias* is unclear, but it suggests some kind of association with England and, judging by his connections to Wycliffite texts, with Lollard–Hussite textual transmission as well.[83] If Šimon of Tišnov is not the "Symon" of Hus' letter, then, he can at least be shown to have frequently crossed paths with those who were associated in some capacity with the dissemination of Wycliffite texts.

As for the other named contact in Hus' reply to Wyche, Hus clearly indicates that Wyche is on familiar terms with Nicholas, a detail which suggests a prior meeting. There is also a suggestion that Nicholas will either be traveling or at least writing to Wyche in the near future. In a statement which is obscure to say the least, Hus writes: "Nicholas, to whom they are writing, shall make mention about other things."[84] We can infer little from the comment other than that unknown parties are writing to someone named Nicholas, a man known to both Hus and Wyche, and that Nicholas will in turn furnish Wyche (in an unspecified way) with more information.[85]

Having exhausted the evidence in Hus' letter, a further suggestion that Faulfiš was in England *c.*1410 emerges when we revise Margaret Deanesly's interpretation of Hus' reference to Faulfiš in his vernacular *postilla*. When Hus wrote the commentary, Faulfiš was already dead.[86] Hus writes:[87]

I heard from a faithful man of good memory, Nicholas, who was known as Faulfiš, that when he was in England, he got to know a certain cook, with whom he boarded; and when the bishop asked [the cook] why he read the Scripture in English against his ban,[88] [the cook] defended himself with Scripture. And then the bishop said to him: "Do you know with whom you are speaking?" He answered that he was speaking with a bishop, [who was also] a man. And the bishop went on: "And do you dare, wretched layman, to speak to me from Scripture?" And [the cook] answered him: "I know that you are no greater than Christ, and as for myself I hope I am no worse than the devil. And because gracious Christ quietly listened to Scripture from the devil, why wouldn't you, as you are less than Christ, listen to Scripture from me, a man?" And the bishop, losing his temper, no longer wanted to speak with him: so that the cook overcame the bishop with Scripture, just as Christ [overcame] the devil.

The story had a long afterlife in Bohemian polemic. Another version appears in a manuscript containing the third part of Mikuláš Mníšek's *Comportatura*, now PNK MS VI.F.17 (*c.*1418–19):[89]

In England it happened that they were keeping the laity from reading the Scriptures in their own tongue. It came to pass that a certain cook, an innocent layman, was studying Scripture in the common tongue and read it often. When the bishop saw him reading, he roared at him: "Why are you reading this?" He replied: "Yet the law was given for the learning of both secular and spiritual men, and Scripture says: 'Let every spirit praise the Lord.'" To which the bishop [replied]: "O, you base man, do you really wish to defend yourself with Scripture?" [The cook] replied: "I believe that you are no better than Christ, nor am I, as I hope, worse than the devil. And why? Christ responded to the devil from Scripture, and on the contrary it was by Scripture that the devil encircled [Christ]. So why do you prohibit me from speaking from Scripture?"

Though the anecdote may not be an instance of verbatim reportage – Faulfiš could have projected onto the figure of a cook a more characteristic enthusiasm among English layfolk for reading the Bible in English – it nevertheless provides a rare insight into the extent of Faulfiš's interaction with the English, and its retelling demonstrates the readiness with which

tidings from England were conveyed to a Bohemian public. If we rely on
Hus' version, Faulfiš seems even to have learned English (unless of course
the cook, if indeed he ever existed, was a *laicus litteratus* like Walter Brut,
and they were conversing in Latin).[90] Deanesly was interested in this
anecdote because of the possibility that the ban which the cook mentions
referred to the *Constitutions* of Thomas Arundel, Archbishop of
Canterbury – a possibility which she dismisses. Since Faulfiš returned to
Bohemia sometime in 1407, and the synod which drafted the *Constitutions*
did not meet until November 7 of that year, Deanesly argues that unless
Faulfiš had his conversation with the cook at the very end of the year,
between the synod and his departure, his reference "would appear to refer
to some earlier edict."[91] She does not, however, suggest what this "earlier
edict" might be, nor have I been able to discover one that fits the cook's
characterization.

Deanesly's interpretation assumes, of course, that Faulfiš was in England
on just one occasion, from 1406–7. But we need not follow her in this
assumption. She is probably correct to doubt that the reported conversation
took place at the very end of 1407, if for no other reason than that the
Constitutions were only issued in 1409, two years *after* they were drafted.[92]
We cannot be certain, but I suggest that if the anecdote refers to an actual
exchange, the cook did refer to the *Constitutions*, and that he held the
conversation with Faulfiš in 1409 or sometime thereafter. Alternatively,
even if the character of the cook was constructed by Faulfiš, a learned
observer, there is no trouble in assuming that knowledge of the
Constitutions had colored his description. That Faulfiš made a trip to
England about the time that the legislation was promulgated is further
substantiated by the fact that on May 8, 1409 Faulfiš, still in Bohemia,
verified that he had received a substantial loan from Šimon of Tišnov
(probably the "Symon" in Hus' letter to Wyche) and several others.[93]
Perhaps Faulfiš intended to use this loan to pay for his next journey to
England.

INTERROGATION, DEATH, AND DECLINE

In 1415, four years after Hus' reply was presumably sent to Richard Wyche,
Hus was on trial at the Council of Constance, and here we find another clue
about the textual exchanges between England and Bohemia. By this point,
Church and secular authorities from a number of regions including England
were catching on to the extent and import of Lollard–Hussite textual
exchange.[94] I mentioned earlier that Hus referred to Faulfiš during his

Constance trial. The occasion for proffering this information arose when an Englishman asked him if he knew who was responsible for bringing the Oxford testimonial concerning Wyclif to Prague. Hus implicated Faulfiš, but it seems that he could do so without jeopardizing the student's safety. When asked, "ubi est ille?" he responded, "Mortuus est alicubi, credo inter Hispaniam et Angliam [He is dead somewhere, I believe between Spain and England]."[95] But Faulfiš did not die on his trip from England to the continent in 1407. And if we are correct to assume (as I think it is safe to do) that he made a second trip to England around 1410, then he survived that trip, too. He was at least alive in early 1411 when Hus received Wyche's letter. Also significant is a dispute over Faulfiš's estate, which places his death somewhere before the end of November 1411.[96] Remembering that Hus' letter to Wyche can probably be dated to 1411 and that in the same letter he had mentioned Nicholas, who (if it is Faulfiš) died later that same year, we must ask what Faulfiš was doing traveling between Spain and England – not the most obvious route between England and Bohemia – before he died. It seems likely that he was either in the process of delivering Hus' letter to Wyche (as well as attending to other business), or on his way back. If so, then Faulfiš died while attempting his *third* trip to England.

Since Hus' letter exists nowhere in the English record, it is difficult to determine whether Nicholas died before or after its delivery. It is interesting to note that John Foxe, a compiler of both English and continental documents, offers a slightly different account of the death of Faulfiš (who is still unnamed). Foxe writes: "Iohn Hus aunswered: I heard say (said he) that *in his returne into England*, he died by the way."[97] Foxe's account is derived indirectly from Peter of Mladoňovice's *Relatio de Magistri Joannis Hus causa*, an eyewitness record of Hus' Constance trial written by one of Hus' proponents, but his immediate source is the edition of that text in the first volume of *Iohannis Hus et Hieronymi Pragensis historia et monumenta*, published by Matthias Flacius when Foxe was in exile on the continent. (Flacius, who also omits Faulfiš's name, writes: "Mortuum postea in itinere esse audiui, quum rediret in Angliam.")[98] It is difficult to say whether Flacius – and through him, Foxe – was relying on a variant reading of Mladoňovice's *Relatio*, or whether he allowed his interpretation of the episode to inform his edition. Neither sixteenth-century version establishes that Faulfiš attempted a return trip to England, but, together with the other details mentioned above, they begin to build a case for such a voyage, as well as presenting an intriguing, but ultimately unreliable detail about the direction of the student's travel.

Evidence in the sixteenth-century historical record may not amount to much, but another letter – this time from John Oldcastle to King Václav IV – provides evidence which supports the possibility not only that the Bohemian student took a third trip, but also that Hus' letter to Wyche was delivered. No one has been able to date this letter with much certainty. It was addressed from London on September 7 to "Wenceslao Romanorum et Boemie regi, Moravie marchioni et principi Luzburgensi [Václav, King of the Romans and of Bohemia, Margrave of Moravia and Prince of Luxembourg]," but with no year provided in the extant manuscript.[99] It could not have been written earlier than 1411, because Václav only became Margrave of Moravia after the death of Jošt, the former incumbent, who died on January 17 of that year. In the letter, Oldcastle also praises Václav for zealously separating the wheat from the chaff, by which he means true and false priests.[100] This has prompted speculation that the letter was written in 1413, the reference alluding to Václav's banishment of Stanislav of Znojmo, Peter of Znojmo, Štěpán Páleč, and other opponents of the Hussites earlier that year.[101] Novotný mentions that Hus was himself in exile at this time, though his relationship with the king was still somewhat favorable. Perhaps, suggests Novotný, Hus wrote to Oldcastle in order to encourage him to write in turn to the Bohemian king, hoping that through Oldcastle's intercession Hus would be able to return to Prague.[102]

The argument is not especially convincing for several reasons. First, there is no indication in Oldcastle's letter which demonstrates his knowledge that Hus and the Bohemian reformers are experiencing anything but the warmest support from Václav. By 1413, the king's relationship with Hus and his friends had deteriorated substantially from what it had been in 1411 – a year which was a high point in the crown's support for the Hussites. Nor does Oldcastle mention his own troubles, which were more pressing in 1413 than two years before. And in fact, Oldcastle was most likely at Cooling on September 7 of that year, not London (where his letter was addressed).[103]

There is no doubt, though, that Oldcastle was writing in response to letters from Hus and others. He writes that the king's reputation for striving to uphold the Gospel has been reported to him "per magistrum Hus, iudicio meo Christi sacerdotum, nec non alios litteratenus [by Master Hus, a priest of Christ in my judgment, as well as others by letter]."[104] Hus' letter has unfortunately been lost, but if we recall what he wrote about the king in his reply to Wyche in 1411 – "Dominus rex noster totaque curia sua, regina, barones et communis populus sunt pro verbo Ihesu Christi [Our lord the king and all his court, the queen, barons, and the common people are in favor of the Word of Jesus Christ]"[105] – it should not seem strange that Hus wrote something very similar to Oldcastle that same year, prompting Sir John to lavish praise on the Bohemian king.

A date of 1411 would clear up several issues, while allowing us to keep speculation to a minimum. Oldcastle's reference to separating wheat from chaff, vague as it is, fits more comfortably with Václav's gradual marginalization of Archbishop Zbyněk in and before 1411, coupled with an increase of secular control over the Bohemian Church – control which included Václav's confiscation of Zbyněk's estates to pay for the Wycliffite books he had burned the previous year.[106] (It would be interesting, in fact, if some of the confiscated money was used in turn to finance the copying of Wycliffite *exemplaria* in England.) In 1411 the archbishop became virtually powerless to enforce excommunications, interdicts, or commands from Rome in Prague. And if we date Oldcastle's letter to 1411, the lack of reference to Hus' or Oldcastle's troubles needs no crafty explanation. In other words, we can allow Oldcastle to mean what he says.

But equally importantly, we have evidence of a possible courier in 1411. It is conceivable that Mikuláš Faulfiš carried Hus' letters to Wyche and Oldcastle sometime before September 7, 1411. We already know that Hus intended to send his reply to Wyche (containing the reference to "Nicolaus"), and that he probably wrote it earlier the same year. If my dating of Oldcastle's letter to Václav (which did make it to Bohemia) is correct, then Hus' response to Richard Wyche, mentioning royal support for the Hussite cause, most likely made it to England after all; it was probably delivered on the same voyage that brought Oldcastle's letter to Prague on the return trip. My proposed scenario cannot determine whether or not Faulfiš personally delivered the letters to Wyche and Oldcastle. As I have already mentioned, Faulfiš died "between Spain and England" in 1411; but the fact that Oldcastle's letter to Václav reached Bohemia indicates that someone else was able to complete the mission, and reported news of Faulfiš's death to Hus.

Just over a decade after Oldcastle wrote to the Bohemian king, Thomas Netter of Walden made the tantalizing claim in his *Doctrinale* (produced in the 1420s), that Hus specifically requested copies of Wyclif's works from John Oldcastle and that Oldcastle fulfilled the request.[107] W. T. Waugh remarked more than a century ago that there is no other evidence to confirm this claim and that, while there would be nothing strange about such a request, "it is equally likely that the story is one of the numerous legends invented to account for the wide dissemination of heterodox views among the Czechs."[108]

It is tempting to speculate that Netter had evidence pertaining to the correspondence which no longer survives. After all, Hus did write to Oldcastle, though whether he asked Oldcastle to send anything is another matter. Or perhaps Netter, referring to an exchange that allegedly transpired several years before, confused (or conflated) Oldcastle with Wyche, whose correspondence with Hus, as we now know, did involve the exchange of other texts ("exemplaria"). Also interesting is a later reference by John Bale, who cites Netter as the source for his slightly embellished claim that "[Oldcastle] caused all the workes of Iohan Wycleue to be written at the instaunce of Iohan huss and so to be sent into Boheme, Fraunce, Spayne, Portyngale, and other landes."[109] The reference may be nothing more than a hyperbolic amplification of Bale's source (which was probably not entirely reliable to begin with), but it is nevertheless intriguing when combined with Hus' claim that Faulfiš died between Spain and England. There is no telling how accurate these later accounts really are, but with more certainty than Waugh, we can at least say that they are based on shreds of fact.

It must be stressed that the conclusions offered in this chapter are what I take to be the most feasible readings of a number of disparate facts. Taken together, the documents cited above suggest that Czech couriers or otherwise ad hoc conveyors traveled between England and Bohemia on a regular basis and that Mikuláš Faulfiš in particular was involved on more than one occasion – perhaps as many as three. Together with Jiří of Kněhnice, he was certainly responsible for conveying three of Wyclif's works to Prague in 1407. Faulfiš's conversation with an English cook, which Hus recounted after the student had died, may be an indication that Faulfiš was also in England in 1409 (or just after), the year that Arundel's *Constitutions* were promulgated. Could he have carried the letters sent from England in 1410, together with, or at least as far as, the "Symon" mentioned in Hus' reply to Wyche? There is also evidence in Hus' letter to Wyche that suggests Faulfiš was on his way to deliver news to Wyche in 1411, and there is reason to believe that he delivered Hus' letter to Oldcastle on the same trip. That he made a third trip is further supported by the fact that he died in 1411, "inter Hispaniam et Angliam."

As was mentioned earlier, however, textual exchange seems not to have continued for long between Lollards and Hussites. Though it is likely that Mikuláš Faulfiš, in his practical capacity as a courier, was responsible for a significant portion (though certainly not all) of the Anglo-Bohemian textual exchanges in the early fifteenth century, he may also have contributed to the silence that ensued after (even as a partial result of) his death. There is little to suggest that the exchange continued later than 1416 (and probably not as late as that),[110] when an over-confident Thomas Lucas apparently tried to send a petition to Sigismund, then in London, containing his opinions about clerical disendowment and soliciting the emperor-elect's support in deposing Henry V.[111] If Lucas had been at all familiar with Sigismund's refusal to enforce Hus' safe conduct at the Council of Constance in 1414, or with Sigismund's increasingly cozy relationship with the churchmen who opposed Hus there, it is hard to believe that he would have bothered to approach him on his trip to England not long after Hus' death. This recklessly optimistic act provides some useful commentary on just how much certain English Lollards may have depended on Hussite couriers – and just how little information they received when the channels of communication closed. The Lollards in Lucas' circle may even have had visions of collaboration with their Bohemian counterparts in more material terms, if we are correct to assume that Lucas believed that Sigismund was a Hussite sympathizer.

While it lasted, however, the Lollard–Hussite fellowship was more than just a network for transmitting Wycliffite texts to Prague, fueling a reform that shared much in common with the English movement. The fact of correspondence – and the sense of community which was fostered by the materiality of this exchange – likewise conditioned the reception and the idea of Wyclif in Bohemia before the Council of Constance, while contributing to the accessibility of his doctrines for a wider audience. Popular outcry on occasions like the Prague book-burning of 1410, then, may have stemmed not only from the perception that cherished doctrinal positions were under attack, but also that a valued relationship, undergirded and "sanctified" by material objects, had been violated.

When we consider the character and extent of Lollard–Hussite communication, we must see Hus' exhortation to Richard Wyche in a new way when he writes: "The church of Christ from Bohemia salutes the church of Christ in England, desiring to be a sharer of the profession of the holy faith in the grace of the Lord Jesus Christ." We should not, of course, overstate the extent to which this "sharing" was manifested in subsequent correspondence and textual exchange. In fact, Hus' closing remarks may be an indication that he was beginning to think in terms of national churches, and less in terms of alliances that would cross regnal boundaries.[112] But in the materiality of the exchange we can still discern a Lollard–Hussite fellowship, one whose participants saw themselves as mutually supportive of each other, if only for a short time.

CHAPTER 4

"Ad regna et loca extranea": diplomacy against heresy, 1411–1416

Audivimus quod spiritus quidam mendacii ad certas partes Christianitatis rumores transvexit ab Anglia, quod opiniones scelerate memorie dudum Johannis Vikleph, sub theologie velamine errorum magistri, clerus Anglie debuit approbasse et ipsum Johannem velud virum katholicum et ascriptum katalogo [sanctorum] predicasse et vestrorum nonnulli huius spiritui fidem dedisse aliqualiter creditivam.[1]

[We have heard that a certain spirit of falsehood has carried rumors from England to certain parts of Christendom, [namely,] that the clergy of England ought to approve the opinions of the late John Wyclif of wicked memory, the master of errors, under the veil of theology, and commend this John as a catholic man, inscribed in the catalogue [of saints]; and how some of your people have believed the spirit of this rumor.]

English officials first learned that Wycliffites from England were in communication with the Bohemians fairly late, by chance, and with considerable embarrassment. By the time they made the discovery, it was clear that the English prosecution had some catching up to do. The kind of communication they discovered was of a particularly troublesome sort, as it employed authenticating forms and signs that were difficult to discredit and, equally importantly, already in circulation within a Bohemian community that was eager to believe its claims. Consequently, the effort to clamp down on the communication was as much a contest to stabilize textual forms as it was a struggle to police the lines of communication themselves.

The effort to combat Wycliffite communication abroad comprises one of the great untold stories of Schism-era religious controversy, the story of how the prosecution of Wycliffism intersected with international reformist contacts. When we think internationally about the prosecution of Wycliffism, it soon becomes clear that the controversy was intriguingly confused and fluid, and that this fluidity had much to do with the situation on the ground in terms of the contingencies and material conditions of textual transmission. The next part of my narrative, then, reveals some important details about late medieval communication, namely, that it was far from centralized, and that Church and secular officials could not boast a clear advantage when it came to dominating the networks of transnational communication. English officials struggled to maintain the fiction that orthodox positions concerning Wyclif and his prosecution were self-evident and authoritative, and this fiction was all the more difficult to uphold when operating outside of insular jurisdictions. The efforts of the English were largely ineffective until they reached a decisive turning point at the Council of Constance during Jan Hus' trial. At Constance, the English showed a remarkable level of concern over the modes, methods, and materials of Lollard–Hussite communication, but more importantly, this highly visible international forum gave them the position they needed to gain narrative control over the Wycliffites during this controversy.

I argue in this chapter that the struggle to police European communication networks before Constance had as much to do with controlling authenticating signs and textual forms as with combating heretical doctrines and sedition. In the pages to follow, I suggest that as heterodox communication intersected with Anglo-Imperial diplomacy, the controversy surrounding Lollard–Hussite communication helped draw the English prosecution of heresy into the orbit of international religious politics. Heresy was not initially a main concern for the Anglo-Imperial missions that preceded the Council of Constance, but the interplay of heresy and diplomacy would be an important effect of this political interaction. And the concern, for English officials, was largely a political one. During the course of the Anglo-Imperial embassies, the issue of Wycliffite heresy, and of its prosecution in England, became linked with English anxiety about their reputation for orthodoxy. Ultimately the Council of Constance would become the primary locus for defending that reputation, but as I show in this chapter, Anglo-Imperial diplomatic missions preceding Constance provided important avenues for gaining narrative control over Lollard–Hussite communication channels by gathering information and circulating official reports of English anti-heresy efforts. An examination of pre-Constance ambassadorial activity provides an important backstory to the eventual English policy toward Wycliffite heresy in its English and Bohemian forms on the floor of a General Council, and brings us much closer to understanding how and why Wycliffite communication with the Bohemians came to a halt at this time.

My story in this chapter begins in the middle of April 1411, when
members of a small embassy left England for Hungary with instructions
to hold talks with Sigismund, who had been elected King of the Romans
late the previous year.[2] It is not entirely clear what happened when they
reached Ofen (Buda),[3] but in general terms the agenda was to include
discussion of an Anglo-Imperial alliance that would reinforce previous
agreements stretching back to the marriage of Anne of Bohemia and
Richard II in 1382. The ambassadors were also commissioned to discuss
the ambiguous matter of "mutual assistance" between the two regions, as
well as economic relations and a number of other issues. A later letter from
Sigismund to Henry IV indicates that the talks also covered the English war
with the French and the idea of a General Council (not yet the Council of
Constance), a primary aim of which would be to end the Great Schism.

The talks in Hungary in 1411 are less important for our purposes, however,
than what happened en route, when the embassy became entangled in
religious politics in Bohemia that seem to have been unrelated to its primary
diplomatic agenda. The ambassadors were John Stokes, a Cambridge licentiate in law, and Hartung von Clux, a mercenary whose name appears often in
Anglo-Imperial diplomatic correspondence. Their mission was in the planning by February 26, 1411 at the latest, when the ambassadors' procuration
was issued,[4] and they were likely back in England by the end of the year, but
certainly by February 1412, as payments are recorded for them at that time.[5]
Stokes and von Clux left England on April 13 and 14, 1411,[6] but the fact of
their departure does not seem to have hindered further communication with
Henry IV. A new set of instructions, for example, was issued for them on
April 29, two weeks after they had left.[7]

The small embassy, then, was met by others from England as it traveled
and, at least in early stages, could maintain a degree of contact with officials
in England as it made its way to Hungary. Others also accompanied them
who were not listed in the procuration or other diplomatic documents,[8]
and, as I shall elaborate below, when Stokes and von Clux stopped through
Prague in September 1411, students of the university reported that "quidam
magistri vel *doctores* de regno Anglie in civitate ista ... pausam facerent
[certain masters or doctors from the kingdom of England were stopping
over in this city]," only one of whom was a certain licentiate in law, John
Stokes.[9]

The point of mentioning all of this continued contact is that about a week
after the ambassadors' second set of instructions was dispatched, Archbishop
Thomas Arundel likewise wrote a letter that now survives in PNK MS VIII.
G.13.[10] The letter, dated May 8, 1411, is addressed "Universis fidei katholice

zelatoribus [To all who jealously protect the Catholic faith]." It is appropriate to mention this letter in the context of the 1411 embassy first of all because the embassy provides a possible means of conveying the letter to Prague, but also because the subject of the letter would resurface during the Stokes–von Clux embassy of 1411 and in English affairs later the same year.

In the letter, Arundel expresses concern that "spiritus quidam mendacii ad certas partes Christianitatis rumores transvexit ab Anglia [a certain spirit of falsehood has carried rumors from England to certain parts of Christendom]," propagated by a group of Oxford masters who assert that John Wyclif should be commended as a catholic man and inscribed in the catalogue of saints. This was nonsense, of course, and as Arundel assures his readers, the clergy of the Province of Canterbury have condemned Wyclif and his followers as heretics. In the closing of the letter, Arundel is also keen to point out the appended seal and the authority it represents – a detail that is not unusual, but nevertheless interesting in light of the letter to which Arundel was responding.

The "spirit of falsehood" that concerned Arundel refers to the contents of a familiar testimonial letter from Oxford, dated October 5, 1406, which was brought to Prague shortly after it was written.[11] That letter claimed that Wyclif's life and writings had been praiseworthy, that he had never been condemned nor suspected of heresy while he lived, but had labored against the blasphemers of Holy Scripture. And of course the idea that Wyclif had ever been condemned, exhumed, or burned was out of the question. "Absit enim," culminates the testimony,

quod nostri prelati tante probitatis virum pro heretico condempnassent qui in logicalibus philosophicis et theologicis moralibus et speculativis inter omnes universitatis nostre ut credimus scripserat sine pari.[12]

[God forbid indeed that our prelates should condemn a man of such virtue as a heretic, who in logic, philosophy, and moral and speculative theology wrote without peer, as we believe, among all our university].

The letter was, I should add, hardly a "rumor" at all, but a document that, fixed with the chancellor of Oxford's seal, was at least in form as authentic as they come.

In fact, Arundel's attempt to characterize the testimonial's narrative as rumor – to distinguish the document as unreliable and malleable, in contrast to his own authoritative letter – reveals not only how mutable documents and their authenticating signs could be during the Middle Ages, but also how the strict dichotomy between rumor and official missive was an imagined distinction. As we shall see, in addition to documents, even

English officials resorted to highly unstable oral messages, whereas the Wycliffites could resort to remarkably convincing documentary forms. By characterizing the testimony of Wyclif as rumor, and thereby setting it off against his own official letter, Arundel betrays the fact that his documents and signs of authenticity were not as stable as he may have liked them to be – and that his ability to control the transnational narrative concerning the English prosecution of Wyclif was hardly guaranteed.

CONFLICTING REPORTS

The Oxford testimony of Wyclif continued to attract controversy long after Arundel attempted to refute it. In England, Thomas Gascoigne alleged that Peter Payne had stolen the Oxford seal and used it furtively to authorize his lies about Wyclif.[13] The notion that the letter had been produced secretly was perhaps suggested to Gascoigne by the slightly earlier and similar account of the episode in Thomas Netter's *Doctrinale* (produced in the 1420s), a copy of which Gascoigne had in his possession (though Netter does not suggest Payne's agency).[14] The accounts by Netter and Gascoigne are of course not entirely reliable; the authors wrote long after the events in question had occurred, and may have felt compelled to force incoherent details into unified narrative sequences.[15] As Gascoigne alleges, Payne may have had a hand in the episode of the testimonial letter; I hasten to point out, however, that his connection to the letter, so often taken for granted, has never been demonstrated. It is also doubtful that Payne (or anyone involved) needed to act in secrecy.[16] There was still in 1406 a substantial amount of freedom to discuss Wyclif's doctrines at Oxford and even those who disapproved of his teachings there may inadvertently have protected the Wycliffites by resisting Arundel's persistent attempts to interfere with the university's privileges.[17]

Of the testimony's transmission and widespread use in Bohemia much more is known. Jan Hus informed the Fathers of the Council of Constance in 1415 that the document had been brought to Prague by two students, one of them Mikuláš Faulfiš and the other whose name Hus claims not to have known, but who must have been Jiří of Kněhnice, Faulfiš's companion in England from 1406–7.[18] Hus does not say when the letter reached Prague, but as it was written in 1406 and brought to Prague by the two Bohemian students who had been in England from 1406–7, the document possibly reached Prague in 1407 or shortly thereafter.

Eventually, Jan Hus and Jerome of Prague used the testimony to punctuate their defenses of Wyclif, but it does not seem to have been employed this way immediately. On more than one occasion between 1407 and 1409, Hus curiously does not mention the letter in defense of Wyclif when doing so would certainly have strengthened his position. In 1408, for example, charges against Hus were brought before Zbyněk, the Archbishop of Prague, one of them alleging that at some point in the recent past Hus had said "quod vellet animam suam ibi fore, ubi est anima Wicleff [that he wished his soul were where the soul of Wyclif is]"; Hus admitted that he had said it, arguing that no one but God can know whether a man was saved or damned – but with no reference to the Oxford letter.[19] Hus made the same argument in his commentary on the *Sentences* in 1409, again without reference to the testimonial.[20] The usefulness of these examples as evidence that Hus was as yet unaware of the letter is ultimately indeterminate. Still, a further example is revealing. In his controversy with John Stokes in 1411 (to which I shall return), Hus again insists that no man can know the lot of Wyclif's soul, using many of the same arguments from Scripture that he had cited in previous defenses. This time, however, he also presents the Oxford testimony to show that Wyclif has not even been condemned by Church officials, as Hus had not done in the examples just cited.[21]

Leaving aside the conspicuous absence of references to the letter in Hus' earlier statements, perhaps the earliest positive evidence of the letter's circulation in Prague comes from a quodlibetal disputation organized by Matěj of Knín at the beginning of 1409. When it was Jerome of Prague's turn to deliver his position (a *recommendatio* of the liberal arts),[22] he used the opportunity to recommend Wyclif's teachings to the younger students in attendance and, as we learn from the records of his trial at Vienna in 1410 and 1412,[23] he accentuated the delivery of his position by producing the Oxford testimonial as a further witness to Wyclif's virtue. Later, at his trial at Constance in 1416, Jerome claimed that, during the 1409 quodlibet, the letter had been handed to him "dum esset in cathedra per quendam juvenem, ut eam publicaret [by a certain youth when he was in the [speaker's] chair, so that he might read it out]."[24] No reference is made to the testimony in the text of Jerome's position from 1409, which absence suggests (as he later claims) that he really may not have known of the letter before he delivered his *recommendatio* to the students that year.

Most commentators since the fifteenth century have regarded the letter as a forgery, a designation which in my view has distracted us from giving it the attention it deserves. What seems more interesting to me is not the question of its legitimacy, but rather how it was used and circulated, and what the controversy it provoked reveals about continental perceptions of England's prosecution of Wyclif. The Oxford testimonial supplements contemporary

narratives of Wyclif's prosecution with a previously unrepresented historiography, one that explicitly calls attention to facts about the prosecution
that the dominant narratives occlude. In this respect, the testimonial joins
attempts like William Thorpe's autobiographical account of his trial before
Thomas Arundel, in which he established what Emily Steiner has called "a
new documentary rhetoric with which to redeem Lollard polemic from the
trial documents of the institutional church."[25] And after all, much of what
the testimony asserts is undeniably true – it *was*, in many ways, the "*spirit* of
falsehood" (to borrow Arundel's phrase) with which its opponents took
issue. They were *trying* to condemn Wyclif (they just hadn't carried it
through yet). By exploiting that middle ground – that truth with a caveat –
the letter gained its potency in circulation. In other words, the Oxford
testimonial extends the truth of the matter, participating in the materiality
and authenticating forms of documentary practice, and circulating in
communities that either accept its claims willingly or find them difficult
to dismiss out of hand. As Alfred Hiatt has recently written, "[t]he success or
failure of forgeries can, perhaps, be gauged by the extent to which they are
able to enter into [the] *parole* of documents – the extent to which they
are received as legitimate, authorized texts that accord with the history of a
person or community."[26] It is not clear, as I have said, that the Oxford
testimonial was a forgery at all, but certainly its participation in the signs
and forms of documentary culture lent it its "performative force"; its ability
to be read and reread during the course of the transnational battle over
Wycliffism.[27]

To those who wanted to be convinced of Wyclif's righteousness, the
testimony was a powerful affirmation, not least because it cast the opposition to Wycliffism as a minority position. Indeed there are many signs that
opponents of the Wycliffites in Central Europe struggled to come to terms
with the letter. A previously unknown copy of the testimony in ÖNB MS
4483 (a Bohemian manuscript), written on a half sheet of paper and bound
into the manuscript, has a note written on the reverse that reveals the
difficulty its author faced in squaring the testimony with other reports he
had heard.[28] The testimony itself is entitled "Bulla rescripta pro Viclef."
Although the suggestion that the letter was "written in response" to something (an earlier letter or request?) cannot be confirmed, it raises the
possibility that information about Wyclif was solicited by someone in
Bohemia or elsewhere, rather than being volunteered by Wyclif's sympathizers at Oxford. In any case, the author of the accompanying note in MS
4483 clearly had trouble dismissing the letter outright, even though he had
heard much to contradict it. He also reveals, unsurprisingly, that many

doubt the validity of the circumstances in which it was written ("videtur ut plures dicunt bulla hec subrepticie scripta est") – although again, not enough to dismiss the letter categorically.[29]

In Vienna, too, Jerome of Prague's accusers found it difficult to dismiss completely the testimonial's account of the English prosecution of Wyclif. In the early weeks of September 1410, and again in 1412, witnesses gathered at the University of Vienna to testify against Jerome, who was not present at his trial. One of these men, the Augustinian theologian Berthold Puchhauser (or Ruchowoser) of Regensburg, was unable to comment on most of the articles that had been drawn up against Jerome – the exception being the eighth, which alleged that on March 20, 1410, Jerome, preaching before the King of Hungary (Sigismund), had said many things against the clerical estate and its liberties.[30] Berthold answered that Jerome, who had stayed with him at some point after the event in question, admitted to saying things of that kind in the king's presence, but beyond that Berthold knew nothing about Jerome.

About John Wyclif, however, Berthold had an interesting story. Around the time that Jerome delivered his suspect sermon, Berthold claimed to have been at Oxford just when the Archbishop of Canterbury was making a visitation of his province:

et tunc fuerit communis fama potissime inter studentes theologie et alios magnos viros in studio Oxoniensi, quod archiepiscopus sic visitando venerit ad ecclesiam parrochialem Wikleph et eiusdem corpus, [quod ibi] noverit sepultum, exhuma-verit propter hereticam pravitatem; quo autem corpus illud pervenerit, nesciat, et dicit, quod exhumacioni non interfuerit, nisi alias in communi fama audiverit, sed archiepiscopum visitare viderit, quia universitas Oxoniensis illi oviam transierit, et sic ipse cum aliis interfuerit.[31]

[and at that time [said Berthold] there was an open rumor particularly among the students of theology and the other great men in the *studium* of Oxford, that the archbishop, on visitation, came to the parish church of Wyclif,[32] and on account of heretical depravity he exhumed his body, which he knew was buried there; what became of that body, however, [Berthold] wouldn't know; and [Berthold] says that he was not present at the exhumation (although he heard of it elsewhere in open rumor), but that he saw the archbishop visit, because the University of Oxford had entrusted the pastoral office to him, and therefore [Arundel] was present with others.]

First to establish the date of Berthold's stay at Oxford: Jerome's sermon in Sigismund's presence, which Berthold addressed before mentioning any-thing about Wyclif, was delivered on March 20, 1410.[33] After commenting on Jerome's sermon, Berthold says that "citra vicesimum secundum fuit in

Oxonia [he was at Oxford around the twenty-second]" – the only reference point for determining the year being Jerome's sermon, just discussed. The record of Berthold's account is undated, but its editor places it in 1410.[34] I am aware of no archiepiscopal visitation like the one in Berthold's account in 1410, but Arundel is known to have conducted a sweeping visitation of his province in the spring and summer of 1411. At this later time, the archbishop traveled extensively in the diocese of Lincoln, where Lutterworth (Wyclif's "ecclesia parochialis" at the time of his death) was located. He set out on the visitation within days of the provincial synod of March 17, when (as I shall elaborate) he received a list of 267 erroneous or heretical articles drawn from Wyclif's writings. Arundel's register reports that he was in Newmarket (in the diocese of Ely) on March 22, by all signs initiating the visitation of his province.[35] There is no other record to confirm Berthold's report of the "open rumor" of Wyclif's exhumation. Berthold was probably wise not to take rumors of this kind too seriously.

Berthold's claim that he was present at Oxford when Arundel and his men visited, however, allows us to fix the date of the Augustinian's stay with more certainty. Arundel visited Oxford at the end of his itinerary that summer. He reached the university on July 26 and stayed until August 11. Berthold's statement that he was there "citra vicesimum secundum" is approximate enough to place him at Oxford perhaps at the very beginning of Arundel's visit (a month after the archbishop was known to have been traveling in Lincoln). He was possibly there just before the archbishop arrived, in time to hear the most recent reports of the visitation that must have been buzzing at Oxford in anticipation of Arundel's arrival. The record of Berthold's testimony at Jerome's trial, then, must come from after that time.

Also unresolved is Berthold's reason for mentioning the Oxford rumor during Jerome's trial in the first place. Though it is not stated in the text (which is, after all, a condensed record of the proceedings), Berthold probably mentioned the rumor as part of a general discussion of the Oxford letter, which was brought up repeatedly during Jerome's trial and which included in its list of claims the assertion that Wyclif was never posthumously burned by the English clergy (nor, by extension, exhumed).[36] Elsewhere, too, we have evidence of Berthold's tremendous concern over the testimonial. Munich, Bayerische Staatsbibliothek Clm. 26676, an autograph manuscript containing the first part of Berthold's lecture on the Apocalypse, also includes a copy of the Oxford testimonial (fol. 2^r). This is followed by a *reprobatio* of the letter (fols. 2^{r-v}), and then a second letter from the chancellor of Oxford, unknown before now, which likewise refutes the testimonial (fols. 2^v-3^r) and is accompanied by a list of Wyclif's condemned articles (fol. 3^r). The refutations are undated, but it seems safe to say that someone (maybe Berthold) had sought from Oxford an opinion on the earlier letter in praise of Wyclif, and that the chancellor's office issued a response.

So had Wyclif been exhumed or hadn't he? Evidently the question was being raised both in England and on the Continent. It should also be noted that at least one of the students who earlier conveyed the testimony to Prague evidently wanted to emphasize this particular part of the letter. We learn from Štěpán Páleč during Hus' trial at Constance that "Faulfiss portavit unam petiam lapidis de sepulcro ipsius Wiclef, quam postea Pragae pro reliquiis venerabantur et habebant [Faulfiš carried a piece of stone from Wyclif's very tomb, which afterwards the Praguers venerated and regarded as relics]."[37] Later proceedings at the Council of Constance confirm, of course, that Wyclif was still in his grave. An order was issued from Constance on May 4, 1415 to correct this – an order that was not carried out until 1428 under the supervision of Richard Fleming, the new Bishop of Lincoln. The order stated that Wyclif's body and bones should be exhumed and cast away from consecrated ground, provided they could be distinguished from the bodies of the faithful buried nearby.[38] A report of the order was also dispatched from Constance to Prague, dated less than three weeks after Hus' execution.[39]

Before Constance, though, the English faced the embarrassing fact that their prosecution of Wyclif had never resulted in Wyclif's formal condemnation or punishment as a heretic – an omission that was easily exploited by Wyclif's supporters. Arundel probably did not know how widespread Lollard–Hussite communication had become by 1411, or how news of the English prosecution of the alleged heresy had been flowing unhindered to Bohemia for years. Of course, his situation was unlike that of Zbyněk, the Archbishop of Prague, in that heterodox texts were not flowing into England the way that Wycliffite texts were being trafficked to Bohemia. Arundel's ignorance of the exchange meant that Wycliffite control over much of the information that reached Bohemia regarding anti-Wycliffite efforts in England could proceed more or less unchecked. Up to the time (in May) that Arundel wrote his letter of refutation, the information that was available in Bohemia pertaining to the English prosecution came almost exclusively from Wycliffite sources, whether written or otherwise reported. This information, moreover, emphasized that most of the major attempts to condemn Wyclif's articles in England could be shown to have mitigating circumstances.

Hus knew, for example, that the Duke of Lancaster, "progenitor Hendrici, regis moderni Anglie [ancestor of Henry, the present king of England]," had in the past acted in Wyclif's defense.[40] Hus was later accused of seducing the people in Prague by claiming that when monks and masters tried to convict Wyclif at St. Paul's in London, thunder and lightning destroyed the gate of the church, and his prosecutors could scarcely escape into the city.[41] Through Wyclif's *Trialogus*, which circulated widely in Bohemia, Hus and his friends also knew of the earthquake that shook London in 1382, which Wyclif attributed to divine retribution for the blasphemies of those who tried to convict him at the Blackfriars Council.[42] In spring 1411, however, Arundel accelerated his drive to remove all doubt about Wyclif's status in the eyes of the English Church – and about the competence of the English clergy in prosecuting heresy – by working to exhume his body. Arundel's discovery of the Oxford testimonial letter, I suggest, was a contributing factor in having the archbishop realize the urgency of such action.[43]

But when did Arundel first learn of the Oxford testimony? There is no evidence that he knew of it before May 1411, when he wrote his letter of refutation. An outside possibility is that news of Jerome of Prague's conspicuous use of the letter eventually reached England, perhaps after the first part of his trial at Vienna in 1410. We know, for example, that Berthold of Regensburg had longstanding ties to Oxford, though his trip to the university, which I discussed above, must have taken place after Arundel already knew of the offending letter. Yet I think that news of the testimony came from closer to home. It is important to recall that 1411 was a key year in the archbishop's campaign to control the University of Oxford.[44] The most intensive period of Arundel's effort to rein in the university between 1406 and 1411 was (as I have said) also a time when Wyclif's doctrines and followers still found a great deal of support there, a solidarity that was emboldened by a common desire even by opponents of Wycliffism at Oxford to maintain the university's independence against the archbishop's efforts to interfere.

A crucial period in this struggle came when the convocation of Canterbury determined in 1407 that a committee of twelve should assess the orthodoxy of Wyclif's theological texts.[45] The committee was originally intended to consist of theologians from both universities, but when Arundel suspected that Oxford was delaying the task of appointing its members, he began to focus less ambiguously on Oxford as an important center of heretical activity. At some point in 1409 the archbishop renewed his call for the committee of twelve – now to be drawn exclusively from Oxford – to begin its investigation and to submit its conclusions to him. Not surprisingly, the committee was a source of resentment and controversy as it slowly performed its duties at Oxford, but on March 17, 1411 it finally submitted its findings – a list of 267 articles – to the provincial synod at St. Paul's.

It is probably not a coincidence, then, that the Oxford testimony of Wyclif likely reached Arundel's attention just as his persistent attempts to discipline and control the university were beginning to produce some cracks in its resistance. Indeed, substantial evidence suggests that the discovery coincided with the committee's report. The list of 267 articles was probably submitted to Arundel on the same day or shortly after it was given to the convocation of bishops at St. Paul's.[46] A series of letters which Arundel wrote subsequent to the committee's report, however, prove most revealing. One of them, the letter that reached Prague, dated May 8, has already been discussed. From a later account by Thomas Gascoigne (writing after the Council of Basel), however, we learn that Arundel also wrote a letter to Oxford the same day, which – as was true of the Prague letter – reported the Canterbury synod's decisions regarding Wyclif's doctrines.

Gascoigne reports seeing this second letter in a large, three-volume paper copy of the *Acta* of the Councils of Pisa, Constance, and Basle (now lost), donated to Durham College, Oxford (the present Trinity College) by Robert Burton, from which he quotes the letter in full:

Archiepiscopus Cantuariensis, Thomas Arundel, in litera sua, quae incipit, "Universis Fidei Catholicae zelatoribus. Thomas, permissione divina," etc. sic scribit, "Vestrae Universitati innotescimus, quod nos, de concilio et consensu suffraganeorum nostrorum et cleri totius nostrae Cantuariensis provinciae, ipsum Johannem Wyclif velut erroneum, et suas opiniones in Theologia ut haereticas, ac in logica et philosophia ut erroneas, exactissimis examinacione et discussione praehabitis, condempnamus, prout merito fuerunt condempnandae, quod ad vestram noticiam deducimus, et deduci volumus per praesentes sigillo nostro consignatas; datum apud Girnkner, octavo die mensis May, anno Domini m° cccc° xi°, et nostrae translacionis anno xv°."[47]

[The Archbishop of Canterbury, Thomas Arundel, in his letter, which begins, "To all who jealously protect the Catholic faith, Thomas, by divine permission," etc. writes thus: "We notify your university that we, from the council and consent of our suffragans and of all the clergy of our province of Canterbury, condemn John Wyclif as erroneous, and his opinions in theology as heretical, and also [his opinions] in logic and philosophy as erroneous, having considered them with the most precise examination and discussion (as they rightly should have been condemned), which we bring to your notice, and we wish this to be shown by these present letters, attested under our seal; posted at Girnkner, on the eighth day of May, in the year of our Lord 1411, and in the fifteenth year of our translation."]

The letter is nearly identical to the one now in PNK VIII.G.13 – a point that has never been made until now. The only significant difference is that the Prague letter alludes to the Oxford testimony of Wyclif ("spiritus quidam mendacii"), while the letter to Oxford does not. And yet the fact that Arundel's letters reporting the provincial synod's decisions (sent to both Oxford and Prague) coincide with a refutation of the Oxford testimony (in the Prague version) suggests that the report of the committee of twelve and the discovery of the testimonial letter were somehow related. Thomas Netter seems to have made this same connection several years later in his *Doctrinale*. Again, Netter's report, written over a decade after the event, may be the result of hindsight historiography, but should be enlisted here as confirmatory evidence. After discussing the Oxford testimony he writes in response:

In hac iterum confusione, Wiclevistarum turba capiendam se sentit, quoniam audietur in mundo, quomodo, per publicum duodecim electissimorum virorum decretum, Oxoniense Studium plusquam ducentarum haeresum ejus dogma delevit, & codices concremavit. Tunc potuit audisse Hussita Bohemus fortitudinem maris, Britannicae scilicet Insulae, dixisse fortem Oxoniam: "Non parturivi, neque peperi juvenes Wiclevistas: non ipsos in sua perversitate nutrivi: nec has stultivagas virgines exaltavi; immo depressi; et, quantum ad me attinet, in Synodo sanctorum Antistitum, aut corripiendas, aut extra Ecclesiae januas excludendas, abjiciendas, et conculcandas penitus postulavi."[48]

[Again in this confusion, the mob of Wycliffites perceives itself about to be seized, because it shall hear in the world how, by the official decree of twelve most elect men, the *studium* of Oxford abolished [Wyclif's] dogma of more than two hundred heresies and burned his books. Then the Bohemian Hussite might have heard the strength of the sea, that is to say, mighty Oxford of the British Isle declare: "I have not brought forth, nor have I begot young Wycliffites: I have not nurtured them in their perversity: nor have I exalted these foolish wandering boys; no indeed, I have suppressed them; and, inasmuch as it fell to me, in a synod of most holy bishops, I asked that they be both censured and shut out from the gates of the Church; cast away and trampled thoroughly underfoot."]

In connection with the Oxford testimony and the report of the committee of twelve, it is appropriate to revisit another of Arundel's letters, this time to Pope John XXIII (antipope). The letter is undated, but was probably written in spring 1411.[49] Following the committee's recommendation, Arundel informed the pope of the committee's activities at Oxford and of the provincial synod's decisions regarding Wyclif's doctrines.[50] The letter accompanied the list of errors which the committee had culled from Wyclif's writings over the previous two years, but at the end of the letter,

Arundel asks for the pope's permission to dig up the bones of the heresiarch and to throw them on the dungheap or burn them.[51] Significantly, this request goes much further than the committee's recommendation, which suggested only that Arundel should forward the list of errors to the pope.[52]

Arundel's request for Wyclif's exhumation is interesting. In his letter to Prague in May, Arundel did not refute the claim that Wyclif had never been exhumed (and of course the charge was irrefutable). The list of 267 errors was enough for the archbishop to seek an exhumation, but the fact that he raised the issue with the pope suggests that he wanted the measure to have wider political resonance – that it was intended to be an unambiguous response to (even an expression that he was aware of) the rumors that had been circulating on the continent regarding Wyclif's status in England. These rumors were likely suggested to him by the Oxford testimonial, which was on his mind at least in May and which emphasized that Wyclif had never been sentenced as a heretic.

By way of a brief aside, it should be noted that nothing in the Oxford letter suggests that it was written exclusively for a Bohemian audience; it could also have circulated in England or elsewhere in Europe, as Thomas Netter seems later to insinuate.[53] We know that at least by 1415 members of the English delegation at Constance had a copy in their possession.[54] Other than the many copies in Bohemian manuscripts,[55] the only other extant copy of the letter in England is the one written in a sixteenth-century hand, now in London, British Library MS Cotton Faustina c.vii, which Wilkins used for his edition. This was not John Foxe's source for his translation of the testimony in the *Actes and monuments*, which he derived from a sixteenth-century continental edition of Hus' *Opera omnia* compiled by Matthias Flacius (Nuremberg, 1558).[56] Earlier references to the testimony by Thomas Netter and Thomas Gascoigne are more difficult to trace, as neither author gives his source for news of the testimony. Perhaps significantly, Netter and Gascoigne do not transcribe or quote directly from the letter. And if the letter did circulate in England outside of Oxford after 1406, there is a good chance that Arundel would have known of it within a very short time. Any copy that remained in England after 1406 was probably not being advertised.

HERESY AND DIPLOMACY

I have been outlining the biography of a document, the Oxford testimony, for what its adventures reveal about textual transmission in Europe in the years before Constance. Up to that time, Wycliffism and Hussitism still maintained strong university ties, which meant that reformists had access to the apparatus of textual production and dissemination – to the means, in other words, of effective propagandizing. It would take the Council of Constance itself, acting as a nexus of communication and center of book production for the whole of Europe, finally to overpower the control that reformists in England and Bohemia were able to hold over the lines of European communication. Before then, however, it was not certain that Church and secular authorities would gain the upper hand. It is in the Anglo-Imperial diplomatic correspondence before Constance, to which we now return, that the first stirrings of transnational cooperation against heterodox correspondence emerge.

In September 1411, the Oxford testimonial became an issue once again during the Stokes–von Clux embassy when the ambassadors passed through Prague on their return from Hungary, where they engaged in controversy with Hus. Information about this episode comes from three documents: Jan Hus' challenge to debate with Stokes, which he posted on the door of the house where Stokes was lodging; Stokes' reply, in which he declined Hus' challenge; and Hus' defense of Wyclif, known to scholars as *Contra Iohannem Stokes*, which he appears to have delivered despite Stokes's refusal to turn up.[57]

From Hus' challenge to debate Stokes we learn that the Englishman had been heard uttering statements touching the virtue of John Wyclif, namely,

quod quicumque legeret libros Magistri Johannis Wikleff vel studuerit in eisdem, eciam sit quomodocumque dispositus a natura vel radicatus in bona fide, ex processu temporis involvetur in heresim.[58]

[that whoever reads the books of Master John Wyclif or studies in the same, even though he may be somehow inclined by nature or rooted in good faith, in the course of time will be entangled in heresy.]

Stokes, in declining to debate (citing his need to return to England), asserted that Hus had misquoted him on certain points, but on the whole he corroborates Hus' charge. In his own words, Stokes claims to have said:

quod si scirem aliquem talem, qui legeret vel studeret in libris Wikleff, vel qui vellet fovere et retinere suas opiniones, ego vellem sibi consulere ex parte dei et ex caritativa dileccione, quam proximus habere tenetur ad proximum, quod desisteret, quia bene cognosco tanta mala ex tali studio, quod vix reperiret hominem eciam bene dispositum ad bonum, quin, si in eisdem continue studuerit, ex processu temporis involvetur in heresim.[59]

[that if I knew any such man who read or studied in Wyclif's books, or who wished to cherish and retain his opinions, I should wish to deliberate with him on behalf of

God and charitable love, as one neighbor behaves to another, that he desist, for
I know well that so much evil [comes] from such a pursuit, that scarcely it finds a
man well disposed to good, but that if he studies these things continuously, in the
course of time he will be entangled in heresy.]

The circumstances in which Stokes made these statements are particularly
interesting, because they suggest that he was aware of the role Wyclif's
doctrines played in the bitter Czech–German rivalry in Prague. Hus begins
his position by describing the conversation in which Stokes spoke ill of
Wyclif. As mentioned above, it became known in the city that "certain
masters or doctors from England" were visiting, and especially a licentiate in
law, John Stokes of Cambridge. When the masters and bachelors of Prague
went to greet Stokes, they found him rather standoffish, too tired for a long
discussion. Later the rector of the university – another of Wyclif's defenders,
Šimon of Tišnov – invited Stokes to the college for lunch, but Stokes, or
rather "a certain knight" (likely von Clux), declined. At some point during
their stay, according to Hus, Stokes and his companions were also heard
saying "multa verba honorem nostrorum regnicolarum tangencia [many
words touching the honor of our kingdom]." Perhaps, considering Hus'
defense, those words had something to do with the charge that Wyclif was
not English, but a German![60] And Stokes was eventually asked whether he
would not like to repeat any of his statements in the presence of a notary.
Evidently he was content only to reiterate his comment about the dangers of
reading Wyclif's books, which I have just cited.

Stokes also writes that "quando erat a me demandatum, quomodo fuerit
de Wikleph et opinionibus suis in regno nostro Anglie, quod ibi habetur pro
heretico; et libri sui quotquot potuerunt inveniri seu reperiri, sunt igne
combusti et cremati; et opiniones sue sunt dampnate ut hereses [when it was
asked of me how it was concerning Wyclif and his opinions in our realm of
England, [I replied] that there he is regarded as a heretic; and however many
of his books they could find or obtain, they were burned in the fire and
reduced to ashes; and his opinions are damned as heresies]."[61] The comment raises the likelihood that the events of March in England – and
perhaps the Oxford testimony of Wyclif – had at some point entered the
discussion. A book-burning like the one that Stokes mentions probably
took place at Carfax in the presence of Oxford's chancellor, Thomas
Prestbury, after the committee of twelve made its report.[62]

It is unlikely, though, that Stokes had enough contact with Hus to give
him an intimation of Arundel's refutation of the Oxford testimony.
(Indeed, Stokes may have been unaware of it.) While Hus does express
some doubt about the credibility of the testimony in his defense of

Wyclif on September 13, it does not seem that he knew of any official attempt from England (other than by Stokes) to discredit its claims. Hus writes that:

Dicit dictus dominus Iohannes Stokes in sua intimacione, quod in Anglia magister Iohannes Wigleff habetur pro heretico. Hoc videtur esse falsum ex litera universitatis Oxoniensis, cui plus est credendum quam sibi. Et si ausus fuerit dicere, quod litera est falsificata, obliget se sub pena ad hoc deducendum; quod si deduxerit, tunc Anglicos Oxonienses falsarios conprobabit, cum tam sigillum quam litere exarate in membrana patefaciunt, quod sint anglicana. Quale ergo Anglicis repatrians afferet gaudium, cum eos falsificatores ostendet literarum![63]

[the said Master John Stokes says that (in his estimate) Master John Wyclif is considered a heretic in England. This seems to be false by reason of the letter from the University of Oxford, which is more to be believed than him. And if he should dare to say that the letter is a forgery, he obliges himself under penalty to explain this; which if he should explain, then he attests that the English Oxonians are false, when both the seal and the letter inscribed on parchment[64] make clear that they are English. With what great joy, therefore, returning to his country, he shall report to the Englishmen, when he exposes them as forgers of letters!]

Hus clearly overestimated the stranglehold that he imagined the testimony would have on Wyclif's English opponents by virtue of its seal. Arundel, as we have seen, was already accusing certain men at Oxford of forging the very same letter, and would later accuse them of bringing scandal to all of England by sending it abroad. Driving all of this, however, was a search for material authenticity. But amidst the confusing abundance of contradictory authenticating signs, the transnational narrative battle over Wyclif would have to be waged through a competition to control the channels of communication.

The testimony from Oxford was just one of a number of the university's infractions in recent years, and yet extremely serious in that it served to widen the scope of the archbishop's controversy with the Wycliffite masters there. In December 1411, perhaps already briefed by the embassy which had recently returned from Hungary, the affair of the Oxford testimony would join the list of charges placed against the university by the convocation of Canterbury.[65] The severity of the infraction, as stated in the charge, was not only that the university seal had been abused to defend a heretic, but that the offending doctors and masters had sent the letter "ad regna et loca extranea [to foreign kingdoms and regions]," thereby bringing scandal to the whole realm of England.[66]

"NON SINE CORDIS AMARITUDINE": EMBARRASSMENT AND REVISION

Events like those surrounding the Oxford testimony in 1411 provide a vital backstory to the English delegation's energetic prosecution of Jan Hus at the Council of Constance, where the letter turns up once again. Peter of Mladoňovice's *Relatio* of Hus' trial, a valuable supplement to the surviving Constance *Acta*, shows that members of the English delegation were remarkably eager and prepared to question Hus on his English contacts. Mladoňovice's account singles out the English for their energetic attacks on Hus perhaps more than the representatives of any other *nacio* in attendance. His text is peppered with the assertions put forth (for example) by "quidam Anglicus [a certain Englishman],"[67] and very often in Mladoňovice's narrative the English are shown to act from a unified – even premeditated – position against Hus during the trial.[68]

At one point during the trial, Mladoňovice tells us, the English presented

copiam cujusdam literae universitatis Oxoniensis Pragam apportatae, quam dicebant magistrum Joannem in sermone publicasse et sigillum pro recommendatione ipsius Wiclef ostendisse. Et cum legissent eam, requisierunt ab eo, si eam pronuntiasset.

[a copy of a certain letter of the University of Oxford that was conveyed to Prague, which they said Master John had proclaimed in a sermon, and the seal of which he had exhibited for the recommendation of Wyclif himself. And when they read it, they asked if he had uttered it.]

Hus replied that he had, citing the seal of Oxford whence two students had brought it to him. Hus was then asked who these students were, and he claimed (as I have discussed) that one of them was Mikuláš Faulfiš, now dead, but that he did not know the second.[69] After learning of the couriers who had brought the notorious document to Prague, members of the English delegation then produced a second letter, also written over the seal of Oxford, which refuted the previous testimony of Wyclif. According to Mladoňovice the new document asserted:

qualiter non sine cordis amaritudine innotescunt, quomodo discipuli et imitatores Joannis Wiclef multos errores ex ejus libris in regno Angliae seminarunt; ideo illi malo universitas volens occurrere, deputavit XII solemnes doctores et magnos theologos, qui libros ejus diligenter revolventes, extraxerunt ex eis CCLX articulos, quos ipsa universitas diligenti examine et matura deliberatione praehabitis judicavit reos igne, sed ob reverentiam fidei et hujus sacri concilii illos huc Constantiam destinavit et transmisit condemnandos, ut in dicta litera continetur.[70]

[how not without bitterness of heart, they have come to know how disciples and imitators of John Wyclif have sown many errors from his books in the kingdom of England; therefore, the university, wishing to oppose this evil, assigned twelve solemn doctors and great theologians, who having diligently perused his books, have extracted 260 articles,[71] which the same university, through scrupulous examination and weighty deliberation, judged [that they] be committed to the fire; but out of reverence to the faith and to this sacred council, selected and carried those condemned books here to Constance, as is maintained in the said letter.]

The letter which Mladoňovice cites in epitome is certainly a later version of the letter submitted by the committee of twelve to the convocation of bishops at St. Paul's on March 17, 1411.[72] Once again, the decision of the convocation in response to the committee's report is here used to refute the claims of the Oxford testimony, as had been the case in Arundel's letter to Prague in 1411. By the time of the Council of Constance, Oxford was much more cooperative with English Church officials than it had been when the testimony of Wyclif was affixed with the university seal in 1406.[73] That same seal was used again this time in an attempt to repair the university's – and England's – damaged reputation for orthodoxy.

Mladoňovice's subtle commentary on the authority of this letter is interesting: the new letter was stamped with the seal of Oxford's chancellor, "ut dicebant [as they said]." Whom could such signs be said to represent? His circumspection may echo Hus' own growing mistrust of the English – a mistrust that would extend not only to his English interrogators, but even to Wyclif himself. When charged during the same session with preaching and defending Wyclif's errors in Prague, Hus is said to have denied it, asserting that

nec Wiclef, nec alicujus alterius praedicavit nec sequi voluit doctrinam erroneam, cum Wiclef non fuerit pater suus nec Bohemus; et si Wiclef aliquos seminavit errores, videant Anglici de illo.[74]

[he wished neither to preach nor to follow the erroneous doctrine of Wyclif, nor of any other man, as Wyclif was neither his father nor a Czech; and if Wyclif had disseminated any errors, let the English see about that.]

Hus' statement was on the one hand clearly a case of self-protectionism, though it also reveals that his struggle all along had been less about Wyclif himself than about following what he believed to be Christ's precepts. If Wyclif had said anything in error, let others who are concerned about the man attend to that; Hus, for his part, was concerned with Christ's laws wherever they may be found. Tragically for Hus, things were not so simple: his successful condemnation would directly enhance England's reputation for orthodoxy, a reputation which Hus had been instrumental in damaging in no small measure by advertising the Oxford letter.

"STUPENDAS ATQUE HORRENDAS NOUITATES DE ANGLIA ANIMADUERTITE"

By way of conclusion, I want to discuss another episode that lay at the intersection of English religious politics and Anglo-Imperial diplomacy, to suggest that English treatment of Wycliffism beyond its own borders before Constance was not an isolated incident. When he came to England in 1416 to negotiate what is now known as the Treaty of Canterbury, Sigismund, who had by then presided over the Council of Constance for more than a year, was aware of the ease with which many tenets of Wycliffite doctrine could be given seditious interpretations, and how Wycliffite challenges to ecclesiastical authority could likewise be turned on the secular arm. This seditious potential was brought to Sigismund's attention, for example, on June 8, 1415, when an exasperated Jan Hus, whose teachings had been linked persistently (if imprecisely) by that time to those of Wyclif, asserted in Sigismund's presence that "qui est in peccato mortali, nec est digne rex coram deo [he who is in mortal sin is not worthily a king before God]"; to which Pierre d'Ailly, the Cardinal of Cambrai, responded (also in Sigismund's presence):

Non sufficiebat tibi, quia statum spiritualem vilipendens conabaris dejicere per tua scripta et dogmata, et jam vis etiam dejicere statum regium et reges a statu suo.[75]

[Because despising the spiritual order by trying to overthrow it through your writings and teachings was not enough for you, now you also wish to overthrow the royal order and kings from their rank.]

How strange it must have seemed to the emperor-elect, then, when during his visit to London the next summer certain Lollards tried to enlist him in their causes of clerical disendowment and royal deposition. Sigismund landed at Dover on May 1, 1416 and his presence in England made a dramatic impression.[76] One purpose of his visit was again to establish the terms of an alliance with the English, and this aim was at last accomplished by the Treaty of Canterbury, signed August 15.[77] On the previous day, however, Thomas Lucas, an English lawyer and by all signs a Lollard,[78] was cited for distributing bills throughout the country as well as a petition to Sigismund, in which he advocated that the religious should neither hold nor enjoy temporal possessions, that Richard II was alive and well in Edinburgh, and that Henry V should be deposed and put to death.[79] From the trial record of two of Lucas' co-conspirators, Benedict Woolman and

Thomas Bekeryng,[80] we learn more specifically the contents of the letter to Sigismund, which alleged:

that the said Richard the Second, late King of England, was in full life, in the parts of Scotland, in the custody of the Duke of Albany, by consent of our said Lord the King, now reigning; who, by consent of the said Duke of Albany, wrongfully, as they asserted, had detained and kept the King of Scotland out of his realm of Scotland aforesaid, and within the realm of England; asking the King of the Romans with a strong hand and powerful arm to bring back the said Thomas Trumpyngtone, whom they so assert to be the said late King Richard, as being such late King, into the realm of England, and raise him to the kingly power in that realm, and to depose our said Lord the King, now reigning, from his regal estate, and so disinherit him and his heirs aforesaid of such realm of England.[81]

Sigismund, as might be expected, promptly handed the letter to King Henry.

The incident of the petition is filled all the more with irony in that it was probably not Sigismund's first encounter with traitorous Lollard conspiracies. On another occasion before the Council of Constance news of a plot in England was conveyed to the Empire through diplomatic channels. Almost immediately after Henry V ascended the English throne in March 1413, Sigismund expressed interest in continuing discussions of a General Council with the new king.[82] The following July, Henry would send a solemn embassy consisting of Walter Hungerford, John Waterton, and Simon Sydenham to Koblenz in Germany,[83] where they met with Sigismund.

That mission was preceded, however, by a lesser-known embassy of Hartung von Clux, whom Henry sent to deliver letters and news to Sigismund and to prepare for the embassy that would set out in July. One of the documents attesting to this earlier mission is the letter of procuration for Hungerford and the other ambassadors, dated July 23, which states that Henry had been informed of Sigismund's desire to enter into "Foedera Amicitiarum et Ligarum [an alliance of friendship and confederacy]" by Hartung von Clux.[84] Many of the details of that earlier discussion are reported by a letter from Sigismund to Henry, which must have been written before Hungerford and the others set out. That letter was carried to England by George von Czedlycz (Sedlec), a knight who probably accompanied von Clux back to London.[85] In it, Sigismund indicates that (as in 1411) he and Hartung had discussed a range of issues, from relations with France to winning the support of the contending popes (at that time three of them) for the upcoming council at Constance. Hartung was in an excellent position to brief Hungerford and the other ambassadors on Sigismund's intentions before they left at the end of July.

More central for us, however, are the signs that Hartung had also discussed matters of a more private nature with Sigismund. Again from Sigismund's letter to Henry we learn that Hartung had been sent in part to assure the emperor-elect of Henry's safety: "Excellentie . . . vestre litteras," writes Sigismund,

dudum de manibus nobilis Hartungi Clux militis et oratoris vestri nostrique fidelis dilecti gratas referentes de vestra incolumitate rumores cum animi iocunditate receptas exultantes in illo et ei gratias referentes, qui regibus dat salutem.[86]

[recently from the hands of the noble knight Hartung von Clux, your orator and our esteemed loyal [servant], letters from Your Excellence, conveying welcome news of your safety, were received with a joyful heart, exulting in [the news] and giving thanks to the one who grants safety to kings.]

Sigismund does not elaborate on the content of these letters. The fact that he calls Hartung "orator," however, suggests that von Clux had additionally delivered a verbal message. Sigismund immediately goes on to say that he has likewise instructed Hartung to relate information to the king by mouth ("vivis relatibus ab ore nostro"). The delivery of oral messages by proctors on such missions, particularly by *nuncii simplices*, was a common practice, and not necessarily a sign of secrecy (and indeed diplomatic letters themselves were often delivered orally).[87] Still, the placement of this detail immediately following the reference to letters conveying reports of Henry's safety suggests that Sigismund's oral message to the English king pertained to the same issue.

So what were the "rumores incolumitate" that Henry conveyed to Sigismund? Considering the timing of Hartung's mission, the news of Henry's safety probably had something to do with the so-called Oldcastle Rising of January 10, 1414.[88] Aspects of Oldcastle's connections with Lollardy, and particularly his correspondence with Hus and his supporters in Bohemia, have been discussed in the previous chapter. After his series of communication with the Hussites and Václav IV in 1410–11, Oldcastle became increasingly notorious as an abettor of the Lollard sect. His previous service to Henry IV and Henry V, together with his noble status, spared him for a time from prosecution, but in June 1413 Henry V no longer could turn a blind eye to the evidence which established Oldcastle's ties to heresy. After a series of unsuccessful attempts to reform him, Henry finally turned Oldcastle over to Archbishop Arundel who, failing to win his confession, excommunicated him and handed him in turn to the secular arm for imprisonment in the Tower. Oldcastle soon escaped and became a fugitive until, according to several accounts, on the night of January 9–10, 1414 he and his accomplices (the names and numbers vary) attempted to implement a plot to murder the king and his brothers, and to attack the religious in London. Ultimately overwhelmed by Henry's forces who already had learned of the plot, Oldcastle evaded capture and remained in hiding until he was discovered and executed three years later.

The suspicion that von Clux may have conveyed news of the rising to Sigismund is supported by two copies of a document that reached the Empire, one of them now in Třeboň, Státní oblastní archiv MS A.16, the other found on a pastedown that was detatched from a book cover in the nineteenth century,[89] the incipit of which – "Stupendas atque horrendas nouitates de Anglia animaduertite [Hear the astounding and dreadful news from England]" – initiates a fascinating and entirely unexamined account of events leading up to and through the Oldcastle Rising of January 1414. The "nouitates" probably reached the Empire shortly after the events they narrate occurred: the narrative begins with an account of Arundel accusing Oldcastle of being the leader of the Wycliffite heresy, which Arundel is said to have done "ante festum Michaelis proxime preteritum [before the feast of St. Michael most recently gone by [September 29, 1413]]." The account ends by reporting the punishment of many of the conspirators and the notice of a reward for the capture of Oldcastle or of members of his sect in the immediate aftermath of the rising. There is no detail, in other words, which would exclude the possibility that it was written in June–July 1414, around the time of Hartung's mission. The narrative differs, moreover, from most other accounts, whose authors benefit from a greater degree of historical distance. This, I suggest, is one of the earliest extant narrative accounts of the Oldcastle Rising.

Most of the details of the narrative are comparable to those found in the familiar versions, but there are some surprises. We are not told, for example, that after Oldcastle was condemned by Arundel he escaped from the Tower and went into hiding. Instead we read that:

baro, post condempnacionem suam de Lundunio recedens, habuit quendam pauperem monachum obuium sibi in campo de Ordine Predicatorum, et eius caput abscidi fecit, dicens: "Tales homines Deo invtiles" et suam sectam magis esse gratam (quia in conuentu Ordinis Predicatorum fuit condempnatus in Lundonio); significans archiepiscopo Cantuariensi quod caput suum abscidere et habere vellet, ut sibi caueret.

[the baron, withdrawing from London after his condemnation, came across a certain poor monk from the Order of Preachers in the field, [and] caused his head to be cut off, saying: "Such men are useless to God," and that his own sect (because it was condemned in London in a convention of the Order of Preachers) was dearer [to God]; signifying to the Archbishop of Canterbury that he [i.e., Oldcastle] wanted to cut off his [i.e., the archbishop's] head and to have it, and that he [the archbishop] should look out for himself.]

And while Oldcastle does appear in the narrative of the rising in St. Giles' Fields (not all of the accounts refer to him as present at that location), much of the action surrounds John Beverly,[90] also described as "lord" and "heresiarch," but whose actions and punishment most closely resemble those of Sir Roger Acton, who in several of the accounts from England is more central to the action than Oldcastle.[91]

The episode which tells of the carpenters who warned Henry of the plot is moreover related in vivid detail, together with a description of their motives and dialogue with the king. Most attention is reserved, however, for Henry's patient attempts to reform Oldcastle, his plans to thwart the plot when it comes to his attention through the workings of divine assistance, and his crushing defeat of the attempted rising – the brainchild (by this account) of John Oldcastle. In terms of emphasis, then, the version of the rising that reached the Empire resembles Walsingham's account in the *Chronica maiora* as well as that of the *Gesta Henrici Quinti*, as would be expected in a Lancastrian-sponsored account of the rising.[92]

But to return to the diplomatic context of the account's transmission, what purpose would it serve for Henry to send such news to Sigismund? The transmission of the text suggests that Henry envisioned the prosecution of heresy – and the matter of conveying his zeal for pursuing heretics – as a problem that had to be approached on a European scale, not localized within the confines of English religious politics. Arundel had earlier realized in the process of routing out heresy at Oxford that the battle against Wycliffism had to be waged on multiple fronts. Most of his attention remained, nonetheless, firmly set on the prosecution of heresy in England, and, after all, he could only hope to control events in his own country.

Could Henry V have taken still more concrete steps by sharing information abroad pertaining to heresy in England?[93] On the one hand, of course, his act of sending the news of Oldcastle to Sigismund was an instance of political posturing; just as he had done in England, Henry actively promoted a narrative of Lancastrian right rule, guided by providence, in support of what was probably the most important alliance of his reign: that with the King of the Romans. It may not be inappropriate here to recall the discussions of "mutual assistance" begun with Henry's father in 1411, and revisited in subsequent embassies. Could this provision have extended to a joint effort finally to condemn Wyclif and Hus at Constance, establishing both Henry's and Sigismund's credentials as Christian princes? The account of the Oldcastle Rising that reached Central Europe suggests that the circulation of news about the prosecution of heretics comprised part of Henry's effort to fight heresy and to defend England's national reputation. Constance became the forum where these efforts were most forcefully realized – but the ground for this was prepared earlier.

We must, of course, stop short of claiming that the two leaders specifically planned a joint campaign against heresy. The references to oral messages between Henry and Sigismund which I have discussed lack the specific details that would reward further scrutiny. An indication of Henry's commitment to fighting Wycliffism writ large may, however, be suggested by the company he kept. It is significant, for example, that Henry's confessor, Thomas Netter, would in the aftermath of the Council of Constance write the only systematic attack by an English author on Wycliffism in its English and Bohemian forms, the *Doctrinale fidei ecclesiae*. Netter may briefly have attended the Council of Constance,[94] but his detailed knowledge of the Bohemian factions, unrivalled by any Englishman until (and perhaps including) John Foxe in the next century, probably came to him by other means. In 1419 Henry sent him at Sigismund's request to negotiate a peace agreement between the Polish king and the Teutonic Knights, and he likely stopped through Bohemia.[95] Importantly, he was accompanied on this embassy by Hartung von Clux, who continued to be a trusted servant to both Henry and Sigismund.[96]

Henry's brother Humfrey, the Duke of Gloucester, whom Henry appointed chamberlain of England after his succession, also appears in connection with a number of personages and events that are relevant to the present study. Humfrey welcomed Sigismund at Dover in May 1416.[97] His interest in the fifteenth-century councils is attested by the books he owned and the coterie with which he associated. He shared books with his friend John Whethamstede, who owned a copy of the *Doctrinale*,[98] and whose *Granarium* (a copy of which Humfrey donated to Oxford)[99] contains entries on Hus and Jerome of Prague. He also owned a copy of the Constance *Acta*, which he obtained from the estate of Thomas Polton, who had been a member of the official delegation at the council.[100] Though Humfrey later nursed a rivalry with Henry Beaufort, his (and Henry's) uncle and papal legate in charge of Martin V's fourth crusade against the Hussites (1427), he was interested in the subsequent conciliar proceedings at Basle, and commissioned Zano Castiglione to procure books for him there.[101] When he died, Humfrey's reputation as a humanist had spread throughout Europe, and he was eulogized by Aeneas Silvius Piccolomini (later Pope Pius II),[102] whose *Historia Bohemica* (1458) leveled an energetic attack against heretics in Bohemia.

An excursus on Henry's associations with men like Netter and Humfrey would soon grow very long. By way of parenthesis, however, I should mention that at least one other figure who was involved directly with the production of diplomatic documents for the embassies I have discussed also participated in the Lancastrian propaganda machine in the wake of the Oldcastle Rising. Thomas Hoccleve, poet and clerk of the Privy Seal, may have written his "Remonstrance against Oldcastle" as part of a delicate but failed effort to bring Oldcastle back into allegiance with Henry V (whom Hoccleve styles "our cristen prince") in 1415.[103] There is no direct way to link Hoccleve or anyone else from the Privy Seal with reports of Oldcastle's rising to Sigismund, but Privy Seal clerks were clearly alert to the gravity of England's relations with the emperor-elect. Hoccleve's formulary as well as that of his associate John Prophete (Keeper of the Privy Seal from 1406–15) both contain many of the documents from which we learn about the embassies that passed between England and the Empire in the years preceding the Council of Constance.[104] The Privy Seal – an office that straddled the divide between domestic and international politics – would have been an ideal instrument for Henry V to employ in lending otherwise domestic issues like the prosecution of Wycliffism a continental scope.

The episodes I have examined in this chapter should change what we see as an effect, if not a purpose, of a number of the embassies that passed between England and the Holy Roman Empire between 1411 and 1414. On the one hand, these embassies were occasions when English religious politics caught up with Anglo-Bohemian heretical communication; when the response to that communication would come to influence English policy toward heresy in the forum of a General Council. On the other hand, the important diplomatic channel between England and the King of the Romans became useful as a way for English officials to control the trafficking of documents and rumors regarding their prosecution of heresy.

A lasting effect of this marriage of diplomacy and religious politics was a fuller understanding for the English that Wycliffism was no longer just an English heresy or a strictly domestic problem. It had become the "doctrina . . . laudata in remotis partibus [the doctrine praised in far off regions]" most elaborately discussed by Thomas Netter just a few years later.[105] This was an understanding that led to repeated attempts to pursue the Wycliffites outside of England during the Hussite Crusades and at the Council of Basle, even if – as was true at Constance – English foreign policy regarding heresy would continue to be determined less by a concern for Wycliffism in its many forms than by a drive to shore up England's damaged reputation for orthodoxy.

CHAPTER 5

The aftermath: Bohemia in English religious polemic before Foxe

> I am the kingdom of Boeme
> I do not tel al men what I do meane;
> For the popes curse I do lytle care
> The more the fox is cursed the better he doth fare.
> Ever sense Wyclif did dwel with me
> I did never set by the popes auctorite.[1]

During the course of the Great Schism, England's sphere of cultural interaction came to include areas of Central and Eastern Europe with which, until that time, it had communicated only sporadically. Yet within a short space of time, a growing sensitivity to heterodox communication (as outlined in the previous chapter) contributed to a hasty restriction of open Anglo-Bohemian cultural exchange, with the exception of confrontational periods during the crusades against the Hussites (1420–c.1434) and at the Council of Basle (1431–45). By the time Basle was convened, it had become clear that Bohemian affairs would not retreat quietly to the margins of Latin Christendom (indeed, as this study has shown, Bohemia was hardly marginal to European affairs in the first place), but would remain a permanent fixture in European – and specifically English – religious politics. That new reality, as I outline in this chapter, was marked in English religious controversy, which served to maintain Bohemia's relevance for the English through the Reformation period.

In the period between the Council of Constance (1414–18) and the Henrician Reformation (1530–38),[2] religious controversialists in England referred to the Bohemian Revolution that erupted in the wake of Constance with striking regularity, suggesting a sustained interest in the situation there. This was a serious matter for the English, arousing the attention of men like Thomas Netter, Reginald Pecock and Thomas Gascoigne in the fifteenth century, and Thomas More, Cardinal Thomas Wolsey and Henry VIII in the sixteenth. At the beginning of this period, not long after Constance,

Thomas Netter emphasized the role that Wyclif's teachings had played in promoting heresy and revolution in Bohemia. Later in the fifteenth century, controversialists complicated the matter, claiming a variety of social ailments (e.g., clerical absenteeism, individualized interpretation of Scripture, etc.) as the primary causes of the Bohemian troubles, and suggesting that if similar trends were not halted in England, the same kind of social upheaval could rear its head there as well.

By the sixteenth century, "Bohemia" had become synonymous with sedition and unchecked revolt in the context of English religious polemic. In the face of a new Lutheran predicament, sixteenth-century Catholic controversialists adapted to their new situation by drawing upon established polemical motifs concerning Bohemia – motifs originating in part from medieval controversy – refurbishing them for their attacks on Luther. And whereas fifteenth-century polemicists seldom acknowledge a clear distinction between Wycliffism and Hussitism, many controversialists similarly blur the line between Hussitism and Lutheranism in the early modern period.

Circumstances surrounding the Council of Constance on the one end and the Henrician Reformation on the other altered the content and agendas of English accounts of Bohemia in significant ways, bracketing off an intervening period of English polemic which had its own distinct characteristics. Before Constance, English interest in Bohemia was mainly restricted to Anne of Bohemia and her entourage – their presence in England in particular – and, as I have discussed in Chapter 4, there were some signs of anxiety about what the spread of Wycliffism to Bohemia was doing to England's reputation for orthodoxy. The Council of Constance shifted the focus to events going on inside Bohemia itself. This was made possible by the unprecedented exchange of texts and information from across Europe, and by the amount of attention which the council, including an influential English contingent, paid to the Lollard–Hussite alliance. On the latter end of the period in question, Henry VIII's establishment of an English church separate from Rome – and his perceived need to legitimize such an autonomous, national church – created institutional support for a new kind of discussion about Bohemia, one which was later popularized by Protestant polemicists like John Foxe in his martyrology, the *Actes and monuments*, which I have discussed periodically in the preceding chapters.

Between these two watershed events, English controversialists realized the gravity of the situation in Bohemia and its implications for England. This realization prompted an increased focus on Bohemian affairs, and from this new attention, Bohemia gained a reputation in England which remained associated with it for over a century. Whether that reputation amounts to an accurate picture – of life in Bohemia, of the nature of influence from Wyclif to Hus, or from Hus to Luther – is another matter. My point is that the notoriety which Bohemia accrued in the context of English religious controversy affected the course of that controversy, as well as having widespread political ramifications. As such, that reputation deserves study in its own right.

FROM CONSTANCE TO BASLE: THOMAS NETTER AND
INTERNATIONAL WYCLIFFISM

Fifteenth-century churchmen in England watched with increasing concern as the situation in Hussite Bohemia worsened from a widening schism with the Church to a protracted revolution. The English were not unique in their concern, as can be gathered from the widespread attention given to the trials of Jan Hus and Jerome of Prague during the Council of Constance, to the Hussite Wars which ensued shortly after, and eventually to the negotiations with the Bohemians at the Council of Basle. When it came to the Bohemians, however, the English were not just one concerned party like all the rest – for the English had also produced John Wyclif and the Wycliffites, and the Wycliffites had much to do (particularly in contemporary estimation) with what was happening in Bohemia. For the English, Bohemian affairs were uncomfortably pertinent.

This awkward association posed unique problems for the English in the fifteenth century. While ecclesiastical and secular leaders from elsewhere in Europe were distressed by the revolution in Bohemia, continental leaders could take some comfort in the fact that at least their countrymen had not contributed to it so directly.[3] The English had no such consolation – a detail which others were keen to point out. Still worse, if English Lollards and Bohemian Hussites (both called "Wyclefistae") had a common root in the teachings of John Wyclif, as was generally assumed, then what would stop revolution from flaring up in England, too? After all, Sir John Oldcastle had attempted a rising in 1414, and churchmen like Thomas Netter were well aware of Oldcastle's communication with the Bohemians (though I have seen no allegation that the Bohemians had anything to do with the 1414 rising).[4] A few decades earlier, the Peasants' Revolt of 1381 had met with more success. The Lollards were not clearly the prime movers of that revolt, but there was plenty of accusation to the contrary. Later in 1431, William Perkins (alias Jack Sharpe) attempted still another Lollard rebellion.[5] Something had to be done, then, not only to preserve reputations – were the English doing enough to combat heresy? – but also to prevent Bohemian-style sedition on English soil. English efforts at Constance would not be enough.

By the end of the 1420s, Thomas Netter had completed his vast work, the *Doctrinale fidei ecclesiae*.[6] This scathing attack on the Wycliffites was so influential because it was both concrete and comprehensive. Netter did not merely undercut the logic of Wyclif's doctrines as men like William Woodford had done. He also cited Church tradition and history to establish precedents for his refutations. By virtue of this historical approach, his work remained influential well beyond the sixteenth century because it continued to be useful in countering Protestantism.[7] And yet Netter's tendency to situate his arguments in historical precedent was not limited to the distant past. Recent and ongoing events in Bohemia provided compelling illustrations of what Netter thought to be the logical extensions of Wycliffite doctrine.

Like many of his contemporaries, Netter believed that the Hussite movement had its origins in John Wyclif's teachings. Wycliffism, according to such thinking, was a broad European heresy, not just an English anomaly. As such, calling attention to the scale of this heresy enhanced the significance of the arguments Netter was making against the English Lollards, his primary adversaries.[8] A continental link suggested that Lollardy was not a contained insular movement, and (equally importantly) neither was its Bohemian offshoot. That is the reason, I suggest, why Netter was so alarmed about events in Bohemia, and why he peppered his text with references to them: if the difference between the movements was essentially one of geographical location, what was to stop similar events from happening in England? Netter understood that in order to eliminate Wyclif's heresy, he would have to redefine the parameters of that heresy, and level an attack on a much broader scale. Indeed, his treatment of the Bohemian crisis is the most detailed of any English account of events in Bohemia before the days of John Foxe.

Netter did not deliberately fabricate a line of direct descent from English to Bohemian reformers; there is every reason to suppose that he believed they were essentially members of the same movement (and there were, of course, many legitimate connections). His knowledge of the precise circumstances of Lollard–Hussite correspondence was incomplete,[9] but this does not change the fact that he knew such correspondence had taken place. Netter's main concern was evidently not to expose the heretics' travel routes or the correspondents who used them. He knew that Wyclif's doctrines had got to Bohemia, and that was what really mattered.

Even if Netter believed that Hussites were essentially Wycliffites by another name, he was informed enough to know that they were not identical in every way. He realizes, for example, that the Bohemians do not necessarily follow Wyclif in his doctrine of the Eucharist. No matter, though, for "Hussitae omnes sunt in Wiclevistarum fonte damnati, quamvis ab eis in haeresi Eucharistiae sint semoti [all the Hussites are damned at the source of the Wycliffites, even if they may be separated from them in the heresy of the Eucharist]."[10] If two trunks grow from the same corrupt root, in other words, does it really matter if they have slightly different crooks in them?

Netter also picks up on the fact that Hus had gained a substantial following for himself after introducing Wyclif's heresies to Bohemia. These days, writes Netter,

Sectatores illius haeresis ibi appellantur Hussitae, amisso nomine principis sui Wicleffi; quemadmodum amisso nomine Donati in Africa, postmodum Sectatores illius Rogatistae dici coeperunt.[11]

[the followers of [Hus'] heresy there are called "Hussites," having done away with the name of his leader, Wyclif; just as, when they did away with the name of "Donatists" in Africa, [Donatus'] followers afterward began to be called "Rogatists".]

For Netter, such heresies are cults of personality more than anything else, invariably tending toward novelty. Admittedly, they participate in a kind of diabolical lineage, and so they are not entirely new; indeed, their descent from heretical forebears is largely what condemns them by precedent. However, one of their defining characteristics is fractiousness, and that tendency is what makes their doctrines and practices particularly volatile.

The fractiousness takes many forms. At one point, Netter claims that the Bohemian reformers – here the "polluted Praguers" ("polluti Pragenses") – prefer their own Mass book, complete "with every Bohemian novelty" ("omni novitate Bohemica"), over the Scriptures.[12] Even among themselves, the Bohemians cannot agree on a liturgy for their new Mass. Netter writes:

Pragensium Wiclevistarum quidam feruntur pro Missae officio Evangelium totum dicere secundum Joannem, *Ante diem festum Paschae*: quidam, *Qui pridie*: quidam aliud.[13]

[For the office of the Mass, some of the Prague Wycliffites are permitted to say the entire Gospel following John, *Ante diem festum Paschae*: certain others [are permitted to say], *Qui pridie*, and still others [are permitted to say] something else.]

For Netter, though, the Bohemians' disorganized doctrine and liturgy is only part of the problem: on a more worrisome scale, the heretics inflict their disorder on the entire kingdom. In the sixth and final book of the *Doctrinale*,

De sacramentalibus, Netter provides a striking illustration of events rumored to be occurring in Bohemia – events which, he claims, expose how savage the Wycliffites really can be, if only they are given the chance:

Hanc persecutionem, religiosi viri damnis rerum, et opprobriis haereticis agitantibus senserunt in Anglia. Sed extremam saevitiam Wiclevistarum ipsi omnes experiuntur in Bohemia, ubi locorum sanctorum eversiones, claustrorum combustiones, violationes virginum, caedes horrendae, sanctorum jugulationes, mactationes sub malleis de membro in membrum, contritiones sanctorum corporum etiam petris molaribus, liquentia item metalla gustant, et exilia vice magnae pietatis gratanter accipiunt: centies acrius sub falsi tituli christianis, quam sub veris Turcis, et Saracenis afflicti.[14]

[In England, devout men have felt this persecution in the form of losses to their property and the agitation caused by heretics' slanders. But in Bohemia the devout are all experiencing the most extreme form of Wycliffite savagery: the ransacking of holy sites, the burning of monasteries, the rape of virgins; terrible slaughters, the butchering of saints, the use of hammers to dismember them limb by limb; even the use of millstones to grind the saints' bodies; they drink molten metals, and willingly accept exile in return for their great devotion. They are afflicted a hundred times more cruelly by "Christians" who bear that name falsely than by actual Turks or Saracens.]

While those who are pious in England have not gone unscathed, Netter implies, the English do not really know what the Wycliffites are capable of doing (again, following his assumption that Lollards and Hussites are all "Wyclefistae"). When combined, Netter's references to Bohemia give the impression that schism is endemic to Bohemian society under the Hussites; doctrinal fissures have become physical violence, a battle of doctrines turned civil war.

Thomas Netter's concern about the Bohemians peaked earlier than that of many in the English Church and secular hierarchies. By 1427, he had already dedicated the first two parts of his *Doctrinale* (books 1–5) to Pope Martin V, who received them warmly.[15] These sections contained several of Netter's references to the Bohemians, though not his most gruesome report (from book 6, quoted above) detailing the Wycliffite savagery in Bohemia. His decision to dedicate portions of the *Doctrinale* to the pope was timely, occurring in the midst of the ongoing crusading campaign against the Bohemian heretics; and as Netter was probably writing the third part of his work, *De sacramentalibus*, tidings from Rome reached the English.

Evidently, it was not with men like Netter in mind that Martin V, in a letter dated October 9, 1428, admonished the English Church hierarchy, roundly warning the prelates of the Bohemian threat to England and criticizing their apparent laxity in routing out heretics in their own land – heretics who (he argued) were fuelling the Bohemian menace. In fact, Netter may have influenced the pope's views on the exchanges between English and Bohemian heretics.[16] Martin V reminds the English churchmen that the Bohemian heresy began in England, and that if the English are to preserve their reputation, they will need not only to recognize this fact, but to act upon it. He points out that whenever the issue is discussed, "mox subjungitur, Ex Anglia eam derivasse [soon it is added that [the heresy in Bohemia] originated in England]"; apparently this is old news to everyone but the English. The pope also writes that

remanserunt ibidem hujus haeresis non parvi surculi, qui nisi celeriter extirpentur, adhuc ita exurgent in altum, quod valde dubitandum est ne Anglia (quod Deus per suam misericordiam avertat) adveniat quemadmodum & Bohemia: quod & si superiori tempore nonnulla indicia apparuerunt, a paucis citra diebus evidentius detectum est; cum in diversis Angliae partibus multi reperti sunt & capti haeretici, quos & fama refert, & valde verisimile est, multos habere participes & magnum sociorum numerum, qui, ut quotidie fieri solet, inficientes & seducentes alios in perniciem totius regni crescent & abundabunt magis, quamdiu vigebit in Bohemia haec haeresis. Et a fide dignis accepimus, & vos certius intellexisse debetis, quod saepenumero a Wicklefistis in Anglia latentibus, in Bohemiam proficiscuntur nuncii, illos in sua perfidia confortantes, & praebentes eisdem auxilii & subsidii spem.[17]

[there have remained [in England] not a few shoots of this heresy which, unless they are quickly rooted out, will continue thus to grow high; so that there is great doubt whether England (may God in His mercy prevent it) may not come to the same fate as Bohemia. Even if no indications appeared in former times, it has been detected more evidently in recent days, when in different parts of England, many heretics have been detected and captured. A rumor reports, and it is very likely, that they have many associates and a great number of allies who (as daily it comes to pass), infecting and seducing others to the destruction of the entire realm, will increase and become more abundant, until this heresy thrives in Bohemia. Similarly, we have been informed by a trustworthy source (and you certainly ought to have perceived) that frequently messengers of the Wycliffites, hiding in England, set out for Bohemia, to encourage [the Hussites] in their faithlessness and provide them with the hope of assistance and support.]

It may seem strange that, at a time when the Lancastrians, in association with the ecclesiastical hierarchy, were very much intent upon stamping out Lollardy, the pope should question the seriousness with which the English were addressing heresy. To understand this apparent irony, however, we should keep in mind that churchmen (especially outside of England, it seems) typically made very little distinction between "Wycliffites" in

England or Bohemia (with Netter as an important exception). The pope, keen on gathering support for his crusading missions, suggests that the English are out of step with the times: if the Lancastrian regime is really serious about Lollardy, it can no longer define it as an English heresy.

English reaction to the papal warning was lukewarm initially,[18] but slowly officials came round to the idea that confronting the Hussites was in their best interest.[19] Still, even after the pope rebuked them, the English were not eager to expand their initiatives against heretics outside of England in material terms – a likely reason being that they were already engaged in war with the French. A diplomatic solution to the Bohemian schism was more attractive than a military one (and surely they knew how poorly the crusades were going). The Council of Basle would provide them with an opportunity to exercise their diplomacy. From the very beginning of the English correspondence with the council, moreover, they made it clear that their primary interest in sending an embassy was to restore the Bohemians to the Church.[20]

"BOHEMIA" AS AN ENGLISH COMMONPLACE

English involvement at Basle brought greater visibility to the Bohemian issue in England. This is one way to account for the proliferation of references to the Bohemian Revolution in the second half of the fifteenth century. Netter's ideas about Bohemia also held currency (at least analogously) in England after Basle, even if his influence over later treatments of the Bohemian Revolution was not always direct.[21] In the second half of the fifteenth century, English assessments of the Bohemian Revolution came from several directions, and as a polemical motif, "Bohemia" became much more adaptable than before. No longer was the emphasis on heretical communication and textual transmission; the tone now was one of alarm over the threat of widespread social upheaval and its potential spread to England. Everyone agreed that something had gone terribly wrong in Bohemia; the reason why this happened was another matter. Many of the suggestions may have had more to do with a particular author's pet issues than with an intimate familiarity with Bohemia, and while feasible explanations were offered, they typically suggest that English discussions of Bohemia were more about England than anything else – but importantly, England vis-à-vis Bohemia.

Reginald Pecock was the next major anti-Lollard polemicist in England after Netter to reference Bohemia for polemical purposes. In his *Repressor of Over Much Blaming of the Clergy* (completed *c*.1455), Pecock was concerned to reveal (among other things) the dangers that would ensue should the "lay parti . . . attende and truste to her owne wittis" in the exposition of Scripture, rather than heeding more "substanciali leerned clerkis."[22] He feared that unregulated interpretation of such a complex and foundational text as the Bible would soon degenerate into backbiting, where people act "as doggis doon in a market, whanne ech of hem terith otheris coot."[23] Pecock worries, though, that things will get much worse than people bickering like "doggis . . . in a market": "eende schulde ther neuere be of her [i.e., the lay parti's] strijf," he claims, "into tyme that thei schulden falle into fiȝting and into werre and bateil; and thanne schulde al thrift and grace passe awey, and noon of her holdingis schulde in eny point be therbi strengthid or confermed."[24] His point is that the confusion which arises from unrestrained interpretation is unlikely to remain on a hermeneutic level; inevitably this confusion finds its way into physical violence on a more destructive scale, making its prevention all the more urgent. After all, Pecock wasn't making this up: "Certis in this wise and in this now seid maner," he recalls, "and bi this now seid cause bifille the rewful and wepeable destruccioun of the worthi citee and vniuersite of Prage, and of the hool rewme of Beeme, as y haue had ther of enformacioun ynouȝ."[25] It was no wonder that "to hem [i.e., the Bohemians] bifille the now seid wrecchid mys chaunce" – this had all been foretold in Christ's prophecy in Luke's Gospel (11.17) *"that ech kingdom deuidid in hem silf schal be destruyed."*[26]

Pecock's logical progression sounds a lot like Netter's. Both men agree that in the absence of some kind of stabilizing oversight, individualized interpretation leads to progressively serious forms of social unraveling. But whereas for Netter the hermeneutic conflict was closely bound up with Wyclif's heresy, not individualized interpretation broadly defined, Pecock does not make the same explicit connection. His ambiguity is consistent with his practice of avoiding terms like "Lollard" in the treatise, probably so that his arguments would appear less confrontational – he wants to bring the Lollards back into the fold through gentle correction, not crushing critique. Pecock still assumes some kind of circumstantial similarity between England and Bohemia ("God for his merci and pitee kepe Ynglond, that he come not into lijk daunce," he prays),[27] but without explicitly referencing the Lollard–Hussite alliance, his warning applies even to those who may not be Lollards, but may nevertheless sympathize with their interpretational practices.

Thomas Gascoigne had other ideas about what caused the troubles in Bohemia. Gascoigne's *Dictionarium theologicum*, compiled throughout much of his life, is an alphabetically arranged preaching guide with entries on a range of theological topics, as well as a lively repository of his views on historical and contemporary issues. Included in the collection are two related issues which aroused his particular scorn: clerical absenteeism and plurality of benefice. So detrimental were these abuses, he claimed, that they were largely responsible for what had happened to Bohemia. In the entry "Appropriacio et non residencia" Gascoigne offers the following assessment of Bohemia's downfall: "Indigna enim promocio inhabilium personarum et appropriacio ecclesiarum parochialium causae fuerunt destruccionis regni Bohemorum, et hereticorum illam patriam et regnum destruentium [Indeed, the unworthy advancement of incapable persons and the appropriation of parish churches were the reasons that the kingdom of Bohemia was destroyed, and that heretics ruined that country and kingdom]."[28] Gascoigne knew that the situation in Bohemia arose from a number of factors. The heretics were allowed to take over the realm of Bohemia because the clerics – who were incompetent and who were not occupying their benefices to begin with – were not around to stop them. Such pastoral negligence reached all the way to Rome, he argues; when the University of Prague sought help from Martin V, no help came to them. No wonder the opportunistic heretics took over: when the Church would send no help, "destructum est regnum Bohemorum et ecclesiae destructae et combustae per Hus hereticorum principem et per Petrum Clark Anglicum [the kingdom of Bohemia was destroyed, and the churches [were] ruined and burned by Hus, the prince of heretics, and by Peter Clark the Englishman [i.e., Peter Payne]]."[29] Gascoigne clearly has no sympathy for the heretics (and least of all for Peter Payne, whom he attacks on several occasions), but he is generous enough to acknowledge that corruption and ineptitude within the Church were just as much to blame for what has happened to Bohemia.[30]

"NEW HERETICS . . . OLD HERESIES": BOHEMIA IN EARLY SIXTEENTH-CENTURY ENGLAND

In early sixteenth-century English polemic, Thomas Netter's historical approach to religious controversy became standard procedure – an obvious difference being that the new heretics of the previous century became the old heretics of the current one. It became a commonplace to mention Luther and Hus in the same breath, without explaining what one had to do with the other. This new association stemmed mainly from comments made during the Leipzig Disputation (1519), where Johann Eck had aimed to link Luther's teachings to several of Hus' condemned positions.[31] Initially, Luther was anxious to deny the charges, but gradually he came to appreciate many of Hus' teachings (particularly his ecclesiology), until Luther finally made the job of his opponents much easier, boldly asserting in 1520 that "sumus omnes Hussitae ignorantes [we are all Hussites without knowing it]."[32]

Several English public figures exploited Luther's wavering attitude toward the Bohemians. In his *Assertio septem sacramentorum adversus Martinum Lutherum* (1521),[33] Henry VIII characterizes Luther as an indecisive opportunist for flattering the Bohemian heretics "whose perfidiousness he before detested."[34] Indeed, writes Henry, "Luther flatters the very scum of the Bohemian commonality: and not without reason . . . for he foresees that the Germans (which he formerly deceived under the form of a simple sheep) would reject him as soon as they should perceive him to be a devouring wolf."[35] Later in the same decade, Thomas More comments in his *Dialogue concerning heresies* (1529) that at one time Luther considered the Bohemians to be "dampnable heretiques" for disobeying the pope; but later "the Bohemes whom he had in hys wrytyngys byfore called dampnable heretykes were good cristen men and all theyr opynyons good and catholyque."[36]

When it came to establishing the relationship between Luther and Hus in more precise terms, English polemicists tended to allow Bohemia's reputation to do the explication for them. John Clerk writes in his preface to Henry VIII's *Assertio* that Luther fled to Bohemia in order to find souls more sympathetic to his teachings than those of the Germans. If the pope had allowed Luther to remain there, however,

what danger, what devouring conflagration had this plague brought to all Christendom let the Hussitanian [*sic*] heresy evince. Which though contented at first with small beginnings, yet through the neglect of Superiors, increased to such a height that at last it turned not only cities and people but also that most populous Kingdom of Bohemia from the Christian Faith, reducing it to that misery under which it now languishes.[37]

Bohemia – which Clerk calls "the mother and nurse of [Luther's] heresies"[38] – is cast as the refuge of heretics, producing as well as sheltering them. The proposition that the "Hussitanian heresy" is able to "evince" the destruction that Luther would have caused if he had remained in Bohemia rests on the argument that Luther is unoriginal – a mere increaser of Hus' inventions (much like what Netter had said of Hus in relation to Wyclif).[39] As an imitator of the condemned Bohemian heretic, Luther furthermore bears all of the baggage that Bohemia has accumulated over the past century in English religious controversy, becoming what William Barlow would later call the "chief captain of new heretics, and bringer forth of old heresies."[40]

Like John Clerk, Thomas More did not define exactly how (other than by analogy) the Lutherans and Bohemians were related groups. More suggests in his *Dialogue* that, severed from the True Church, the people of Saxony and Bohemia have become increasingly sectarian as a result of widespread disagreement:

> For in Saxony fyrst and amonge all the Lutheranes there be as many heddes as many wyttes. And all as wyse as wylde gees. And as late as they began yet be there not onely as many sectes almost as men but also the maysters them selfe chaunge theyr myndes and theyr oppynyons euery day and wote nere where to holde them. Boheme is also in the same case. One fayth in the towne another in the felde. One in prage another in the nexte towne. And yet in prage it selfe one faythe in one strete an other in the nexte. So that yf ye assygne it in Boheme ye muste tell in what towne. And yf ye name a towne yet must ye tell in what strete.[41]

More intends for this passage to explain why none of the sects in Saxony or Bohemia can rightly claim to be the "True Church." To be dignified as such, he argues, a sect has to demonstrate a certain degree of continuity with that Church throughout history, which these groups cannot do (just look at how they squabble amongst themselves already!). More establishes an alternative lineage for the Lutherans by way of the Hussites, but one which, as we have seen before, has novelty as its identifying characteristic.

The assumed connection between Luther and Bohemia stems, as I have said, from the recent controversy at Leipzig (even Luther made the association); but less directly, the implications of a Lutheran–Hussite connection are informed by the reputation Bohemia had gathered over the past century in the course of English polemic. Once the link between Luther and Bohemia has been suggested in the accounts quoted above, the remaining amplifications run very much along the lines of what we have come to expect in discussions of Bohemia from the fifteenth century.[42] At the same time, religious polemic (old and new) was not the only source of information about the situation in Bohemia. News of Bohemia traveled freely from the continent to England, and of course there was communication between Bohemia and the rest of Europe in the sixteenth century. The wide correspondence of Erasmus, who acted as a nexus of pan-European communication, is a case in point. Erasmus was party to a series of epistolary exchanges with several of his Czech admirers. These letters make it clear that aspects of the English references to Bohemia I have been discussing form part of a wider European – and not exclusively Catholic – discussion of Bohemia as a fallen land.[43]

In 1519, Erasmus mentions some interesting details in his reply to Jan Šlechta, a Bohemian nobleman, in the process of refusing a warm welcome to Prague, which was accompanied by promises of safe conduct. "I do not care for countries in which convoy of this kind is necessary," he writes:

Here I am free to go where I please, even by myself. Not that I have any doubt of finding in your part of the world, as you say in your letter, plenty of good scholars and religious men, not polluted by the vices of schism. But it surprises me that none can be found to bring this whole division to an end.[44]

Erasmus provides a valuable perspective because, unlike the others we have been examining, he is not necessarily opposed to, or even in favor of, any of the factions in the troubled Czech lands. Instead he argues that "it is better to have concord on conditions that are not wholly fair than perfect fairness and divisions," without clearly suggesting which party is in the best position to provide and enforce such concord.[45]

In other letters, Erasmus shows considerable sympathy for the Bohemian Brethren, though he never advocates a break with Roman Catholic tradition. Still, he is disgusted by the danger and division in Bohemia, and says as much without ever having traveled there. Erasmus' references to Šlechta's letter (now lost) show that English anecdotes about Bohemia were not mere fabrications, written in bad faith for polemical purposes. And considering Erasmus' close communication with Englishmen like Thomas More, Cardinal Wolsey, and John Fisher during this same period, many of the English accounts cited in this chapter may have been influenced by Erasmian attitudes, as well as by English polemical tradition.[46]

As Henry VIII's "great matter" began to take shape not just as a marital, but also a political and religious issue, many of his advisers worried that his former opposition to Luther was beginning to slacken. In the *Life and death of Cardinal Wolsey* (composed 1554–8; first printed edition 1641), George Cavendish reports a conversation between Cardinal Wolsey and Sir William Kingston which took place when Wolsey was on his deathbed (1530). Wolsey requests of Kingston that, if Kingston was made a member of Henry's Privy Council (which was likely), he should be sure "that [the king] haue a vigilent eye" so as not to allow the Lutheran sect to grow within his dominions. Wolsey cites the Bohemians as a warning of what could happen to England if Henry does not take the Lutheran threat seriously. The troubles in Bohemia began, he says, because the Bohemian king failed to subdue his commoners, then "enfected with wycklyfes heresies," who, feeling at liberty to "spoyell and murder the sperytuall men & Religious persons of hys Realme" in a "frantyke rage," gathered such courage by turns that they "disdayned ther prynce and souerayn lord with all other noble personages And the hed gouerners of the Contrie." They gathered such force, in fact, that they "slewe the kyng the lordes & all the gentilmen of the Realme," who could not withstand their strength in battle; "by means of whiche slaughter," says Wolsey, "they haue lyved euer synce in great mysery & pouertie with out an hed or gouernor but lyved all in Comen lyke wyld bestes abhorred of all Cristyan nacions."[47]

Once again, the connection between the Lutheran sect and the Bohemians is tacitly assumed. Bohemia's reputation still carried weight at the time of Wolsey's death, and it would not lose this reputation any time soon. But with times changing as they were, this version of the story would only be preserved in certain circles.[48] The characterizations of Bohemia by both Henry VIII and Cardinal Wolsey – stated less than a decade apart – serve as a gauge of Henry's changing attitudes toward Protestant reform. Far from the person he was when the *Assertio* was printed, at the time of Wolsey's death, Henry has become, Wolsey suggests, wilfully ignorant of the encroaching reform, or even sympathetic with it. And indeed, the next major account of the Bohemians in England would be written by a Protestant. For John Foxe, whose antiquarian activities were conditioned by the shifting affiliations of the English Crown, "the story of the Bohemians" would be characterized not by schismatic violence, but by an apocalyptic struggle for purifying reform, ushering in the seventh age.

Afterword

This book has told a story of how complex communication networks developed in response to the Great Schism of the Western Church. And while this protracted crisis gave rise to a number of new communication channels and impacted existing ones in new ways, I have chosen to examine the activities of those specific networks which connected England with Bohemia. This decision was informed in part by the contingencies of my own historical and academic perspective, but also by my conviction that the momentous period of Anglo-Bohemian contact has been insufficiently understood. Through the course of this book, we have seen the rise and fall of Wycliffite communication with the Bohemian Hussites; but importantly, heterodox communication is not really where the story began. I have argued that England's alliances with Bohemia during the Ricardian and early-Lancastrian periods brought a variety of English texts into wider European circulation, and that this dynamic of textual transmission contributed not only to the spread of Wycliffite texts and ideas, but also to the widening in scope of England's prosecution of heresy. I could scarcely have told that same narrative if my aim had been to understand medieval reformist relations as they looked forward to the Reformation, or even if my task had been to examine late-medieval Wycliffite–Hussite communication in a more limited sense. When we reorient the discussion, viewing Anglo-Bohemian cultural contact against the backdrop of European religious crisis in the later Middle Ages, a variegated landscape of textual circulation begins to emerge.

We began by revising the long-held implication that Anne of Bohemia's position at the English court directly facilitated Wycliffite communication with the Bohemian reformists. I chose instead to outline Anne's symbolic availability for the English in a broader sense, examining her position at the center of a Ricardian court in which varying strands of reformist and mainstream devotion held currency, and in which a number of overlapping and competing narratives accrued around the figure of Queen Anne. This dynamic can be discerned, as we have seen, in the complicated transmission histories of eulogies about the queen, and in the many and varied narratives (literary, reformist, political) that crystallized around Anne in the wake of her death in 1394. We have likewise seen in the transmission of Richard Rolle's writings to Bohemia how trends in English devotional reading were also reflected in the exchange. The group of Rolle's texts that made it to Bohemia can be linked in part to the politics of devotion in Rome, but there are also indications that some of them may have been associated with the Wycliffites. And of course, the complicated arena of religiosity and reform in Europe at this time did include the Wycliffites and the members of the dynamic reform movement in Bohemia. Amidst the wider exchange between England and Bohemia, members of these movements made contact and capably came to dominate the lines of transnational communication in the early fifteenth century. Their success was attributable in part to their institutional affiliations, to the authenticating forms of the documents they used, and to the Hussites' use of sanctioned spaces for preaching and disputation in disseminating news from England to large audiences. All of this made it enormously difficult for Church and secular authorities to counter Wycliffite news and propaganda with their own narratives.

Some observations come to the fore: first, Wycliffite textual transmission did not initially define the exchange between England and Bohemia. This very important strand of communication, which did indeed come to dominate, began to develop alongside, and in competition or conjunction with, other channels of exchange. And second, English communication with Bohemia was not a centralized affair; it did not require royal patronage or centralized planning to proceed. As I suggested in the introduction, communication at this time was a contingent, localized practice, mediated and conditioned by ad hoc personal contact and documentary forms that were far from stable. In a manuscript culture, the material conditions of communication and textual dissemination afforded authorities little advantage over the propagandizing projects of competitors, particularly when it came to crossing regnal boundaries, and particularly, too, when competitors laid mutual claim to authenticating modes and forms of documentation. It would take the Council of Constance to lend its platform and resources to disseminating a centralized response to heterodox missives, and we witness the early signs of this response as it mobilized in the diplomatic correspondence between England and Emperor-elect Sigismund in the years immediately preceding that council. Until Constance, however, communication channels were enormously difficult to police.

Where does this story leave us? I mentioned in the Introduction that I wanted to conduct the thought experiment that the Reformation never happened, which would encourage me to frame different questions about Schism-era communication than we are used to asking. But surely, Protestant historiography and antiquarian activity have informed this project at almost every stage, in integral ways, and so it was never really possible to leave off with these early modern developments anyhow. What we can do is to resist applying facile models to medieval textual transmission, admitting instead a more nuanced approach that takes in the complexities of communication in a manuscript culture. And indeed, the result may be, as has been the case in this study, a story that "disregards linear regularity,"[1] involving unexpected turns, narrative irruption, cross-currents and convergent transmission. After all, we are dealing with humans engaged in the practice of communication – a practice which is inherently localized, materially conditioned and only sometimes governed by intentionality and advanced planning. This is how communication tends to proceed in a manuscript culture. It is my hope that I have conveyed a sense of that practice in the story I have told.

Three verse eulogies of Anne of Bohemia: an edition

The following edition uses PKMK D.12 as the base text for "Anglica regina," except when the readings from D.12 are clearly corrupt. All variants are supplied in the apparatus to that poem where, unless otherwise indicated, the first item refers to the D.12 copy (*D*) and the second to H.15 (*H*). The decision to give preference to D.12 is based on the fact that it is less corrupt, giving better readings on several occasions (exceptions are marked accordingly in the apparatus). However, the heading printed above "Anglica regina" in the following edition appears only in H.15. F. M. Bartoš edited this poem from D.12 only (he was not aware of the poems in H.15) in *Časopis Musea Království českého* 93 (1919): 203–4. Considering my discovery of a second copy, and the fact that Bartoš's edition gives some mistaken readings, I have considered it appropriate to provide a fresh edition of the poem. The second and third poems, which have not been edited before, are based on H.15, the sole witness.

In the edition below, expanded portions of words are italicized. All punctuation is of course editorial. The few instances where I have emended a word are usually indicated in angled brackets. This has been done when, for instance, the scribe seems to have omitted an abbreviation and the sense would otherwise be obscured. Other emendations and textual problems are explained in the apparatus following each poem. Textual and historical references are discussed in the Textual and explanatory notes section. English translations of the poems are also supplied at the end of the Appendix.

A.1 ANGLICA REGINA

PRAGUE, KNIHOVNA METROPOLITNÍ KAPITULY,
MS H.15, FOL. 90ʳ

PRAGUE, KNIHOVNA METROPOLITNÍ KAPITULY,
MS D.12, FOL. 217ʳ⁻ᵛ

[fol. 90ʳ]

[Heading:] Epitaphium de Anna Regina Anglie filia Imperator*is* Karoli de Boemia

     Anglica regina, nu*n*c Anna iacet Libiti*n*a.
     Dum vixit domi*n*a, fuit Anglis nulla ruina.
     Inclita filia cezaris *et* pia *con*iuga regis,
     Sp*re*verat impia fecit *et* om*n*ia *con*sona leg*is*.
5   Rixas sedavit, discordes pacificavit,
     Mansuetis favit, p*ro* tristib*us* ista rogavit –
     Londonie*n*sibus hinc m*ihi* testib*us*, acta p*ro*bando,
     Na*m* fuit om*n*ib*us* in g*ra*vitatib*us* hiis ministrando.
     Paup*er*ib*us* prona *semper* fuit add<e>re dona:
10 Distribue*n*do bona, no*n* vivit tanta patrona.
     Hinc Alma*n*ia, tota Boe*m*ia corde dolebunt:
     Sed mag*is* Anglia iu*n*ctaq*ue* Valia pro nece flebu*n*t.
     Pregna*n*tes pe*n*a m*u*lieres vissit amena,
     Et p*er* eam plena q*ue*vis releva*tur* egena.
15 Diluit asp*er*a cu*n*ctaq*ue* p*ro*sp*er*a fecit adesse.
     Det *sibi* mun*er*a cu*n*ctipotens Era, V*ir*gula Yesse.
     Toto *fer*vore Sacratu*m* Neuma decore
     De solito mo*re* cum corde colebat *et* ore:
     Hinc pia pecto*re* Neumat*is* affo*re* luce p*ro*batur.
20 Mortua corp*ore*, postea marmo*re* subpedita*tur*,
     Cum nulla cu*ra* fiet morte*m* fugitura
     Ulla creatu*ra* nu*n*c ens nec in orbe futura.
     Dulc*is* in om*n*ib*us* *et* pia morib*us* h*e*c generosa.
     Nec putret ymbrib*us* *et* sua v*er*mib*us* *est* caro rosa.
25 Hinc ut debem*us* qui tanta m*a*t*re* carem*us*,
     P*ro*pt*er* eam dem*us* lacrimas *et* sepe rogem*us*
     Sit sibi g*ra*c*ia*, q*uo*d bona sit via qua sit itura,
     Su*mm*aq*ue* gaudia, celica p*re*mia, sint sua iura.

---

2 Anglis *H*] Anglic*is* *D*   3 cezaris] cesaris   4 Sp*re*verat] Sprevere   5 sedavit] cedavit   6 ista] ipsa   8 ministrando *H*] miserando *D*   9 add<e>re] addare *DH*   10 bona] dona   11 Hinc] Ha*n*c   12 Valia] Vallia   13 Pregna*n*tes *H*] Pugna*n*tes *D*   14 releva*tur* *H*] relevan*tur* *D*, where titulus over *a* incorrect. *D* scribe has corrected from "revelan*tur*"   15 cu*n*ctaq*ue*] m*u*ltaq*ue*   16 Det] Sed Era] Hera   19 p*ro*batur] p*ro*bata   20 subpedita*tur*] subpedita   24 Nec] Nunc putret *H*] putet *D*   27 sibi] t*ibi* via] vita   28 Su*mm*aq*ue*] Su*mm*amque

A.2 FEMINA FAMOSA

PRAGUE, KNIHOVNA METROPOLITNÍ KAPITULY,
MS H.15, FOL. 90ᵛ

[fol. 90ᵛ]

[Heading:] Obiit Anna R*egina* septima die Junii, a. d. m° ccc xc iiii

Femi*n*a famosa, iac*et* h*ic* m*uli*er ge*n*erosa.
Imp*erator* f*rate*r rexerat atq*ue* pater.
Anna vocaba*tur*, qua*m* plebs me*r*ito venera*tur*:
Na*m* n*ulli* nocuit plu*r*ib*us et* placuit.
5   Munda fuit mu*n*do Riccardo nupta Secu*n*do.
Fida fidem tenuit, ergo tene*n*da fuit.
Hec *et* regnor*um* fuerat regi*n*a duor*um*:
Anglia testa*tur*, Francia ju*r*e da*tur*.
Hec ded*it* egrotis victu*m*, peditando remot*is*;
10   Quod regem latuit pauperib*us* patuit.
Visere la<n>guentes voluit, partu*m* pacientes,
Et male vestita: sepe meavit ita.
Neumat*is* Almifici voluit Missa*m* sibi dici;
Misse dando fidem continua*vit* idem.
15   Ha*n*c inspiravit, ha*n*c Spi*r*it*us* Alm*us* amavit,
Quod p*r*obat apta quies, mors bo*n*a, digna dies:
In Pe<n>tacoste regi*n*a recessit ab hoste,
Vincere que*m* meruit hu*n*c quia deseruit.
Vos qui transit*is*, ani*m*am relevare vellit*is*
20   Ut superata nece, sic rep*ar*ata p*r*ece.

11 la<n>guentes] laguentes, without titulus over *a*   17 Pe<n>tacoste] Petacoste, without titulus over
initial *e*

A.3 NOBIS NATURA FLOREM

PRAGUE, KNIHOVNA METROPOLITNÍ KAPITULY,
MS H.15, FOLS. 90ᵛ–92ʳ

Seq*uitur*

Nobis n*atur*a flore*m* p*r*odux*it* ad ortu*m*,
Qui m*od*o i*n* mort<e> marcid*us* ecce cadit.
Floruit i*n* regno q*uod* d*icitur* esse Boemu*m*.
Flos ca*m*pi de quo sc*r*ibim*us* Anna fuit:
5   Felix ille locus ta*m* felix gig*n*ere ge*r*me*n*
Qui potuit, de quo sing*ul*a regna canu*n*t.
Si genus ips*ius* p*r*ict<i> orb*is* pompa tonabit,

2 mort<e>] mort*is*   7 *pict*<i>] pict*is*

Hoc probitas matris *et* patris ipsa sonat.
Nam pater *et* mater rex *et* regina fueru*n*t

10   De quib*us* est orta nobilis hec m*u*lier.
No*n* possu*m* sane cu*m* ta*n*ta laude tac*ere*:
Y*m*mo loquar plus, ne maxi*m*a laus p*er*eat.
Su*m*m*us* i*n* I*m*perio fuit ellect*us* pate*r* Anne,
In quo felices fecerat ips*e* dies.

15   Anne su*n*t ecia*m* duo f*ra*tres sceptra g*er*ent*es*:
P*ri*mu*m* Roma t*e*net, alt*er* i*n* Hunga*ri*a
Regnat; t*er*cius *et* f*ra*te*r* no*n* defuit Anne:
Dux Gorlie*ns*is, belliger atq*ue* ferox.
Dic*ere* nemo p*otest* q*uod* maior nobilitas sit

20   Sa<n>guinis i*n* mu*n*do femi*n*a qua*m* te*n*et hec.
Et sic i*n* laude p*ro*lis, genitor genit*ri*xq*ue*
Extollu*n*t*ur* e*n*i*m* laudib*us* eximiis:
Na*m* de se gignu*n*t A*n*na*m*, q*ue* no*m*ine ta*n*to
Digna voca*ri* sit, "g*ra*ti*a*" q*uod* resonat.

25   Cog*eri*s asserere q*uod* g*ra*ti*a* fulsit i*n* Anna,
In qua fulseru*n*t spes, pietas *et* amor:
Spes pecata fugat, pietas succurrit egeno,
Regna mere*ri*q*ue* celica fecit amor.
Claruit h*ec* m*u*li*er* i*n* st*ir*pe ducu*m* gen*er*osa;

30   Claruit i*n* se plus p*ro*p*ri*a p*er* m*er*ita.
Anne no*n* tenuit fama*m* sua pat*ri*a ta*n*tu*m*,
Immo sed ad nos fu*n*dit*ur* suus odor.
Et q*uia* Ricard*us*, Edwardi P*ri*ncipis h*er*es,
Rex illust*ri*s erat co*n*iugeq*ue* caruit,

35   Opta*tur* vi*r*go reg*is* complexib*us* apta
Concilio proce*ri*s ne pereat. Proceres
Lustra*n*t*ur* regna, sub millite calcar acutu*m*,
Ut rex sit spo*n*sus, cu*rre*re cogit equos.
Sponse su*n*t vise va*ri*e va*ri*os decea*n*tq*ue*

40   Reges, sed n*ost*ro tradit*ur* A*n*na place*n*s.
Tande*m* rex noster regina*m* fecerat A*n*na*m*,
Qua*m* despo*n*savit eclesie facie.

Sic p*er*felices, rex A*n*naq*ue* plurib*us* a*n*nis
Co*n*iu*n*xe*re*; dies comple*n*s digna fuit.
45   A*n*nam mors rapuit post h*ec* ab p*ri*ncipe n*ost*ro,

---

20 Sa<n>guinis] Saguinis, without titulus over *a*   32 fu*n*dit*ur*] eff*un*dit*ur*

De quo rex doluit. Plu*r*ima sig*na* doce*nt*:
M <anno> c, *ter* lx decesserat A*n*na
(Si te*r*denos *et* quatuor anume*r*es).
Ip*s*a na*m*que die qua S*a*nctu*s* Spiritu*s* om*n*es
50   Discipulos docuit, ip*s*a recessit abhinc.
Ip*s*ius i*n* morte tu*r*ba*tur* machi*n*a mu*n*di:
Eclips*im* pati*tur* Anglia tota simul.
Et q*uia* q*uod*q*ue* suu*m* pet*it*, A*n*nam te*rr*a requ*i*rit:
Te*rr*am p*r*o requie dat sac*er* iste loc*us*.
55   Tales exequie no*n* sunt vise muner*is* hui*us*,
Qu*oni*am plebs orat cler*us* *et* officiat,
Primates adera*n*t, bini cu*m* plesule pluri,
Quos *n*um*er*o c*on*stat siste*r*e q*u*inq*u*edecim.
Qu*i*nq*u*aginta vi*r*i varii dicti mo*n*achor*um*
60   Abbates assu*n*t: splendida tu*r*ba fuit.
Addas xv quos nove*r*is esse p*r*iores:
Cu*m* reliquo clero psalle*r*e suffragia.
Ex alio late*r*e sec*u*lar*is* *et* alta potestas
Affuit: obtulit mune*r*a p*r*ecipua.
65   Tresq*ue* duces comitesq*ue* dece*m*, qu*i*b*us* *et* dab*is* unu*m*
(Si plac*et* exp*r*ime*r*e sub brevitate, potes);
Et de millitib*us*, si o*m*nes nosce*r*e qu*o*t su*n*t,
Qu*i*nge*n*tos esse publica fama refert.
De reliquo vulgo no*n* arbitror esse loque*n*d*um*
70   Qua*n*tus erat popul*us*: dice*r*e nemo val*et*.
O qua*m* luge*n*da p*r*imevi culpa pare*n*t*is*,
Qua quo*n*da*m* o*m*nes ca*r*ne deficiu*n*t!
Infelix gusta*n*s, cui*us* gustu mo*r*ia*n*tur
O*m*nes qu*os* radix toxica progenuit.
75   Flam<m>a vorax mors est gladi*us* qu*i* vastat *et* om*n*es:
Indignos dignos opp*r*imit arte pari.

[fol. 92ʳ]

No*n* honor i*n* solio nec corpore*us* vigor orb*is*
Mort*is* decretum ru*m*pe*r*e q*u*isq*ue* pot*est*.
Si t*ibi* blandi*tur* ge*n*us aut facu*n*dia ve*r*bi,
80   Mors tame*n* i*n*vadit fortia castra tua.
Si t*ibi* fortu*n*a v*e*l fallax glo*r*ia mu*n*di
Arridet, tame*n* noxia mors sequi*tur*.
No*n* extolla*r*is: te laudat publica fama?

47 <anno>] duo, which must be a scribal mistake   55 muner*is*] MS corrupt. Scribe seems to have written "mulier*is*," but canceled the *l*   57 plesule (*sic*)] read "presule." Postconsonantal substitution of *l* for *r* is occasionally attested in medieval Latin texts. See Peter Stotz, *Handbuch zur lateinischen Sprache des Mittelalters*, III, § 236.2.   61 xv] line scans if read "quindecim"   64 obtulit] letters after "ob" cancelled, corrected in marg. to "tulit"   75 Flam<m>a] Flami*n*a   78 q*u*isq*ue*] apparently "quisque"="quisquam"

Captivat*us* eris mort*is in* exilio.
85   Turba stiparis lacta*ris et* ube*re* dulci?
Morte loque*nte* t*ibi* sing*u*la se retrahe*nt*.
I*n* forma rutilas? Resplende*nt* pi<n>guia me*n*se?
Ge*mm*e te dita*nt*? O*mn*ia mors abicit.
Curva*ntur* genua, d*o*min*u*m te p*re*dicat orbis:
90   De te*rr*a, te*rr*am mors ho*min*e*m* refficit.
Turbid*us* est host*is* q*ui* nulli p*ar*ce*re* cu*r*at,
O*mn*es expugna*ns*, nec tacet i*n*sidians.
Est atrox bellu*m* cu*m* quo via nulla salut*is*:
Mors cogit cunctos subd*ere* colla sibi.
95   Quid loquar a*m*plius <. . .> n*isi* q*ui*sq*ue* p*re*ce<tur>
Q*uod* Sanct*us* Michael Ang*e*l*us* ha*n*c capiat
I*n* luce*m* sa*n*ct*a*m q*ua* gaud*et* q*ui*sq*ue* be*a*t*us*,
*Et Christu*s cuiq*ue* glo*ri*a qua*m* meruit.
Qui leg*is et* tra*n*s*is*, rogo sis mot*us* pietate,
100   *Et* p*ro* regina, q<u>ero, fu*n*de p*re*ces.

87 rutilas] rutilās. Titulus over *a* incorrect   pi<n>guia] piguia, without titulus over initial *i*
95 n*isi*] MS *n* or *r* plus suspension. Reading is doubtful; line metrically defective (as indicated by <. . .>)
p*re*ce<tur>] p*re*cet
100 q<u>ero] MS corrupt. Seems to read "qeto," where *o* has been corrected from *s*

TEXTUAL AND EXPLANATORY NOTES

A.I ANGLICA REGINA

l. 1   *Libitina*: goddess of funerals. The sense is that Anne lies as the property of Libitina. By transferral, *Libitina* was also used to mean "death." Alternatively, the term could be translated "on the bier," if taken in the ablative. See *Dictionary of Medieval Latin from British Sources*, s.v. "Libitina."

l. 3   *Inclita filia cezaris*: Anne was the daughter of Charles IV, Holy Roman Emperor from 1355–78.

l. 7   *Londoniensibus hinc mihi testibus, acta probando*: two years before Anne died, she and Richard made their triumphant re-entry into London, where Richard's reconciliation with the Londoners (who had earlier refused him a substantial loan) was enacted through elaborate pageantry, most fully related in Maidstone's *Concordia*. Throughout the pageantry, Anne assumes the role of *mediatrix* between Richard and the Londoners, pleading on their behalf for Richard's forgiveness. Line 7 probably alludes to this event.

l. 9   *Pauperibus prona semper fuit add<e>re dona*: cf. Anne's epitaph in Westminster Abbey: "Pauperibus prona semper sua reddere dona."

l. 12   *Valia*: Wales.

l. 13   *Pregnantes pena mulieres vissit amena*: cf. Anne's Westminster epitaph, where Anne is said to have relieved pregnant women ("pregnantes relevavit"). See also the discussion in Chapter 1 for the possibility that these references were designed to associate Anne of Bohemia with St. Anne, the patron of pregnant women.

ll. 17–19   *Toto fervore Sacratum Neuma decore / De solito more cum corde colebat et ore: / Hinc pia pectore Neumatis affore luce probatur.* Anne died at Pentecost, which in 1394 fell on June 7.

l. 25   *tanta matre caremus*: in keeping with the hagiographic terms in which the eulogy casts Anne, the deceased queen is here presented as the mother of those who mourn for her, bestowing on Anne a kind of spiritual motherhood.

A.2 FEMINA FAMOSA

I. 2   *Imperator frater rexerat atque pater*: Anne's father, Charles IV, was crowned Holy Roman Emperor on April 5, 1355, a title which he held until his death on November 29, 1378. Václav (Wenceslaus) IV, one of Anne's brothers, was technically speaking never emperor, although as King of the Romans, he was the emperor-elect until being deposed from that position in 1400. Many medieval texts (from England for example) do not make the distinction between emperor and king of the Romans, as was also the case for Sigismund of Hungary, who was often called emperor before his formal coronation by Pope Eugenius IV in 1433. Walsingham (*St. Albans Chronicle*, 573) remarks that Wenceslaus called himself "Emperor" in his letters, though the title was not legitimately his.

l. 5   *Munda fuit mundo Riccardo nupta Secundo*: cf. Anne's Westminster epitaph: "Dum vixit mundo, Ricardo nupta Secundo."

ll. 13–18   *Neumatis Almifici voluit Missam sibi dici, etc.*: i.e., the Mass of the Holy Spirit, or Pentecost. Anne in this passage is said to have been devoted to the Holy Spirit, on account of which she was given a particularly appropriate day of death (Anne died at Pentecost, as l. 17 reports). Cf. "Anglica regina," ll. 17–19.

l. 15   *Spiritus Almus*: one of the many names for the Holy Spirit, attested for example in several of the offices for the Feast of Pentecost. In mentioning that the Holy Spirit inspired Anne ("Hanc inspiravit"), the poet also recalls the role of the Third Person of the Trinity in inspiring the prophets and apostles, mentioned in similar terms, for example, in the York Missal ("Prophetas tu inspirasti"). See Henderson, *Missale ad usum insignis ecclesiae Eboracensis*, 1.153.

A.3 NOBIS NATURA FLOREM

l. 4   *Flos campi*: cf. Canticum canticorum (Ct.) 2.1: "ego flos campi et lilium convallium." The "flower of the field" was often associated with the Virgin Mary. See for example Dreves and Blume, *Analecta hymnica*, xx.165 no. 209, 173 no. 225, and 203 no. 280. The "Nobis natura" poet continues to draw from the Song of Songs, for example in l. 32 ("ad nos fu*n*di*tur* suus odor").

l. 9   *Nam pater et mater rex et regina fuerunt*: Anne's father, as I have discussed in previous notes, was Emperor Charles IV. Her mother, Elizabeth of Pomerania, was especially dear to Richard II, who maintained a regular correspondence with his mother-in-law. See Perroy, *Diplomatic Correspondence*, nos. 35, 57, 62, and 140. In 1393, Richard ordered a requiem Mass to be said for Elizabeth at St. Paul's. See Saul, *Richard II*, 92 n. 35.

ll. 15–17 *duo fratres sceptra gerentes, etc.*: Václav (Wenceslaus) IV, King of the Romans; Sigismund, King of Hungary.

l. 18   *Dux Gorliensis*: Jan Zhořelecký, Duke of Görlitz, youngest son of Charles IV.

ll. 23–5 cf. Maidstone's *Concordia*, ll. 431–6 (quoted in Chapter 1).

l. 32   *ad nos funditur suus odor*: see note to l. 4 above.

l. 33   *Edwardi Principis heres*: Edward of Woodstock, Prince of Wales (the Black Prince), was Richard II's father.

ll. 37–8 *Lustrantur regna, sub millite calcar acutum, / Ut rex sit sponsus, currere cogit equos*: the reference is probably to the embassy of John Burley and Michael de la Pole. Initially they had been sent, together with George Felbrigg, to conduct marriage negotiations with the Visconti family of Milan on Richard's behalf. The eruption of schism in 1378, however, precipitated a change of plans. Burley and de la Pole continued on to Rome and then to Prague, where they took steps to form an Anglo-Imperial bloc in support of Urban VI through the marriage of Richard II and Anne of Bohemia. See Saul, *Richard II*, 83–107, esp. 83–8.

l. 39   *Sponse sunt vise varie varios deceantque*: cf. the similar instances of wordplay in Maidstone's *Concordia*, for example in l. 251: "Femina feminea sua dum sic femina nudat." For discussion, see also *Concordia*, 37.

ll. 47–8   *M <anno> c, ter lx decesserat Anna / (Si terdenos et quatuor anumeres)*: cf. Maidstone's dating in *Concordia*, ll. 15–16: "M cape, ter quoque C, deciesque novem duo iunge / (Hunc numerum anni supputo dando notis)." Dating formulas such as these appear elsewhere in Anglo-Latin literature. See for example Gower's *Chronica tripertita*, ll. 1–2 (*Complete Works of John Gower*, IV.314): "Tolle caput mundi, C ter et sex lustra fer illi, / Et decies quinque cum septem post super adde." For additional examples, see *Concordia*, 33 n. 92.

ll. 49–50   *Ipsa namque die qua Sanctus Spiritus omnes / Discipulos docuit, ipsa recessit abhinc*: Pentecost, the day that Anne died (June 7, 1394).

ll. 51–2   *Ipsius in morte turbatur machina mundi: / Eclipsim patitur Anglia tota simul*: I am not aware of other reports of natural phenomena at the time of Anne's death. The reference may allude to the eclipse during Christ's crucifixion, based on the accounts in Matthew 27.45, 51–4; Mark 15.33; and Luke 23.44–5.

l. 54   *iste locus*: seems to refer to Anne's tomb in Westminster Abbey.

l. 66   *Si placet exprimere sub brevitate, potes*: the poet here appears to refer to his system of numbering, by which he at times uses Roman numerals, while at others chooses to spell out the numbers. Cf. ll. 47, 61.

TRANSLATIONS

A.1 ANGLICA REGINA

An epitaph of Anne, Queen of England, daughter of Emperor Charles of Bohemia

The English queen Anna now lies dead.[1]
While this lady lived, the English flourished (experienced no decline).
Celebrated daughter of the emperor and pious consort of the king,
She spurned wickedness and did all in accordance with the law.

5   She allayed disputes, pacified the quarrelsome,
       Favored the gentle, pleaded for the distressed –
       Thus the people of London testify to me, confirming her acts,
       For she ministered to all of them in their oppressions.
       She was always eager to give gifts to the poor:
10   There never lived a patroness so great in her bestowal of goods.
       Henceforth Germany and all Bohemia will grieve at heart:
       But more will England, and with it Wales, weep for her death.
       Cheerful, she visited pregnant women in their suffering,
       And any pregnant woman in need is comforted by her.
15   She cleared away adversities and brought about all prosperity.
       May the Almighty Lady, the Tree of Jesse, reward her.
       With all ardor she fittingly worshipped the Holy Spirit
       With heart and mouth out of constant habit:
       Thus it is granted to her, devout of heart, to have parted on Pentecost.
20   Dead in body, she is afterwards endowed with marble,
       Since no creature now existing or to come in this world
       Will, by any provision, escape death.
       This noble woman was pious and sweet in every way.
       Her flesh is rosy, nor will it rot with rains and worms.
25   Hence, as we ought who lose such a mother,
       Let us shed tears for her and often pray
       That grace may be upon her, that the path she is about to travel may be
          good,
       And that the highest joys, heavenly rewards, may be her due.

A . 2   F E M I N A   F A M O S A

Queen Anne died on the seventh day of June, AD 1394

       Here lies a renowned lady, a noble woman.
          Her brother reigned as emperor, and also her father.
       Anna she was called, whom the people rightly adore:
          For she harmed no one and pleased many.
5   Pure, she was married to the pure Richard II.
          She kept the faith, and so was considered faithful.
       She was also the queen of two realms:
          England bears witness, France is granted [to her] by right.
       She gave nourishment to the sick, going to them on foot, however far off;
10   What she concealed from the king, she extended to the poor.
       She wished to visit the ill, those enduring childbirth,
          And [she did so] poorly dressed: often she went about this way.
       She wanted the Mass of the Holy Spirit to be said for her;
          In putting faith in this mass, she carried forth the faith.
15   The Holy Spirit inspired her, loved her,

As is proven by her apt rest, good death, worthy day:
   On Pentecost the queen withdrew from the enemy,
   Whom she deserved to conquer because she forsook him.
You who pass by, please comfort her soul
20   So that, though overcome by death, she may thus be made whole by prayer.

A.3 NOBIS NATURA FLOREM

Nature brought forth a flower for us,
   Which now, behold, falls withered in death.
It flowered in the kingdom which is said to be Bohemia.
   The flower of the field of which we write was Anna:
5   Happy the place which can beget such a happy bud,
   About which all the kingdoms sing.
If the glory of the map trumpets her lineage,
   So too does the virtue of her mother and father proclaim it.
For her father and mother were the king and queen
10   From whom was sprung this noble woman.
Certainly, I cannot keep silent with such praise:
   No indeed, I shall say more, lest the greatest praise die.
Anne's father was chosen the highest in the Empire,
   In which he made the days happy.
15   Also carrying scepters are Anne's two brothers:
   Rome holds the first, the other in Hungary
Reigns; and Anne did not lack a third brother:
   The Duke of Görlitz, warlike and fierce.
No one can say that there is greater nobility
20   Of blood in the world than this woman possesses.
And so in praise of this offspring, her mother and father
   Are extolled indeed with exceptional praises:
For from themselves they brought forth Anna, worthy to be called
   By such a name, which resounds "grace."
25   You will have to admit that grace shone forth in Anne,
   In whom shone hope, piety and love:
Hope drives away sins, piety runs to the aid of the destitute,
   And love caused [her] to win heavenly kingdoms.
This woman grew bright in a noble line of dukes;
30   She grew brighter still in herself through her own merits.
Not only did her own country possess Anne's fame,
   But rather to us wafts her odor.
And because Richard, the heir of Prince Edward,
   Was an illustrious king and lacked a wife,
35   A suitable maiden is chosen for the king's embraces
   By a council of nobles, lest he go to waste.
Nobles traverse kingdoms, the sharp spur under the knight

Compels the horses to run so that the king may be a husband.
Various spouses are seen which would befit various kings,
40   But Anne, pleasing, is bequeathed to ours.
At last our king made Anne his queen,
   Whom he betrothed in the eyes of the Church.
So very happy, the king and Anne for many years
   Were married; fulfilling her days she was worthy.
45   After this, death snatched Anne away from our prince,
   About which the king grieved. Many signs show this:
In the year M, three times C, LX Anna died
   (If you add three times ten and four).
And on the very day that the Holy Spirit taught
50   All the disciples, she passed away from here.
In her death, the fabric of the world is disturbed:
   All England at once endures an eclipse.
And because everything desires its own, the earth seeks Anne:
   This sacred place gives the earth for her respite.
55   For the service at hand, such a funeral was never seen,
   For the commoners pray, and the clergy officiates,
The primates were there, both with many bishops,
   Whose number is agreed to be fifty.
Some fifty different men titled abbots of monks
60   Are present: there was a splendid crowd.
Add XV whom you know to be priors:
   They chanted intercessions with the other clergy.
And from the other side the high power of the secular arm
   Was there: it offered special tributes.
65   And there were three dukes and ten counts, to which you shall add one
   (If you like to express it briefly, you can);
And of the knights, if everyone recalls how many there are,
   Popular report has it that there were five hundred.
Of the remaining crowd I do not think it can be said
70   How many people there were: no one is able to say.
O, how lamentable the fault of the primeval parent,
   By which all eventually perish in body!
Unhappy the one who tastes, by whose tasting all die
   Whom the poisonous root has begotten.
75   Death is a ravenous flame, the sword which wastes all men:
   Unworthy and worthy it oppresses with equal cunning.
Neither any dignity upon the throne, nor any bodily vigor in this world
   Can destroy the decree of death.
If noble birth or eloquence of speech favors you,
80   Death still invades your strongholds.
If fortune or the false glory of the world
   Smiles upon you, still noxious death follows.

Be not puffed up: does public fame praise you?
  You will be captive in the exile of death.
85 Are you surrounded by the crowd, and nursed by a sweet breast?
  Each of these will withdraw itself when death is speaking to you.
Do you shine with beauty? Are the fat meats of your table splendid?[2]
  Do gems enrich you? Death casts them all aside.
Knees are bent, the world praises you as lord:
90   From earth, death turns man back into earth.
Wild is the enemy who cares to spare no one,
  Conquering everyone, nor is he quiet, lying in wait.
The war is cruel by which there is no way of deliverance:
  Death forces all to subject their necks to it.
95 What more can I say, except that everyone should pray
  That St. Michael the Angel may receive this woman
Into the holy light in which whoever is blessed rejoices,
  And in which Christ will be the glory of every person who has merited it.
You who read and pass by, I ask that you may be moved by piety,
100   And for the queen, I ask, pour out your prayers.

News of the Oldcastle Rising, 1414: an edition

Text *T* below was transcribed from Třeboň, Státní oblastní archiv, M S A.16, fol. 157^{r-v}. There are significant differences between this copy and text *S*, which is why I do not conflate the two. In the edition of *T*, expanded portions of words have been italicized. Emendations, which have been made only to correct grammatical issues, are enclosed in angled brackets and explained in the apparatus which accompanies the Latin text. Additions, likewise explained in the apparatus, appear between square brackets. All punctuation is editorial. Lengthier textual and historical notes are discussed in the Textual and explanatory notes section, and correspond to the line numbers of the Latin transcription.

Text *S* is derived from the edition by Jodok Stülz (*Sitzungsberichte der Philosophisch-Historischen Classe* 5 [1850]: 64–7), which was transcribed from the inside of a pastedown that had become separated from a manuscript or early printed book, the identity of which Stülz unfortunately does not specify. Because the edition has escaped the notice of scholars of the 1414 Oldcastle Rising, and because Stülz offers little comment and some confusing editorial decisions, I have decided to reprint it here with editorial changes, notes, and a translation. Emendations, which have been made mainly to correct grammatical problems, are indicated by angled brackets, and are explained in the apparatus accompanying the Latin text. Square brackets have been used to supply missing words, and are as they appear in Stülz' edition, with the exception of the alterations to lines 5, 16, and 96. Because it has been impossible to identify the original manuscript, I have been unable to indicate where words have been expanded, or to offer emendation of Stülz' edition other than in cases where I have disagreed with his punctuation (which I have silently emended), or with the occasional problems he raised with the Latin (he marks with "[*sic*]" several items which are in fact unproblematic). I have also emended in instances where Stülz likely mistook "W" for "B" (as in "Bicleff," l. 5, which I have emended to "Wicleff") or "u/v" for "b" (as in "Boborle," l. 31, which has been changed to "Bouorle"). Stülz' readings in these instances have been recorded in the apparatus accompanying the Latin edition. Where Stülz and I agree that the grammar is defective, I have emended the Latin in every case (whereas Stülz does not emend the text). More involved textual and historical issues, for example the apparent confusion of the names of important places and people in *S*, are addressed in the Textual and explanatory notes section, and correspond to the line numbers which I have provided for the Latin text.

B.1 TŘEBOŇ, STÁTNÍ OBLASTNÍ ARCHIV MS A.16, FOL. 157^{r-v} (*T*)

[fol. 157^r]
[Heading:] Nouitates de Anglia de Wikleph

Stupendas atq*ue* horrendas nouitates de Anglia animadu*er*tite. Factu*m* est an*te* festu*m* Michaelis *pro*xime *pre*te*r*ito q*uod* quida*m* nobilis et *pre*pote*n*s baro de regno Anglie, D*omin*u*s* Joh*ann*es de Oltkastel, Cobham alio no*mine* d*i*ctus, *per* archi*epi*scopu*m* Cantu*ar*iens*em* accusat*us* fuit regi Anglie tamq*uam* caput Wikleff
5 et erro*rum* suo*rum* h*er*eticaliu*m* *et* illis i*n*her*er*e vole*n*tib*us* tutor et defe*n*sator; quem rex ad accusa*c*io*n*em archi*epi*scopi vocauit eu*m*q*ue* beniuole a*m*monuit ut a *pre*dictis erro*r*ib*us* desist*er*et; qui, monit*is* reg*is* no*n* acq*ui*escens, iter*um* modico i*n*t*er*uallo elapso *per* regem vocat*us* fuit *et* monit*us*. No*n* desistit, *sed* p*er*tinaciter institit, errores dictos fouendo et i*n* sua p*er*tinacia p*er*seu*er*ando. Rex, videns eu*m*
10 induratu*m*, *pro*hibuit *pr*imo ne ad ei*us* cam*er*am ampli*us* acced*er*et, postea ma*n*dauit sibi ne curia*m* a*ut* capella*m* sua*m* a*m*modo visitaret. Iste baro, ad om*n*es accusa*c*iones archi*epi*scopi no*n* desistens, iter*um* regi accusat*ur* ab arch*i*epi*scopo* satis *im*portune. Rex, se excusans, dixit: "Ego feci q*uod* i*n* me fuit, ad *pr*esens iudicii v*es*tri int*er*est corrig*er*e et *pro*ced*er*e ordine iur*is* co*n*tra t*a*les ut decet."
15 Archi*epi*scop*us*, h*abi*ta lice*n*cia reg*is*, co*n*uocauit suffraganeos ep*i*scop*os*, doctores [et] *pre*latos, et co*n*cilium fecit; et citauit istum Joh*ann*em Cobham Barone*m* et brevit*er*, obseruatis t*er*minis t*r*ibus a*ut* pluribus, ut h*er*eticum iudiciali*ter* co*n*dempnauit. Pop*u*lus co*m*mu*n*is de secta sua, co*n*dempnacio*n*em egre ferens, co*n*uenciones et co*n*spiracio*ne*s occ*u*ltas co*n*tra regem *et* cler*um*
20 om*n*esq*ue* religiosos feceru*n*t. Ide*m* ecia*m* baro, *post* co*n*dempnacio*n*em sua*m* de Lundunio recedens, h*abu*it que*n*da*m* paup*er*em mo*n*achu*m* obviu*m* sibi i*n* ca*m*po de Ordine P*re*dicato*rum*, [et] ei*us* caput abscidi fecit, dice*n*s: "Tales ho*m*ines Deo i*n*vtiles" et sua*m* secta*m* mag*is* esse grata*m* (quia i*n* co*n*ue*n*tu Ord*in*is P*re*dicato*rum* fuit co*n*dempnat*us* in Lu*n*d*on*io); significans archi*epi*scopo
25 Cantu*ar*iens*i* q*uod* caput suu*m* abscid*er*e *et* h*abe*re vellet, ut sibi caueret. Ist*is* sic sta*n*tibus, d*ic*tus baro malicia*m* sua*m* in regem ac cler*um* deduc*er*e conat*us* est et co*n*spiracio*n*em occulta*m* co*n*spiracion<e> cum*u*la<tus> tanta*m* fecit *et* ad

27 co*n*spiracion<e>] *co*nspiracioni   cum*u*la<tus>] cum*u*lans

effec*tum* pe*r*duxit: q*uod* i*n* ciuitate Lundon*iensi et* ex*tra* ciuitate*m* [de] secta
Wikleff i*n* p*re*urbio Lundon*iensi* in vigilia Epiphanie secrete co*n*gregau*erat*
30 viginti milia armator*um*, inte*r* q*uos* plu*res* clerici Wyklefiste fuerant *et* vn*us*
p*re*cipue h*er*esiarcha no*mine* Joh*annes* Beuerle; et voluer*unt* illa nocte expug*n*are
munic*i*one*m* reg*is* p*ro*pe Lundonie*n*se*m* ad duo p*ar*wa miliaria theut*on*icalia, q*ue*
vocat*ur* Eltam, in qua rex erat *et* solem*p*nis a*m*basiata reg*is* Francie cu*m* eo, missa
a rege Fra*n*cie. *Et* ibi om*nes* cu*m* rege occidere volueru*nt* ipsis i*n* so*m*pno p*ri*mo
35 *pro*funde dormientib*us*, suppone*ntes* q*uod* rex ibi cu*m* ambasiatorib*us* let*us*
exist*er*et *et* eos ho*n*oraret co*n*uiuio.

[Heading:] Hic se*quitur* quo*modo* rex Dei p*ro*uide*ntia* factum disposuit.

Contigit q*uod* rex p*ri*us [disposuisset] ante aliquot me*n*ses q*uod* vellet edificare
vna*m* domu*m*, et ad illud edificiu*m* p*er*ficie*ndum* m*ul*tos artifices conuocauit
carpenta*rio*s de Lundonia. Factu*m* est q*uod* duo carpentarii de secta Wikleph *et*
40 societate dicti baronis ad dictam domu*m* edifica*ndam* fuer*un*t ecia*m* vocati qui in
illis *tem*po*ri*b*us* qua*ndo* baro istas congrega*cio*nes genciu*m* fecerat; et eis
exposi*tum* fuit quo*modo* rege*m et* suos occide*re* vellent illa nocte, v*idelicet in*
vigilia Epyph*anie*, *et* co*n*seque*nter* vellent i*n*trare Lundoniense*m* alt*er*a die *et*
occide*re* om*nes* ep*iscop*os *et* p*re*latos ac religiosos p*er* totam ciuitatem.

[fol. 157ᵛ]

45 Isti carpentarii, ut breuit*er* credit*ur*, diu*initus* inspirati int*er* se *et* ista*m* materia*m*
tracta*ntes* cogitaba*nt* qua*ntum* malu*m* istud ess*et* regnu*m* destrue*re et* rege*m*
destitue*re* et tanta*m* strage*m* in clero *et* ecclesia Dei facere. Co*n*cluser*unt* s*i*ne
mora *tr*ansire et rege*m* visitare, ne tanta mala in eu*m* co*m*mitt*er*entur. Quibus ad
Eltam munic*i*one*m*, vbi rex fuerat, venie*ntibus* magna i*n*stancia petieru*nt*
50 accessu*m* regum, q*uod* co*n*cessu*m* eis fuit; et de toto malo *et* co*n*spiraco*n*e rege*m*
instruxer*unt*. Rex v*er*o, no*n* de facili ad v*er*ba eor*um* motus, *re*spondit: "Videat*is*
ne me*n*tiami*ni*: si no*n* rep*er*iam ut dicit*is*, capitib*us* vest*ri*s p*re*uabimi*ni*." Qui
co*n*senser*unt*: "S*i*c sciat*is*, q*uia* ista nocte p*ro*pe Eccl*es*ia*m* S*an*cti Egidii ex*tra*
muros Lundonie*nses* co*n*gregabu*ntur*, et d*i*ctus Joh*annes* Beuerle h*er*esiarcha
55 eor*um* volens videre exercitu*m* et a*n*imu*m* ipsum et co*n*fortare."

Breuit*er*, rex audiens, finxit se ire dormitu*m* et sedit in vna*m* p*ar*vam
nauicula*m et* p*er*tra*n*siuit flumen q*uod* p*ro*pe munic*i*one*m* in qua erat cucurrit; et
ex alia p*ar*te transmisit Lundoniense*m* occulte p*ri*mo p*ro* legist*is*, in quib*us*
maiore*m* co*n*fide*n*cia*m* habuit, et exposuit eis factu*m*; qui subito ordi*n*aueru*nt*

---

28 secta Wikleff] secta et Wikleff   30 marg. 20 m*ilia*   32 p*ar*wa (*sic*)   34 p*ri*mo] followed in MS
by "dormientib*us*," which is deleted by subpunction   37 [disposuisset]] verb missing in MS. Supplied
from S   50 accessu*m* regum (*sic*)] The common collocation is "accessum regis"   53 Eccl*es*ia*m* S*an*cti
Egidii] Ecc*le*sia*m* S*an*cti Egedii co*n*gregabu*ntur*. No sign of deletion, but "congregabuntur" is clearly
redundant

*qui*nque milia armator*um*, qui statim ad reg*em* vener*un*t, de quo m*ultum* gauis*us* fuit. Post misit ad ciuitat*em* Lundonien*sem* secrete *et* congregauerunt xx milia; sic q*uod* no*n* p*ost* m*ul*tas horas xxx milia armator*um* h*a*buit. Et exiuit p*ro*pe Ecclesia*m* S*an*cti Egidii extra muros vbi Wiklefiste *pro*posueru*n*t co*n*uenire, et p*re*uenit eos *et* expectauit; et expectans modicum congregac*io*ne*m* sua*m*, misit quem*dam* milite*m* ad p*re*vrbiu*m* ex illa p*ar*te vbi Joh*ann*es Beuerle stabat ad suis, suscitando eu*m* *et* voc*a*ndo eu*m* cu*m* suis, ut subito ve*n*iret extra ad campu*m* vbi Ecclesia S*an*cti Egidii erat, dice*n*s q*uod* d*omin*us suus, v*idelicet* baro esset ia*m* cu*m* suis gentib*us*, et vellent sermone*m* ibi h*a*be*re* i*n* campo; quib*us* Joh*ann*es h*er*esiarcha illu*m* milite*m* secut*us* est, credens ire ad barone*m*, et miles duxit eu*m* cu*m* ducen*tis* ad faciem reg*is*; et rex cum suis circu*m*dedit et tenuit. Postea veneru*n*t centu*m*, p*os*tea pauc*i*ores sic, q*uod* t*a*lit*er* rex m*ul*tos arripuit. Postea iter*um* venit vna turma seu rotha, quib*us* venit vn*us* obuia*m*, qui euasit a rege et dixit, om*n*es esse traditos, q*uia* rex esset in ca*m*po cu*m* magna turba, [et] q*uod* reuerter*en*tur. Subito sic m*ul*ti detenti fueru*n*t et baro vix solus euasit ad pauc*is*, v*idelicet* Joh*ann*es Baro de Cobhaym. Sic rex tenuit illu*m* ca*m*pu*m* tota die Epipha*n*ie D*omi*ni *et* nocte, antequ*a*m recessit p*ro*pter ciuitate*m* Lundonien*sem*, ne ibi subito fuisse*n*t rumores. Postea, p*ost* paucos dies, rex fecit execuc*io*nem. De illis captiuis xxxvii trahi p*er* ciuitate*m* ut traditores et suspe*n*di, et denuo cu*m* patibulo ut h*er*eticos co*n*cremari. Joh*ann*em Beuerle iii et septem vt h*er*eticos cremari qui p*re*sbiteri erant; et p*ost* paucos dies C et L occisi su*n*t et multi incarcerati.

Item fecit rex p*ro*clamar<i> p*er* p*re*cones i*n* om*n*ib*us* strat*is*, q*uod* quicu*m*que sci*re*t regi dicere vbi ille Baro Cobhaim esset, vellet sibi dare xv c noblor*um*; et quicu*m*que eu*m* adduc*er*et vel int*er*ficeret tria milia noblor*um*. Et *sic* est *fi*nis. Gregorius

---

60 marg. 5 m*ilia*   61 marg. 20 m*ilia*   62 marg. 30 m*ilia*   66 suscitando eu*m* *et* voc*a*ndo] suscitando eu*m* ut *et* voc*a*ndo. No sign of deletion, but "ut" redundant   82 p*ro*clamar<i>] p*ro*clamare

B.2 STÜLZ (*S*)

Stupendas atque horrendas nouitates de Anglia animaduertite. Factum est ante festum Michahelis proxime preteritum quod quidam nobilis et prepotens baro de regno Anglie, Dominus Johannes de Oltchastel, Baro de Echaym alio nomine dictus, per Archiepiscopum Cantuariensem accusatus fuit regi Anglie tamquam caput Wicleff [et] errorum suorum hereticorum et illis inherere volentibus tutor et defensator; quem rex ad accusationem archiepiscopi vocauit et beniuole ammonuit ut a predictis herresibus desisteret; qui, monitis regiis non acquiescens interuallo temporis, iterum per regem vocatus et monitus. Non destitit, sed pertinaciter institit, errores dictos fouendo et in sua pertinacia perseuerando. Rex, videns eum induratum, prohibuit primo ne ad eius cameram amplius accederet,

---

5 Wicleff] *S* Bicleff

postea mandauit sibi ne curiam et cappellam suam ammodo intraret.

Iste baro, ad omnes accusationes huiusmodi non desistens, iterum regi accusatur ab archiepiscopo satis importune. Rex, excusans se, dixit archiepiscopo: "Ego feci quod in me fuit, ad presens iudicii vestri interest corrigere et procedere ordine iuris contra tales ut decet." Archiepiscopus, habita licencia regis, conuocauit suos suffraganeos episcopos, doctores [et] prelatos, et concilium fecit; et citauit istum Johannem de Eckhaym Baronem et breuiter, obseruatis omnibus terminis et pluribus, ut hereticum iudicialiter condempnauit. Populus communis de secte sua, condempnacionem egre ferens, conuenciones et conspiraciones occultas contra dictum regem et clerum omnesque religiosos fecerunt. Idem eciam baro, post condempnacionem suam de Lundonio recedens, habuit quendam pauperem monachum obuium in campis de Ordine Predicatorum, cuius caput abscidi fecit, dicens: "Tales homines Deo inutiles" et suam sectam Deo magis esse gratam (quia in conuentu Ordinis Predicatorum fuit condempnatus in Lundonio); significans archiepiscopo tantum: quod suum caput abscidere et habere vellet, ut sibi caueret. Istis sic stantibus, dictus baro maliciam suam in regem et clerum deducere conatus est et conspiracionem occultam conspiracione cumulatus tant<a>m fecit et ad effectum perduxit: quod in ciuitate Lundoniensi et extra de sua secta et Wicleff in preurbio Lundoniensi in vigilia Epiphanie Domini secrete congregauerat viginti milia armatorum, inter quos plures clerici Wicleuiste erant et vnus precipuus eorum heresiarcha nomine dictus Bouorle; et voluerunt ista nocte expugnare vnam mvnicionem regis prope Lundoniam ad duo parua miliaria teutonicalia, que vocatur Elchaym, in qua rex erat, et solempnis ambasiata regis Francie ibidem secum fuerat, ad eum missa de Francia. Ibi regem et omnes secum existentes occidere volebant in nocte ipsis in primo sompno profunde dormientibus, supponentes quod ibi rex cum ambasiatoribus regis Francie letus esset et eos honoraret conuiuia et epulas ordinando.

Contigit quod rex prius disposuisset ante aliquot menses quod vellet edifficare vnam domum, et ad illud edifficium perficiendum vocari fecit plures carpentarios de Lundonio. Factum est quod duo carpentarii de secta Wicleff et societate dicti baronis ad dictam domum edifficandam sunt eciam vocati qui in illis temporibus quando baro istas congregauerat gentes eciam uocati fuerunt; et eis expositum fuit quomodo regem et suos occidere vellent in illa nocte, videlicet in Epiphania Domini, et consequenter vellent intrare Lundoniam altera die et occidere omnes episcopos et prelatos ac religiosos per totam ciuitatem existentes vbique. Illi carpentarii breuiter diuinitus, ut creditur, inspirati inter se istam materiam tractantes et voluenteste cogitabant quantum istud malum esset regnum destruere regi<s> et stragem tantam in clero et ecclesia Dei facere. Inter multa argumenta habita concluserunt sine mora transire et regem auisare, ne [a] barone tanta mala et periculosa in eum committerentur. Quibus ad Eltkhaym, ubi rex constitutus fuerat, quantocius venientibus cum instancia magna petiuerunt

---

28 tant<a>m] tantum   29 Wicleff] *S* Bicleff   30 Wicleuiste] *S* Bicleuiste   31 Bouorle] *S* Boborle   40 Wicleff] *S* Bicleff   48 regi<s>] regi

accessum ad regem, quod eis concessum fuit. Breuiter, regem de tanto malo et
tractatu et conspiracione facta auisant. Rex autem, non de facili advisatione eorum
motus, respondit: "Videatis ne mentiamini: si non reperiam rem ut dicitis, capite
vos puniam." Illi responderunt: "Domine, si non volueritis credere in hiis que
diximus vobis, non decapitabitis nos, sed committatis hoc aliis: quia vos non eritis
viuus, quasi dicerent; vos videbitis quod ita veniet: quod interficiamini cum
vestris, ideo non poteritis nos decapitare." Dixerunt eciam regi quomodo
Wiclefiste in preurbio Lundoniensi congregati deberent omnes post medium
noctis convenire prope Basilicam Sancti Egidii extra muros Lundoniensi<s> in
campis; et ibidem dictus baro et dictus Johannes Bouorle eresiarcha eorum vellent
videre exercitum et examinare eos et confortare.

Breuiter, rex finxit se ire dormitum et personaliter sedet super vnam
nauiculam paruam et pertransiuit flumen quod prope mvnicionem erat; et ex alia
parte transiuit Lundoniam et misit occulte pro legistis, in quibus maiorem
fiduciam habuit, exponens ipsis factum; qui subito ordinauerunt II° milia
armatorum, qui ad regem secrete venerunt, de quo multum gauisus fuit. Demum
misit ad ciuitatem Lundoniensem secrete et congregauerunt XX milia armatorum;
sic idem in non multis horis habuit extra in campo et in ciuitate quasi XXX milia
armatorum. Et exiuit ad locum prope Ecclesiam Sancti Egidii extra muros vbi
Wicleffiste proposuerunt conuenire, et preuenit eos et expectauit; et expectans
modicum congregationem suam, misit vnum militem ad preurbium ex illa parte
vbi Dominus Johannes Bouorle stabat cum suis, suscitando et vocando eum, quod
subito veniret extra ad campum ad Ecclesiam Sancti Egidii, vbi dominus
suus fidelis baro esset cum gentibus suis, et vellet sermonem habere in campo; qui
Dominus Johannes heresiarcha illum militem secutus est, credens ire ad baronem,
et miles duxit eum cum ducentis ad faciem regis. Ille, credens ibi esse et stare
socios suos, regi presentatus est, quem rex cum suis circumdedit et tenuit. Postea
veniunt centum, postea pauciores sic, quod taliter rex multos arripuit. Postea venit
vna rotta, cui venit vnus obuiam, qui euasit a rege et dixit, omnes esse traditos,
quia rex esset in campo cum magna gente, quod auerterentur. Et subito multi
detenti sunt et baro vix solus affugit, videlicet Baro de Elckhaim. Sic rex
tenuit illum campum tota die Epiphanie Domini et nocte, antequam recessit
propter ciuitatem Lundoniensem, ne ibi subito facti fuissent rumores. Postea, die
XIIII mensis Januarii, rex fecit execucionem. Et fecit de illis captiuis XXXVII
trahi per ciuitatem ut traditores, et postea suspendi et postea cum patibulis ut
hereticos concremari. Dominum Johannem Boorle [cum] septem ut hereticos
concremare fecit, qui septem omnes prespiteri erant; et post paucos dies facta est
execucio successiue sic, quod iam centum et iam L occisi sunt et multi
incarcerati. Item fecit rex proclamari per precones publice in omnibus stratis,

---

59 Wiclefiste] *S* Biclefiste   60 Lundoniensi<s>] Lundoniensium   61 Bouorle] *S* Boborle
71 Wicleffiste] *S* Bicleffiste   73 Bouorle] *S* Boborle   80 rotta] read "turba." See Du Cange,
Glossarium ad scriptores mediae et infimae latinitatis, s.v. "rotta"   82 Baro de Elckhaim] Baro de
Kobha de Elckhaim, with "de Kobha" under erasure   87 Boorle (*sic*)] read "Bouorle"

quod quicumque sciret dicere in quo loco esset Baro de Elckhaim, illi vellet dare quingentas et habere deberet libras Anglianenses que faciunt in moneta quindecim decentena nobilorum; qui autem posset eum interficere aut ad presenciam regis ducere deberet habere mille libras Anglianenses, que faciunt tria milia nubilorum.

95 Item generalem fecit proclamacionem, quod quicumque aliquem inveniret de illa secta, quod ipsum abque iudicio interficeret, si esset ita potens, [et quod si] non posset eum interficere, quod tunc denunciaretur regi et ipse vellet facere execucionem. Et rex dixit per illum se velle modo illam sectam extirpare.

Wilhelmus Canonicus Ecclesie Olomucensis

96 si esset] et si esset

TEXTUAL AND EXPLANATORY NOTES

1. TŘEBOŇ, STÁTNÍ OBLASTNÍ ARCHIV MS A.16, FOL. 157^{r-v} (*T*)

ll. 1–2 *Factum est ante festum Michaelis proxime preterito*: the Feast of St. Michael, or Michaelmas, falls on September 29. The event in question, then, occurred just before September 29, 1413, and the qualification "proxime preteritum [most recently gone by]" indicates that this account was written or delivered orally before the end of September 1414. See Chapter 4 for discussion.

ll. 18–20 *Populus communis . . . fecerunt*: plural verbs were by this time commonly used with singular nouns which are collective in sense. See Peter Stotz, *Handbuch zur lateinischen Sprache des Mittelalters*, IV, § 79.2.

ll. 21–2 *habuit quendam pauperem monachum obvium sibi in campo de Ordine Predicatorum*: i.e., a Dominican friar.

ll. 23–4 *in conuentu Ordinis Predicatorum fuit condempnatus in Lundonio*: i.e., the Blackfriars Council of 1382 which condemned twenty-four conclusions drawn from Wyclif's writings. This was not technically a Dominican convention, but one held at their main London house.

l. 29 *in vigilia Epiphanie*: Epiphany falls on January 6, with the vigil, of course, being January 5.

ll. 30–1 *vnus precipue heresiarcha nomine Johannes Beuerle*: see *S*, n. to l. 31.

ll. 33–4 *solempnis ambasiata regis Francie*: I am aware of no reference to a French embassy in other accounts of the 1414 Rising.

B.2 STÜLZ (s)

ll. 1–2   *Factum est ante festum Michahelis proxime preteritum*: see *T*, n. to ll. 1–2.

l. 3   *Dominus Johannes de Oltchastel, Baro de Echaym*: the scribe (Wilhelmus) seems confused by names in the account, which is not entirely surprising, since foreign names were often altered or rendered beyond recognition when copied in medieval texts. Oldcastle was Lord Cobham, not "Echaym" (Eltham). The scribe may have heard the correct title at some point, as is suggested by the fact that in l. 82 "de Kobha" is erased, and replaced with "de Elckhaim." The alteration is particularly confusing in this account because Henry V's royal palace is at Eltham – an accurate historical description. Names in *T* are much clearer.

ll. 18–20   *Populus communis . . . fecerunt*: see *T*, n. to ll. 18–20.

ll. 21–2   *habuit quendam pauperem monachum obuium in campis de Ordine Predicatorum*: i.e., a Dominican friar.

ll. 24–5   *in conuentu Ordinis Predicatorum fuit condempnatus in Lundonio*: see *T*, n. to ll. 23–4.

l. 29   *in vigilia Epiphanie Domini*: see *T*, n. to l. 29.

l. 31   *heresiarcha nomine dictus Bouorle*: as I discuss in Chapter 4, n. 90, the identity of "Bouorle" is puzzling. Compounding the confusion are the many contradictory accounts of the 1414 Rising found in England. Bouorle's actions and punishment most closely resemble those of Sir Roger Acton in some other accounts. At the same time, Bouorle's designations as a "lord" and "priest" match the description of John Beverly in one of the English anecdotes. The account in *S* also introduces Bouorle as a priest (ll. 30–1) and mentions that he was executed among seven other "prespiteri" (ll. 87–8). His name, "Bouorle," furthermore bears a resemblance to "Beverly," and indeed the account in *T* confirms that "Beverly" is meant. For references to Acton and Beverly in other records, see Kingsford, *English Historical Literature*, 284–5, 292–3, and 324–5.

l. 33   *Elchaym*: see note to l. 3 (above).

ll. 33–4   *solempnis ambasiata regis Francie*: see *T*, n. to ll. 33–4.

ll. 43–4   *in Epiphania Domini*: this copy of the text is somewhat indecisive as to whether the event in question happened on the vigil of Epiphany (Jan. 5), or on the day of Epiphany itself (Jan. 6).

ll. 55–8   *Domine . . . decapitare*: the scribe of *S*, or that of his exemplar, has
produced a substantially more detailed and lively account of the
carpenters' dialogue with the king than we see in *T*. Here they
seem far more bold and confident in the king's presence.

TRANSLATIONS

B.I TŘEBOŇ, STÁTNÍ OBLASTNÍ ARCHIV MS A.16, FOL. 157 ^r–v^ (*T*)

Hear the astounding and dreadful news from England. It happened
before the feast of St. Michael most recently gone by [Sept. 29, 1413]
that a certain noble and very powerful baron from the kingdom of
England, Lord John Oldcastle, also called Cobham, was accused by the
Archbishop of Canterbury to the King of England of being a chief of
Wyclif and of his heretical errors, and protector and defender of those
willing to adhere to them; whom the king summoned on the archbishop's accusation and benevolently admonished to desist from the
aforesaid errors; who, not acquiescing to the king's admonishments,
when a moderate interval had passed, was summoned and admonished
by the king a second time. He did not desist, but obstinately pressed on,
fostering the said errors and persevering in his obstinacy. The king,
considering him obdurate, first forbade him to approach his chamber
any longer, and afterwards commanded him henceforth not to visit his
court or chapel.

This baron, not heeding all of the archbishop's accusations, was again
accused by the archbishop to the king importunately enough. The king,
excusing himself, said [to the archbishop]: "I have done my best, and now it
lies in your judgment to correct and proceed by the order of law as is fitting
against such a man." Having considered the king's authorization, the archbishop called together the suffragan bishops, doctors, [and] prelates, and
formed a council; and he cited this John, Baron of Cobham, and briefly,
after considering three or more conciliar rulings, legally condemned him as
a heretic. The common people from his sect, scarcely considering the
condemnation, held secret assemblies and imagined conspiracies against
the king, the clergy, and all the religious. And furthermore the baron,
withdrawing from London after his condemnation, came across a certain
poor monk from the Order of Preachers in the field, [and] caused his head
to be cut off, saying: "Such men are useless to God," and that his own sect
(because it was condemned in London in a convention of the Order of
Preachers) was dearer [to God]; signifying to the Archbishop of Canterbury

that he [i.e., Oldcastle] wanted to cut off his [i.e., the archbishop's] head and to have it, and that he [the archbishop] should look out for himself. And so the said baron endeavored to bring his malice against the king and the clergy when they were resting, and in conspiracy he amassed such a secret plot and put it into effect: [namely,] that in the city of London and outside the city, he secretly gathered together twenty thousand armed men from Wyclif's sect on the outskirts of London on the vigil of Epiphany [Jan. 5, 1414], among whom were many Wycliffite clerics, and one [of them] in particular was the heresiarch named John Beverly; and on that night they wanted to assault the king's fortification about two short German miles near London, which is called Eltham, in which was the king, and with him a solemn embassy of the King of France, sent by the French king. And there they wanted to murder everyone with the king when they were fast asleep in the first watch, supposing that there [at Eltham] the king with the ambassadors would be cheerful and that he [the king] would honor them with a banquet.

Here follows how the king managed the affair by the providence of God.

It turned out that the king had determined several months earlier that he wanted to build a house, and to complete that construction, he called together many skilled carpenters from London. It so happened that two carpenters from Wyclif's sect and of the aforesaid baron's company were likewise summoned to the construction site who [were also summoned] at the same time when the baron had brought forth his gatherings of people; and it was explained to them how on that night, namely, on the vigil of Epiphany, they wanted to murder the king and his companions, and consequently they wanted to enter London the next day and slay all the bishops and prelates and the religious throughout the whole city. In short, those carpenters, divinely inspired between themselves, as it is believed, were hauling lumber and were thinking how evil it was to destroy the kingdom and to forsake the king and cause such a massacre against the clergy and the Church of God. They concluded without delay to go over and visit the king, lest such evil should be committed against him. When they had come to the fortification of Eltham, where the king was, with great urgency they begged access to the king, which was granted to them; and they informed the king about the great evil and conspiracy. The king, however, not easily moved by their words, responded: "See that you do not speak falsely: if I do not discover [the affair] to be as you say, you will be punished with your heads." They agreed[, saying]: "Thus you will know, for on this night they will be gathered near the church of Saint Egidius [i.e., St. Giles] outside the walls of London, and also the said John Beverly their heresiarch [will be there] wanting both to examine the army and to comfort their spirits."

In short, hearing this, the king pretended to go to sleep, and he sat in a small boat and crossed the river which flowed quickly near the fortification in which he was staying; and from the other side he first sent secretly to London for messengers, in whom he had utter confidence, and explained to them the [planned] affair. The messengers immediately ordered five thousand soldiers, who came at once to the king. There was much joy about that. After that he sent secretly to the city of London and gathered together twenty thousand soldiers; so that after not many hours he had thirty thousand soldiers. And he moved near the church of St. Egidius outside the walls where the Wycliffites proposed to convene, and he preceded and awaited them; and, anticipating their congregation for a short while, he sent a certain soldier to the outskirts [of the city] from the side where John Beverly was standing by his men, rousing and calling upon him [i.e., Beverly] with his men, [saying] that he should come immediately out into the field where the church of St. Egidius is, [and] saying that his lord, namely the baron, is already [there] with his people, and that they want to have a word there in the field. Lord John [Beverly] the heresiarch followed this soldier to them, thinking to go to the baron, and the soldier led him with two hundred men into the presence of the king; and the king with his men surrounded and apprehended him. Afterwards a hundred came, and then fewer, so that in this way the king arrested many men. Afterwards there came a mob or crowd again, and a man who had evaded the king came up to them [i.e., the crowd] and said that all are handed over, for the king is in the field with a great company, and that they should turn back. So in no time at all many were detained, and the baron scarcely managed to flee by himself with just a few men, namely, John the Baron of Cobham. Thus the king held the field the whole day and night of the Epiphany of the Lord, until he withdrew near the city of London, lest in a short time rumors would arise there. Afterwards, after a few days, the king held an execution. Of the captives, thirty-seven were drawn through the city as traitors and hanged, and in turn burned with the gibbet as heretics. [He had] John Beverly and three and seven [others] burned who were priests. And after a few days one hundred and fifty were killed and many imprisoned.

Also the king had it proclaimed by the criers in all the streets that anyone who knows the whereabouts of the Baron of Cobham to report to the king, he will give him 115 nobles; and that whoever leads him [to the king] or kills him [will be given] 3,000 nobles. And so that is the end. Gregory

B.2 STÜLZ (*s*)

Hear the astounding and dreadful news from England. It happened before the feast of St. Michael most recently gone by [Sept. 29, 1413] that a certain noble and very powerful baron from the kingdom of England, Lord John Oldcastle, also called Baron of Eltham [*sic*; read "Cobham"], was accused by the Archbishop of Canterbury to the King of England as being a chief of Wyclif and of his heretical errors, and protector and defender of those willing to adhere to them; whom the king summoned on the archbishop's accusation and benevolently admonished to desist from the aforesaid heresies; who, not acquiescing to the royal admonishments within an interval of time, was summoned and admonished by the king a second time. He did not desist, but obstinately pressed on, fostering the said errors and persevering in his obstinacy. The king, considering him obdurate, first forbade him to approach his chamber any longer, and afterwards commanded him henceforth not to enter his court and chapel.

This baron, not heeding any such accusations, was again accused by the archbishop to the king importunately enough. The king, excusing himself, said to the archbishop: "I have done my best, and now it lies in your judgment to correct and proceed by the order of law as is fitting against such a man." Having considered the king's authorization, the archbishop called together his suffragan bishops, doctors, [and] prelates, and formed a council; and he cited this John, Baron of Eltham [i.e., Cobham], and briefly, after considering all the conciliar rulings and more, legally condemned him as a heretic. The common people from his sect, scarcely considering the condemnation, held secret assemblies and imagined conspiracies against the said king, the clergy and all the religious. And furthermore the baron, withdrawing from London after his condemnation, came across a certain poor monk from the Order of Preachers in the fields, whose head he caused to be cut off, saying: "Such men are useless to God," and that his own sect (because it was condemned in London in a convention of the Order of Preachers) was dearer to God; signifying this to the archbishop: that he [i.e., Oldcastle] wanted to cut off his [i.e., the archbishop's] head and to have it, and that he [the archbishop] should look out for himself. And so the said baron endeavored to bring his malice against the king and the clergy when they were resting, and in conspiracy he amassed such a secret plot and put it into effect: [namely,] that in the city of London and outside [the city], he secretly gathered together twenty thousand armed men from his and Wyclif's sect on the outskirts of London on the vigil of the Epiphany of the Lord [Jan. 5, 1414], among whom were many Wycliffite clerics, and one of them in particular was the heresiarch named Beverly; and on this night they wanted to assault one of the king's fortifications about two short German miles near London, which is called Eltham, in which was the king, and there with him was a solemn embassy of the King of France, sent to him from France. There they wanted to murder the king and all who were there with him at night, when they were fast asleep in the first watch, supposing that there [at Eltham] the king with the ambassadors of the King of France would be cheerful and that, ordering the courses, he [the king] would honor them with a banquet.

It turned out that the king had determined several months earlier that he wanted to build a house, and to complete that construction, he had many carpenters summoned from London. It so happened that two carpenters from Wyclif's sect and of the aforesaid baron's company were likewise summoned to the construction site who were also summoned at the same time when the baron gathered together his people; and it was explained to them how on that night, namely on the Epiphany of the Lord, they wanted to murder the king and his companions, and consequently they wanted to enter London the next day and slay all the bishops and prelates and the religious living everywhere throughout the whole city. In short, those carpenters, divinely inspired between themselves, as it is believed, were hauling that lumber and were thinking ponderously how evil it was to destroy the king's kingdom and to cause such a massacre against the clergy and the Church of God. Among many reasoned arguments they concluded without delay to go over and advise the king, lest such evil and perilous things should be committed against him by the baron. When they had come as quickly as possible to Eltham, where the king was located, with great urgency they begged access to the king, which was granted to them. In brief, they advised the king about the great evil and pact and conspiracy which had been made. The king, however, not easily moved by their advice, responded: "See that you do not speak falsely: if I do not discover the affair to be as you say, I shall punish you with your head." They responded: "Lord, if you do not wish to believe these things which we have said to you, you shall not decapitate us, but you shall forfeit this [i.e., your own head] to others: for you shall not remain alive, as they declare; you shall see that it will happen thus: that you are killed with your companions, and therefore you shall not be able to decapitate us." They also told the king how all the Wycliffites should be gathered on the outskirts of London after midnight to converge near the Basilica of Saint Egidius [i.e., St. Giles] in the fields outside the walls of London; and there the said baron and the said John Beverly their heresiarch want to see the army and to examine and encourage them.

In short, the king pretended to go to sleep, and he personally sat upon a small boat and crossed the river which was near the fortification; and from the other side he crossed over to London and sent secretly for messengers, in whom he had utter confidence, explaining to them the [planned] affair. The messengers immediately ordered two thousand soldiers, who came secretly to the king. There was much joy about that. Finally he sent secretly to the city of London and gathered together twenty thousand soldiers; and so in not many hours he had outside in the field and in the city about thirty thousand soldiers. And he moved to the place near the church of St. Egidius outside the walls where the Wycliffites proposed to convene and he preceded and awaited them; and, anticipating their congregation for a short while, he sent a soldier to the outskirts [of the city] from the side where Lord John Beverly was standing with his men, rousing and calling upon him [i.e. Beverly], [saying] that he should come immediately out into the field, to the church of St. Egidius, where his faithful lord the baron is with his people, and wants to have a word in the field. Lord John [Beverly] the heresiarch followed this soldier, thinking to go to the baron, and the soldier led him with two hundred men into the presence of the king. He [i.e., Beverly], thinking that his accomplices were standing there, was presented to the king, whom the king with his men surrounded and apprehended. Afterwards a hundred came, and then fewer, so that in this way the king arrested many men. Afterwards there came a mob, and a man who had evaded the king came up to it and said that all are handed over, for the king is in the field with a great company, and that they should turn back. And in no time at all many were detained, and the baron scarcely fled by himself, namely the Baron of Eltham [i.e., Cobham]. Thus the king held the field the whole day and night of the Epiphany of the Lord, until he withdrew near the city of London, lest in a short time rumors would arise there. Afterwards, on the fourteenth day of the month of January, the king held an execution. And of the captives, he had thirty-seven drawn through the city as traitors, and afterwards hanged and then burned with the gibbets as heretics. He had the Lord John Beverly with seven others burned as heretics, which seven men were all priests. And after a few days an execution was held like this successively, so that now a hundred, and now fifty were killed and many were imprisoned. Also the king had it publicly proclaimed by the criers in all the streets, that anyone who knows the whereabouts of the Baron of Eltham [i.e., Cobham] to report [to the king], he will give him five hundred English pounds to keep, which makes 1,500 nobles in coin; but anyone who can kill him or lead him into the presence of the king would have a thousand English pounds, which makes 3,000 nobles. Also he made a general proclamation that whoever finds anyone from that sect should kill him according to his own judgment, if he is so able, and that if he was not able to kill him, he [i.e., the heretic] should then be denounced to the king, and he would do the execution himself. And the king said by this that he himself wants to root out the sect in this way.

William, Canon of the church of Olomouc

Notes

INTRODUCTION

1. Concerning texts that reached England from Bohemia, my research has identified only diplomatic correspondence and evidence of letters sent from reformists in Prague to the Wycliffites Richard Wyche and John Oldcastle.
2. *Von der Handschrift zum gedruckten Buch.* See especially diagram 38b in II.657 ("Die absolute Handschriftenproduktion in Europa, 1250–1530"). For the breakdown of manuscript production in the Empire, see *ibid.*, 619 (diagram 5).
3. *Ibid.*, 657 (diagram 38b) and 619 (diagram 5).
4. Vojtěch Raňkův of Ježov, for example, studied at Paris in the 1340s and became procurator there of the English *nacio.* In the 1350s he seems to have traveled to Oxford, where he may have met Richard FitzRalph, Archbishop of Armagh, and received an autograph manuscript (still extant) of FitzRalph's *De pauperie Salvatoris.* Shortly before he died in 1388 he established a scholarship for Czech students to study theology or philosophy at either university, provided that the students were Czech-speaking and of Czech descent. Jerome of Prague may have been one of the beneficiaries, and it seems safe to suggest that the practice of *peregrinatio academica* was a contributing factor in the initial transmission of Wyclif's texts to Bohemia. It has also been suggested that Vojtěch was the author of a text known as *Tetragonus Aristotelis*, which includes a dialogue in the form of a fictional epistolary exchange between the universities of Prague, Oxford, and Paris, in which Prague and Oxford vie to save the University of Paris from destruction by the schismatics after 1378. University ties, both real and imagined, continued into the Schism period, and would even be influential in facilitating reformist textual exchange. For a recent discussion of Vojtěch's career, see Herold, "Vojtěch Raňkův of Ježov" (for the details discussed here, see esp. 73–4, 77). Bartoš edited *Tetragonus Aristotelis* as *Tetragonus Aristotelis: konciliaristický projev s počátku velikého církevního rozkolu.* The text is also discussed in Swanson, *Universities, Academics and the Great Schism*, 55–6.
5. *Austerlitz*, 100–1.
6. *Graphs, Maps, Trees*, 1.
7. *Ibid.*, 3, quoting Krzysztof Pomian.
8. *The Logic of Practice*, 82–3.
9. Moretti, *Graphs, Maps, Trees*, 4.

10. Rymer, *Foedera*, VII.291.
11. See, for example, the documents in *ibid.*, 283 and 290–5.
12. *Ibid.*, 291.
13. See, for example, Mugnai, "La *Expositio reduplicativarum* chez Walter Burleigh et Paulus Venetus," 318–20.
14. I borrow the term "internationale" from discussions of Waldensian–Hussite contacts in the fifteenth century by Amedeo Molnar ("L'Internationale des Taborites et des Vaudois") and Giovanni Gonnet ("L'Internationale Valdo-Hussite").
15. *Pedagogy, Intellectuals, and Dissent*, 185.
16. *Wycliffite Heresy*, 210–11.
17. *Vox Dei*, 229.
18. Here I must disagree with Ralph Hanna's fairly strict distinction between vernacular and Latinate book production, a distinction which is not borne out in my research. See, for example, Hanna's "Miscellaneity and Vernacularity: Conditions of Literary Production in Late Medieval England," esp. 48. It should be noted, however, that when Hanna refers to Latin books, he is thinking of books produced in affiliation with monasteries, schools, and so on, which is not uniformly the situation with the Latinate books I discuss in this study. Still, by the later Middle Ages, I am not convinced that a strict distinction existed between vernacular and Latinate book production, the latter being more "fixed" than the former.
19. See the discussion in Hobbins, *Authorship and Publicity before Print*, 193ff and the notes therein.
20. *Von der Handschrift zum gedruckten Buch*, II.657.
21. *Authorship and Publicity before Print*, esp. ch. 5, "The Schoolman as Public Intellectual: Implications of the Late Medieval Tract."
22. On the dissemination of Constance *Acta* to England, see esp. Crowder, "Constance Acta in English Libraries."

CHAPTER 1: "THE OCCASION OF QUEENE ANNE"

1. From *A compendious olde treatyse, shewynge howe that we oughte to haue ye scripture in Englysshe* (1530). Edited by Bühler in "A Lollard Tract: On Translating the Bible into English," 178–9.
2. The most recent studies of Anne of Bohemia include Andrew Taylor, "Anne of Bohemia and the Making of Chaucer"; David Wallace, "Anne of Bohemia, Queen of England, and Chaucer's Emperice" (adapted from ch. 12 of his *Chaucerian Polity*); Paul Strohm, "Queens as Intercessors" (ch. 5 of his *Hochon's Arrow*); John Bowers, *The Politics of Pearl*, passim; Alfred Thomas, *Anne's Bohemia*, passim; and Thomas, *A Blessed Shore*, esp. ch. 1 and 2.
3. Cole, *Literature and Heresy*, 46; Hanna, *Pursuing History*, 9.
4. *Actes and monuments* (1583), 507.
5. *Ibid.*, 588.

6. *Ibid.* Foxe seems to have encountered figures from the early Bohemian reform in his source material, though the extent of his knowledge of the native movement is unclear. I have found only one reference to an early Bohemian reformer, Milíč of Kroměříž (*ibid.*, 20). It should however be borne in mind that his narrative trajectory is determined from the start: his title page indicates that the work is a "Vniuersall history" of the Church, but also makes it clear that the *telos* is always "this Realme of England and Scotland." Such a history does not call for an elaboration of Bohemian affairs before the introduction of Wyclif's doctrines.

7. *An apologie for Iohn Wickliffe*, sig. K4^r.

8. Thompson, *Chronicon Angliae*, 183.

9. *An apologie for Iohn Wickliffe*, sig. K4^r.

10. *A compleat history*, 468–9 (italics original).

11. Luther's letter to Spalatin is dated February 14, 1520, and is printed in *D. Martin Luthers Werke, Kritische Gesamtausgabe. Briefwechsel*, II.40–2.

12. Milton's statement is from *Of Reformation*, 525.

13. The idea for this thought experiment arose from a conversation with David Mengel, to whom I am grateful.

14. Rymer, *Foedera*, VII.291.

15. *Actes and monuments* (1563), 1556: "A notable proofe assuredly of the prouidence and pleasure of God in sowing the gospell, was that comminge of the Boheminans [*sic*] vnto vs, to thintente to heare Wicklyfe, of whom wee spake before, who at that time red openly at Oxforde: and also the going of our men to the sayde Bohemians, when persecution was raysed agaynst vs."

16. Foxe prints the tract in the 1563 edition on 452–5.

17. Edited in Bühler, "A Lollard Tract."

18. For Hudson's discussion of the tract, see "The Debate on Bible Translation."

19. The anecdote first appears in isolation in Foxe's 1570 edition.

20. Note also the entry in Foxe's 1563 index, "bohemians learned the Gospell in England," which refers to the passage transcribed in n. 15 (above).

21. For Wyclif's reference, see *De triplici vinculo amoris*, 168: "Nam possibile est, quod nobilis regina Anglie, soror cesaris, habeat ewangelium in lingwa triplici exaratum, scilicet in lingwa boemica, in lingwa teutonica et latina, et hereticare ipsam propterea implicite foret luciferina superbia." It seems that Foxe must have known of Wyclif's claim at least indirectly. Elsewhere (448–9 in the 1583 edition of *Actes and monuments*), Foxe quotes a lengthy passage from Hus' *Contra Iohannem Stokes*, which he presumably translated from Matthias Flacius' 1558 edition of Hus' *Opera omnia*. In this defense of Wyclif against Stokes, Hus quotes frequently from Wyclif's *De triplici vinculo amoris*, including the passage on Anne's alleged trilingual Bible. Foxe does not, however, include this particular reference in his translation of Hus' defense. The other reference to Czech vernacular Scriptures from the Prologue to the Lollard Bible is edited in Hudson, *Selections from English Wycliffite Writings*, 71: "Also Frenshe men, Beemers [Bohemians] and Britons han þe Bible and oþere bokis of deuocioun and of exposicioun translatid in here modir

langage." Robert Crowley also printed the reference in *The true copye of a prolog* (1550).

22. For discussion of the legends which developed around John Wyclif, see: Aston, "John Wyclif's Reformation Reputation"; Crompton, "John Wyclif: A Study in Mythology"; and Mudroch, *The Wyclyf Tradition*, esp. 4, 9–10.

23. The varying accounts of the episode are discussed in Stow, "Richard II in Thomas Walsingham's Chronicles," 90 and his n. 104.

24. I refer here to Nigel Saul's discussion of Richard's later years, from *Richard II*, particularly his comment on 388: "Unity – that is, peace – was incompatible with dissent; what the king required was unquestioning acceptance of his rule and submission to his will."

25. For chroniclers' eulogies of the queen, see for example Walsingham, *St. Albans Chronicle*, 961; the Evesham Chronicler's account in Stow, *Historia vitae et regni Ricardi Secundi*, 134; and *Chronicle of Adam Usk*, 18.

26. For discussion, see Wallace, *Chaucerian Polity*, 371–2.

27. Bowers' discussion of *Pearl* as a eulogy for Anne is discussed most fully in ch. 8 of *The Politics of Pearl*, 151–86.

28. There are several references in the chronicles and elsewhere to the so-called Bohemian fashion of shoes with long "pykys," often attributed to the coming of Queen Anne to England. See for example the Evesham Chronicler's remarks (Stow, *Historia vitae et regni Ricardi Secundi*, 134): "Cum ista regina uenerunt de Boemia in Angliam abusiones ille execrabiles, sotulares scilicet cum longis rostris, Anglice 'cracows' uel 'pykys,' dimidiam uirgam largiter habentes, ita ut oporteret eos ad tibiam ligari cum cathenis argenteis, antequam cum eis possent incedere." It is interesting to note, however, that similar references to this kind of shoe were made long before Anne's arrival in England in 1381 (and the term "cracows" would suggest a Polish origin, not Bohemian). See for example Haydon, *Eulogium*, III.231 (reference for 1362); Tait, *Chronica Johannis de Reading*, 167 (for 1365); John Gower has a similar reference in his *Mirour de l'Omme*, in *The Complete Works of John Gower*, 1.258, ll. 23393–4. The references persist in England until at least the 1420s, though the association with Bohemians falls away. See the Wycliffite treatise *Of Antecrist and His Meynee* in Todd, *Three Treatises*, cxxxviii; and *The Castle of Perseverance* (1400–25?), in Eccles, *The Macro Plays*, 34/1059. For further discussion, see Green, "Jack Philipot, John of Gaunt, and a Poem of 1380," esp. 331 and his n. 3; Eccles' note in *The Macro Plays*, 190/1059; and Scattergood, "Fashion and Morality," passim.

29. Fols. 1ʳ–89ʳ.

30. Fols. 95ᵛ–96ʳ. One of these is in verse, beginning: "Tu Ihesus est testis, ubi Christoforus memoratur." The poem is Walther, *Initia*, no. 19480 (where "Ihesus" is "Deus"), although Walther lists only Oxford, Trinity College MS 7 (which does not seem to have been the source for the poem in Prague, Knihovna Metropolitní kapituly (PKMK) H.15).

31. Fol. 95ᵛ.

32. Fol. 96ʳ. As with many renditions of St. Christopher carrying the Christ Child, this sketch also depicts the aquatic life swimming around the saint's feet, here

represented by a lobster and a fish. The lobster motif is less common than others, but nevertheless circulated fairly widely. It appears elsewhere in the Middle Ages, for example in England and in Poland, as well as in the Bohemian region, notably in the painting of the scene (though perhaps from a slightly later date) at the east end of St. Barbara's Cathedral in Kutná Hora.

33. His description of France is on fols. 92^{r-v}.

34. The section describing England is on fols. 92^{v}-93^{r}.

35. See *A Survey of London*, 1.25: "In the yeare 1395. on S. Georges day, was a great iusting [jousting] on London bridge, betwixt Dauid Earle of Craford of Scotland, and the Lord Wels of England. In the which the Lord Wels was at the third course borne out of the saddle, which hystorie proueth, that at that time the Bridge being coaped on either side was not replenished with houses builded thereupon, as since it hath beene, and now is." Compare the Bohemian traveler's account written not long after 1395 (fol. 92^{v}): "et est pons in quo sunt domus magne sicut una placea et habet testudines XXI."

36. Whether more than three of them once existed is impossible to determine from the account. In the discussion which follows, I shall refer to the eulogies, which I edit in Appendix A, by their first lines.

37. See in particular the Introduction to Hanna's *Pursuing History*.

38. Printed in *An Inventory of the Historical Monuments in London*, 1.31. I have altered the punctuation as printed in the *Inventory*.

39. Rymer, *Foedera*, VII.795–6 (for Yevele and Lote) and 797–8 (for Broker and Prest).

40. *Ibid.*, 798.

41. Cf. Lindley, "Absolutism and Regal Image," 292 n. 49. A commission is not, of course, evidence of royal authorship, as Bowers seems to suggest. See *Politics of Pearl*, 20, where the tomb has become "inscribed with an epigraph of the king's own invention."

42. The epitaph is edited and discussed by Rossell Hope Robbins in "An Epitaph for Duke Humphrey."

43. The Duke of York's epitaph is edited by Richard Firth Green, who also discusses this funerary practice, in "An Epitaph for Richard, Duke of York."

44. *Ibid.*, 221.

45. From *Riverside Shakespeare*.

46. Lindley, "Absolutism and Regal Image," 62.

47. For discussion, see Rigg, *History of Anglo-Latin Literature*, 15–16, and the references therein.

48. See Chapter 4 for discussion.

49. Gaunt's will, printed in Armitage-Smith, *John of Gaunt*, 420–36, stipulates the burial site as follows (420): "En primes jeo devise m'alme a Dieu et a sa tresdouce miere Seinte Marie et a le joy du ciel, et mon corps a estre ensevelez en l'esglise cathedral de Seint Poule de Londres, pres de l'autier principale de mesme l'esglise, juxte ma treschere jadys compaigne Blanch illeoq's enterre." John Stow (*A Survey of London*, 1.336) attests that in the late fifteenth and early sixteenth centuries Gaunt's tomb (destroyed in the 1666 fire of London) was located "on the north side the Quire, beside Blanch his first wife."

50. Harvey, *English Mediaeval Architects*, s.v. "Yeveley, Henry."
51. *An Inventory*, II.121.
52. There is a remote possibility that the traveler found the poems on Anne's hearse, which would of course have contained the queen alone, nearer to the time of the funeral itself, rather than finding them later, situated on or around the joint tomb. Judging by some of his other descriptions which I discuss here, however, most notably the description of Westminster Hall, I suggest that he found them after the joint tomb was already in place at Westminster.
53. Cf. Bowers, *Politics of Pearl*, 156.
54. Cf. n. 25 (above) and the discussion below.
55. Further discussion of "Anglica regina" and "Femina famosa" is found in the notes to the edition in Appendix A.
56. Maidstone's and Gower's use of the elegiac couplet is discussed by Rigg, *History of Anglo-Latin Literature*, 285 and 287. All citations from Maidstone's *Concordia* are taken from Maidstone, *Concordia: The Reconciliation of Richard II with London* (Rigg and Carlson edition).
57. I refer to the opening of Book VIII when, after Venus reminds Amans of his old age, Amans swoons and, in a dream vision, gazes on famous lovers. His description includes what appears to be an allusion to the Ricardian court of an idealized past, essentialized by the image of Bohemian clothing. See *Confessio amantis*, in *Complete Works of John Gower*, III.453, ll. 2462–72: "I sih wher lusty Youthe tho, / As he which was Capitein, / Tofore alle othre upon the plein / Stod with his route wel begon, / Here hevedes kempt, and therupon / Garlandes noght of o colour, / Some of the lef, some of the flour, / And some of grete Perles were; / The newe guise of Beawme there, / With sondri thinges wel devised, / I sih, wherof thei ben queintised."
58. ll. 36–40: "Proceres / Lustrantur regna, sub millite calcar acutum, / Ut rex sit sponsus, currere cogit equos. / Sponse sunt vise varie varios deceantque / Reges, sed nostro traditur Anna placens."
59. Bale (*Scriptorum illustrium Maioris Brytanniae catalogus*, 1.499) lists *In Cantica canticorum* among Maidstone's writings. The commentary is not known to survive, if indeed Maidstone ever wrote one. Andrew Kraebel kindly informs me that the hand of the commentary which Stegmüller attributes to Maidstone in Paris, Bibliothèque nationale de France, lat. 13198 is much too early.
60. *Chronica maiora of Thomas Walsingham*, 170–1.
61. NASA's eclipse website (http://eclipse.gsfc.nasa.gov) lists no eclipse (solar or lunar) for 1394 or for the years immediately surrounding it. I thank Daniel Hobbins for bringing this resource to my attention.
62. See for example the pseudo-Augustinian sermon *De annuntiatione Dominica* (Migne, *Patrologia Latina*, vol. XXXIX, cols. 2104–5): "Adest nobis, dilectissimi, optatus dies beatae ac venerabilis semper virginis Mariae: ideo cum summa exsultatione gaudeat terra nostra, tantae Virginis illustrata die solemni. Haec est enim flos campi, de qua ortum est pretiosum lilium convallium, per cujus partum mutatur natura, protoplastorumque deletur et culpa."
63. All Chaucer citations come from the *Riverside* edition (ed. Benson).

64. *Philippe de Mézières' Campaign*, 27–8.
65. The Anne/*gratia* association is ubiquitous in the texts associated with her feast as well. The offertorium for the Hereford Rite, for example, calls for *Diffusa est gratia*. See Henderson, *Missale ad usum percelebris ecclesiae Herfordensis*, 290.
66. Knighton also records the scene. See *Knighton's Chronicle*, 549.
67. This and all translations from *Concordia* are by A. G. Rigg.
68. Wormald, *English Benedictine Kalendars*, ii.24.
69. Scase, "St. Anne," 83.
70. Stow, *Historia vitae et regni Ricardi Secundi*, 134: "Sepulta est itaque cum maxima solennitate in ecclesia de Westmonasterio, in die Sancte Anne sequente; cuius festum, ut in ecclesia Anglicana solennius celebraretur, ista regina a domino papa impetrauit."
71. Dickinson, *Missale ad usum insignis et praeclarae ecclesiae Sarum*, cols. 825–6.
72. Henderson, *Missale ad usum percelebris ecclesiae Herfordensis*, 290.
73. Hanrahan, "'A straunge succesour'," 335.
74. For discussion of St. Anne as the patron of pregnant women, see Brandenbarg, "Saint Anne: A Holy Grandmother and Her Children."
75. For discussion, see Parsons, "Burials and Posthumous Commemorations of English Queens."
76. Walsingham, *St. Albans Chronicle*, i.961.
77. Cf. Hudson's statements in *Premature Reformation*, 417.
78. *Actes and monuments* (1583), 507.
79. Wyche writes: "Et omnes fideles legis dominice amatores ex intimis meis precordiis nunc saluto, et specialiter vestrum in ewangelio coadiutorem Jacobellum, rogans, quod pro me ad dominum interpellent et universali ecclesia Ihesu Christi." The letter is edited by Novotný, *M. Jana Husi korespondence*, 78.
80. References to Wyclif appear, for example, in Hus' lecture on the *Sentences* and his *De libris haereticorum legendis*.
81. Read: "sterne"?
82. The line is metrically defective.
83. l. 38 (fol. 218^r): "scopis" (shops); l. 264 (fol. 221^v): "pyed freres" (pied friars). I have elsewhere seen evidence that at least one other Wycliffite text containing English words was either sent to Bohemia or copied by a Bohemian scribe who omitted the English passage. In Prague, Národní knihovna (PNK) X.C.23, fol. 195va, in reference either to Wyclif's *Epistola missa ad simplices sacerdotes*, or to his *De demonio meridiano*, the scribe remarks: "verba sunt Anglica," presumably indicating the presence of an English passage in his exemplar.
84. The poem has been edited twice (though never from PKMK D.12): from London, British Library MS Cotton Cleopatra B.ii, fols. 60^r-63^r by Wright, *Political Poems and Songs*, i.53–63; and collated from the Cleopatra MS and Vienna, Österreichische Nationalbibliothek (ÖNB) 3929, fols. 223^v-225^r by Lechler, *Johann von Wiclif*, ii.621–32. A further copy (as yet unedited) is in Vatican, Pal.lat. 994, fols. 159^v–160^r. For recent discussion of this poem and its possible authorship, see Hudson, "Peter Pateshull," 167–83; Scase, "'Heu! quanta'"; and Scase, *Literature and Complaint*, 95–8.

85. The other manuscripts are: Oxford, Bodleian Library MS Bodley 861; Oxford, Corpus Christi College MS 193; and Dublin, Trinity College MS 153. Cf. Allen, *Writings Ascribed to Richard Rolle*, 150.

86. In addition to the poems discussed below, the manuscript's other contents include Albertano of Brescia's *Liber de doctrina dicendi et tacendi* and Hildegard of Bingen's *Prophetiae de futuris eventibus*.

87. *Actes and monuments* (1583), 588.

CHAPTER 2: COMMON GROUND: RICHARD ROLLE AT THE EDGES OF ORTHODOXY IN ENGLAND AND BOHEMIA

1. From the *Regulae* of Matěj of Janov. Printed in *Regulae veteris et novi testamenti*, II.225.

2. From Walter Hilton, *Scale of Perfection*, I. 20.

3. *Writings Ascribed to Richard Rolle*.

4. The shelfmarks are as follows: *Incendium amoris* (with the *Oleum effusum*): PNK V.A.23 and ÖNB 4483; *Latin Psalter:* PNK IV.E.I, PNK V.D.4, PNK X.D.3, PKMK B.32.1, PKMK B.32.2, PKMK B.32.3, Kraków, Biblioteka Jagiellońska DD.XIV.2, and Schlägl, Stiftsbibliothek MS Plagensis 105; *Emendatio vitae*: PKMK B.6.3.

5. For Allen's discussion of Jenštejn, see *Writings Ascribed to Richard Rolle*, 43, 47–8, 168 and 221.

6. *Ibid.*, 168.

7. "Carthusian Participation," 115.

8. See for example, Hughes, *Pastors and Visionaries*, 221: "It is even possible that the Hussites were taking Rolle's works out of the country: one version of the *Incendium* ends with a colophon giving the approbation of the future Innocent VII, found otherwise only at Prague; this copy occurs in a paper volume containing a compilation, also unique to Prague, and many works connected to the Hussites." Hughes bases his comment on Allen, *Writings Ascribed to Richard Rolle*, 39–40, though at no point does Allen say that Hussites may have been taking Rolle's writings out of England. It should be emphasized, furthermore, that Jan of Jenštejn, mentioned in the explicit of the Bohemian copies of Rolle's *Incendium*, could not have been a Hussite, nor was he ever known to have been in England.

9. "Wycliffism and Lollardy," 445. See also J. Patrick Hornbeck's application of Wittgenstein's family resemblance theory to the development of religious controversy over time in late medieval and early modern England in *What is a Lollard?*, esp. ch. 1.

10. See Doyle, "Carthusian Participation," for discussion.

11. This copy of the *Incendium* was listed (without discussion) by Marzac, *Richard Rolle de Hampole*, 186 (no. 266 *ter*).

12. Spěváček, *Václav IV*, 711.

13. *Ibid.*, 709.

14. For Cosmato's various titles, see Perroy, *Diplomatic Correspondence*, 59 (no. 90), 60 (no. 91), and 207–8 (n. to no. 85).

15. Weltsch, *Archbishop John of Jenstein*, 11.
16. *Ibid.*, 60–1.
17. Vatican City, Biblioteca Apostolica Vaticana, Vat.lat. 1122, fols. 99^v–110^v. For the dedication, see Bloomfield, *Incipits*, no. 5167.
18. For discussion of the development of the feast, see Pfaff, *New Liturgical Feasts*, 62–83. See also Biasiotto, *History of the Development of Devotion to the Holy Name*.
19. For discussion, see Watson, *Richard Rolle*, 55.
20. Margaret Deanesly first designated the versions of Rolle's *Incendium* as "short" and "long" texts. See her edition of the *Incendium Amoris*, where she discusses the versions (passim, esp. 60ff.).
21. All quotations listed below are taken from PNK V.A.23.
22. For discussion of the *Quandoque tribularis* compilation, see Allen, "Some Fourteenth Century Borrowings," 1–8; Allen, *Writings Ascribed to Richard Rolle*, 218; Sargent, "Transmission," 232; and Sargent, "A Source," 535–9.
23. Unprinted. The text is a compilation of Part IV of Rolle's *Super Canticum canticorum* and extracts from the *Incendium*.
24. The text is also found in the earliest manuscript of Tynemouth's *Historia aurea*, Oxford, Bodleian Library MS Bodley 240. Horstmann describes this section of the manuscript as a continuation of the *Historia*, drawn in part from Tynemouth's earlier writings. For discussion, see Horstmann, *Nova legenda Anglie*, 1.lvii–lix.
25. For Odo of Cluny's corresponding passage on Anthony, see Migne, *Patrologia Latina*, vol. CXXXIII, col. 0623D.
26. Suso, *Heinrich Seuses Horologium sapientiae*, 596/7–597/17.
27. Migne, *Patrologia Latina*, vol. CLXXXIII, col. 0855A–B.
28. *Ibid.*, cols. 0846D–0847D.
29. Allen (*Writings Ascribed to Richard Rolle*, 221) also transcribes the PNK V.A.23 colophon, but with some incorrect readings. I provide a corrected transcription here. The slightly different colophon in PKMK D.125 is as follows: "Finis libri optimi qui valet pro viris contemplativis, cuius copia concessa fuit per reverendum in Christo patrem dominum Cosmatem cardinalem dignissimum Bononiensem pro Johanne cardinali in Curia Romana. Incendium amoris divini nuncupatur, per quemdam nobilem et sanctum virum Anglicum heremitam compositus revelacione divina in spiritu. Laus Deo."
30. I thank David R. Holeton for sharing his extensive knowledge of Bohemian liturgy with me. For the *Litoměřice Gradual*, see Barry Graham, *The Litoměřice Gradual of 1517*. The difference between Utraquist and Roman graduals is not extreme, the main variation being the former's inclusion of items concerning the martyrdom of Jan Hus.
31. The 1393 copy of Suso's *Horologium* and *Cursus* is PKMK MS C.81. Later copies (not always complete, and not always including the *Cursus*) are found in PNK MS I.D.25; PNK I.E.39; PNK V.A.19; PNK X.B.13; PNK XII.E.11; and PNK XIII.D.6.
32. The text is edited from the extant manuscripts in Weltsch, *Archbishop John of Jenstein*, 218–32.

33. *Ibid.*, 76 and his n. 145.
34. Fols. 19^r–21^v. The sermon is not part of the group of passages on the Holy Name which circulated with Bohemian copies of the *Incendium*. The text borrows heavily from Scripture and several authors, particularly Bernard of Clairvaux. Some, though not all, of the excerpts from Bernard are also found among the selection of texts accompanying the *Incendium*, but the author clearly had more than just this compilation at hand.
35. The text is unedited. My discussion relies on Weltsch, *Archbishop John of Jenstein*, 110–12. Jenštejn's *De divinis nominibus* survives only in Vatican City, Biblioteca Apostolica Vaticana, Cod. Vat.lat. 1122, fols. 287^r–293^v.
36. *Writings Ascribed to Richard Rolle*, 48.
37. For Cosmato's appointment to England by Urban VI in 1379, see *Calendar of Entries in the Papal Registers*, IV.257. For the reference to "late the pope's collector," see *Calendar of Close Rolls, Richard II*, III.554.
38. Duchesne, *Le Liber pontificalis*, II.531.
39. For the former, see Rymer, *Foedera*, VII.355; the later letter is printed in Chitty and Jacob, "Some Winchester College Muniments," 13.
40. Richard releases Cosmato from paying customs on exports on a number of occasions. See, for example, Rymer, *Foedera*, VII.356 (for 1382); and *Calendar of Close Rolls, Richard II*, III.232 (for 1387).
41. It is perhaps significant, however, that in 1390 Richard II wrote to Boniface IX in support of William of Wykeham, Bishop of Winchester, who sought privileges for his new foundations of Winchester College and New College, Oxford. Another letter, nearly identical to the one addressed to Boniface, was sent to Cosmato, asking for his support in furthering Wykeham's suit at the Curia. In the letters, the king recommends the petition "on account of the tremendous devotion which [Wykeham] is recognized to have to the glory and honor of the Name of the Crucified, [and] of His mother the Blessed Virgin Mary [propter deuocionem pregrandem quam ad gloriam et honorem nominis Crucifixi, beatissime Marie Virginis matris eius ... habere dinoscitur.]" The copy of the letter which was sent to Cosmato was furthermore signed by Anne of Bohemia, representing the only known example of her signature to survive. Chitty and Jacob edit and discuss the letters in "Some Winchester College Muniments."
42. For Allen's discussion and transcriptions, see *Writings Ascribed to Richard Rolle*, 39–43.
43. *Ibid.*, 43.
44. It is possible, of course, that the "monachus" and "doctor" from England are the same person. Admittedly, it would be strange for the same annotator to refer to one source with two separate titles (as opposed to, say, "predictus doctor de Anglia"), but as I indicate here, the annotations in MS 4483, while apparently written in the same hand, are copies of notes from a lost exemplar which may originally have been written by more than one scribe, or annotated on separate occasions.
45. *Ibid.*, 42.

46. Discussed in Harvey, *The English in Rome*, esp. 166, 170–1.
47. See my discussion in n. 41 (above).
48. *Chronicle of Adam Usk*, 154.
49. My summary of Jenštejn's involvement in the Feast of the Visitation is based on Weltsch, *Archbishop John of Jenstein*, 88–91. The fullest account of the feast's development is Polc, *De origine Festi Visitationis*. See also his "La Festa della Visitazione e il Giubileo del 1390."
50. Printed in Tomassetti, *Bullarum*, IV.602–4.
51. For Easton and Bramfield, see Harvey, *English in Rome*, 202–3. See also Polc, *De origine Festi Visitationis*, 76ff.; and Pfaff, *New Liturgical Feasts*, 43–4.
52. Easton's office is printed in Dreves, *Analecta hymnica*, XXIV.89–94. Easton's is followed by nine other offices in the edition, 94–122. Jenštejn's office is partially printed in *ibid.*, XLVIII.427.
53. During the same period when Easton participated in establishing the Feast of the Visitation, however, the newly rehabilitated English Cardinal also resumed his efforts to promote Bridget of Sweden's canonization (discussed in Harvey, *English in Rome*, 204 and Minnis, *Fallible Authors*, 202–7). There can be little doubt that Easton's interest in promoting Bridget's case reached Jenštejn's attention while he was in Rome, and indeed a detail in his *Vita* suggests that Bridget attracted his interest. In 1396, as I mentioned earlier, Jenštejn traveled to Rome to relinquish his archbishopric into the hands of Boniface. His intention was to retire to his castle at Helfenburg, and to spend his last days living a solitary and eremitic life. Unable to maintain himself, however, he set out for Rome once again, where ultimately Boniface granted him the honorary title "Patriarch of Alexandria." According to his *Vita*, after failing to maintain himself as a hermit, Jenštejn decided to travel to Rome as a pilgrim, "like Saint Bridget, who was at that time canonized as a saint [ut sancta Brigitta pro tunc canonisata]" (Truhlář, *Život Jana z Jenšteina*, 466). However, the reference may be proof less of Jenštejn's own devotion to Bridget than of his would-be hagiographer's interest in casting him in the likeness of Christendom's most recent saint (that is, the most recent saint to be canonized before Jenštejn's death in 1400. The English Augustinian John Thwing of Bridlington was canonized in 1401), and so the instance offers no certain evidence of a closer link between Jenštejn and Easton.
54. Thompson, *Carthusian Order*, 220. Cf. Pfaff, *New Liturgical Feasts*, 43.
55. For Easton's library, see Ker, *Books, Collectors and Libraries*, 243–72. See also Harvey, *English in Rome*, 222–4.
56. See n. 53 (above) for discussion.
57. My discussion of this episode summarizes Hudson's more detailed account in "The Survival of Wyclif's Works in England and Bohemia," 31–7.
58. This does not mean, of course, that other copies did not exist in the sixteenth century. Those which now survive only in this manuscript are Štěpán Páleč's *Quaestio utrum universale sit aliquid extra* (fols. 61ᵛ–67ʳ) and Stanislav of Znojmo's Romans commentary (fol. 249ʳ⁻ᵛ). See Spunar, *Repertorium*, 1.327 (for Páleč's tract) and 286 (for Znojmo's commentary).

59. The sermon is Thomson, *Latin Writings*, no. 200.
60. The testimonial is not included in the modern pagination, but is listed on the original table of contents. I discuss the letter extensively in Chapter 4.
61. Tříška, *Životopisný slovník*, 279.
62. The annotations are printed in Sedlák, *Miscellanea Husitica*, 289–97 nn.
63. *Korrespondence Josefa Dobrovského*, 1.188.
64. For Raňkův's opposition to the feast, see Weltsch, *Archbishop John of Jenstein*, 88. For the reference to Kuneš of Třebovle and the Feast of the Visitation, see ÖNB 4483, fol. 47^r.
65. Raňkův also brought to Prague a codex containing autograph copies of FitzRalph's *De pauperie Salvatoris* and *Defensio curatorum contra fratres mendicantes*, now ÖNB MS 1430. FitzRalph was furthermore a favorite *auctor* for the Lollards during their own controversies with the mendicants. For FitzRalph's influence on subsequent antifraternal polemic, see Scase, *Piers Plowman and the New Anticlericalism*, passim, esp. 7–11. Katherine Walsh has also discussed the place of FitzRalph's writings in Lollard and Hussite controversy in her "Die Rezeption der Schriften des Richard FitzRalph."
66. Hanna, *Pursuing History*, 7. Caution must be exercised, of course, when analyzing manuscript compilations as a whole, as their current form and ordering of texts may not always be the result of decisions made at the time, or even the period, of production.
67. For Allen's discussion, see *Writings Ascribed to Richard Rolle*, 168.
68. *Ibid.* The manuscript in question is Gdańsk, Biblioteka Gdańska Polskiej Akademii Nauk, MS Mar. F.152.
69. Spěváček, *Václav IV*, 734.
70. PKMK B.32.1; PKMK B.32.3; PNK X.D.3; and Kraków, Biblioteka Jagiellońska DD. XIV.2.
71. The primary material which fills the manuscript pertains to the disputes in Prague in the years immediately preceding the Council of Constance (1414–18). The inclusion of Hus' *Sermo de pace* (fols. 181^r–189^v), which Hus intended to deliver at Constance, together with texts pertaining to Lollard–Hussite correspondence (which, as I shall suggest in Chapter 3, does not seem to have lasted much beyond 1414), also support a dating of *c*.1414 as a probable year of compilation. The presence of Hus' *Quaestio de sanguine Christi* (fols. 174^r–176^v), written in 1414, lends further support to this dating. The colophon mentioning Jakoubek, who, together with Hus, may have been in communication with the Lollards (and thus may have been interested in the Lollard material in D.12), could mean that the manuscript was intended as a gift for Jakoubek, perhaps presented to him by Hus around the time of Hus' departure for Constance on October 11, 1414. In the end, however, this suggestion remains entirely speculative.
72. Hudson, *Selections*, 24.
73. Wyclif's ever-broadening anticlericalism occasionally included the hermits, though it is not always clear that his criticism categorically targeted the anchoritic way of life per se. See, for example, *Trialogus*, 437: "Unde

Eremitae nisi haberent suam fundationem a Domino et a Baptista, forent rationabiliter proscribendi." See also *De officio regis*, 202: "Unde quantum ad fratres anagoritas et heremitas exproprietarie viventes non dubium quin sint homines legii regum terre, cum propter prodicionem, depopulacionem, occi-sionem, vel aliam foris facturam enormem oportet eos convictos de crimine patriis legibus subiacere." When Wyclif criticizes hermits, however, he often has the Augustinian friars (the "Eremitae Augustinenses") in mind. Since the Magna Unio of 1256, large numbers of eremitic communities were adminis-tratively combined to form the order of *fratres eremitarum sancti Augustini*. The new order, though its members retained their original designation as hermits, in practice became increasingly integrated to urban and university settings. For an account of the Magna Unio of 1256, see Andrews, *The Other Friars*, 83–90.

74. Cited in n. 1 (above).

75. Somerset, "Wycliffite Spirituality," 378–86.

76. For the text of *De amore*, see Wyclif, *Opera minora*, 8–10. The five questions, as they appear in *De amore*, are as follows (8): "primo quid sit amor; secundo ubi sit amor; tercio quomodo Deus veraciter est diligendus, quarto quomodo fidelis potest cognoscere quod diligit Deum suum et quinto in quo statu potest homo congruencius diligere Deum suum." For editions of the Wycliffite *Five Questions on Love*, see Arnold, *Select English Works*, III.183–5; and Winn, *Wyclif: Select English Writings*, 110–12.

77. This is not to be confused with Rolle's Latin commentary on the Psalter. As Professor Hudson confirms for me, Lollard familiarity with the *Latin Psalter* has not been demonstrated. More detailed discussion of the Lollard revisions of Rolle's commentary must await Hudson's much anticipated edition, *Two Revisions of Rolle's Psalter Commentary*, forthcoming with the Early English Text Society (in three vols.).

78. For Everett's discussion of this text, see "The Middle English Prose Psalter of Richard Rolle of Hampole" (pts. 1–3). Other studies of the textual history of Rolle's *English Psalter* include: Hudson, *Premature Reformation*, 259–64, 421–2; Gustavson, "Richard Rolle's *English Psalter* and the Making of a Lollard Tract"; Kuczynski, "Rolle among the Reformers: Orthodoxy and Heterodoxy in Wycliffite Copies of Rolle's Psalter"; and Muir, "The Influence of the Rolle and Wyclifite Psalters upon the Psalter of the Authorised Version."

79. The prologue is in Oxford, Bodleian Library MS Laud Misc. 286, fol. 1ᵛ (printed in Rolle, *Psalter*, 2): "Copyed has þis Sauter ben, of yuel men of Lollardry: / And afterward hit has bene sene, ympyd in wiþ eresy. / They seyden þen to leude foles, þat it shuld be all enter, / A blessyd boke of hur scoles, of Rychard Hampole þe Sauter. / Thus þei seyd, to make þeim leue on her scole thoro sotelte, / To bring hem in, so hem to greue, ageyn þe feyth in grete fole, / And slaundird foule þis holy man."

80. Hudson discusses the textual history of the *Riwle* in *Premature Reformation*, 27–8.

81. For Brady's primary studies of *Pore Caitif*, see: "The Pore Caitif: An Introductory Study"; "Rolle's 'Form of Living' and 'The Pore Caitif'"; "Rolle

and the Pattern of Tracts in 'The Pore Caitif'"; and "Lollard Sources of 'The Pore Caitif'." See also Hudson, *Premature Reformation*, 425.

82. For discussion see Pyper, "An Abridgment." Cf. Hudson, *Premature Reformation*, 425 and her n. 150.

83. Pyper, "An Abridgment," 309.

84. For evidence, see, for example, the reading circle discussed in Hudson, "Wyclif Texts in Fifteenth-Century London."

85. Hilton, *Scale of Perfection*, i.i.

86. i. 20 of Hilton's *Scale of Perfection* (also quoted in the epigraph to this chapter, and in the main text above) contains some of his most indignant statements about the hypocrisy of heretics.

87. Clanvowe, *Two Ways*, ll. 503–13.

88. The notion that Clanvowe was one of the Lollard knights comes initially from Walsingham but also seems to be corroborated by Clanvowe's many associations with other suspected Lollard knights. McFarlane was convinced of Sir John's Lollardy (see Part 2 of *Lancastrian Kings*, passim). More recent studies, including the present chapter, have been less concerned than McFarlane with making clear distinctions between orthodoxy and heresy, or between orthodox and heterodox manuscripts, a distinction which does not always reflect the concerns of late-medieval readers.

89. For discussion, see McFarlane, *Lancastrian Kings*, 207–20; Catto, "Sir William Beauchamp," 46–8; and Tuck, "Carthusian Monks," 155.

90. See, for example, *Walter Hilton's Mixed Life*.

91. Catto, "Sir William Beauchamp," 43–6. The Vernon manuscript is Oxford, Bodleian Library, MS Eng. poet. a. 1. For discussion of the relationship between the Vernon and Simeon manuscripts, see Doyle, "The Shaping of the Vernon and Simeon Manuscripts."

92. Catto, "Sir William Beauchamp," 43–4.

93. *Ibid.*, 46–7.

94. Knowles, *English Mystical Tradition*, 65.

95. Kerby-Fulton, *Books under Suspicion*.

96. Szittya ("Sedens," 34) has claimed that there is a relationship between "Sedens" and "Quis dabit." Rigg (*History of Anglo-Latin Literature*, 272) also discusses the association. Cf. Scase, "'Heu! quanta'," 31.

97. *Ibid.*, 30. Wyclif's sermon is printed in *Iohannis Wyclif sermones*, ii.121. The relevant passage is as follows: "Et videtur multis fidelibus quod fratres tam singulariter a templo Salomonis et factis suis culpabilibus in suis edificiis exemplum accipiunt, quia vellent ad status regios aspirare, ut dicit metricus: Quod in suo animo / Vellent esse reges, / Sed absit hoc a seculo / Ne confundant leges."

98. Scase, "'Heu! quanta'," 24ff. Hudson has suggested that the author of "Heu quanta" was Peter Pateshull, who once owned Oxford, Bodleian Library MS Digby 98, the manuscript which contains the only copy of the poem in England. See "Peter Pateshull," 171–2, 175–6.

99. Transcribed from PKMK D.12, fol. 218^r, ll. 43–8.

100. Text edited by Salter, *Snappe's Formulary*, 130–2. The relevant passage, adapted from Lam. 1.1–5, is as follows: "Et quomodo nunc sedet sola civitas plena populo, et facta est quasi vidua domina gentium, princeps provinciarum facta est sub tributo, plorans ploravit in nocte, et lacryme eius in maxillis eius; non est qui consoletur eam ex omnibus caris eius, et omnes amici eius spreverunt eam facti sunt ei inimici; omnes persecutores eius apprehenderunt eam inter angustias; sacerdotes eius gementes et parvuli sui ducti sunt in captivitatem ante faciem tribulantis."

101. PKMK D.12, fol. 194^v, commenting on Lam. 1.6.

102. *Ibid.*, fol. 200^r, commenting on Lam 4.1.

103. Another copy of "Heu quanta" is also found in ÖNB 3929 (fols. 223^v–225^r), and there is a fragment of the *Lament of the pauperculi sacerdotes* in ÖNB 3932 (fols. 89^v-90^r). Both manuscripts are Bohemian.

104. Kerby-Fulton, *Books under Suspicion*, passim.

105. It is interesting to note, however, that Jan Hus cited Hildegard in a position which he delivered in 1412 as part of his controversy with Štěpán Páleč and Stanislav of Znojmo. The position is a defense of several of Wyclif's articles which had been condemned in Prague in 1403. In the second part of his defense, "De ablatione temporalium de clericis," Hus cites a passage "ex prophecia Hildegardis virginis" which entirely overlaps with the extract in MS D.12. The passage is in Hus, *Defensio articulorum Wyclif*, 193–4. The parallel may suggest that Hus was associated with MS D.12. Other texts from the longstanding controversy between Hus and his former friends Páleč and Znojmo are likewise copied into the manuscript, and the book was eventually dedicated to Hus' friend Jakoubek.

106. For discussion, see Scase, "'Heu! quanta,'" 34–5.

107. The colophon reads, "pro Magistro Jacobo de Strziebro."

108. The copies of most of the Wycliffite texts in PKMK MS B.6.3 have been dated to 1421 (Thomson, *Latin Writings*, nos. 300, 414, 415, and 432). It is impossible to determine whether their present arrangement in combination with Rolle's *Emendatio* reflects the original circumstances of transmission to Bohemia. Rolle's text is furthermore incomplete, missing most of its twelfth and final chapter. However, the scribe seems to have expected to access an exemplar for this last section: he breaks off in the middle of the word "contemplativa," but has written a note just beneath which seems to say "quere cum anteriori litera 'R'." He has also left ample space before the next text (Wyclif's *De demonio meridiano*) to fill out the remainder of the *Emendatio*.

109. Catto, "Sir William Beauchamp," 42–3.

110. The manuscript containing the students' transcriptions is now ÖNB MS 1294.

111. *Actes and monuments* (1583), 507.

112. In the F Prologue to the *Legend of Good Women*, for example, Chaucer includes the couplet (ll. 496–7): "And whan this book ys maad, yive it the quene, / On my byhalf, at Eltham or at Sheene." Chaucer's F Prologue to the *Legend* is filled with elaborate allusions to the queen. For discussion of the dating of Clanvowe's poem and the possibility that the "Quene" to which it

refers is indeed Anne, see, for example, V. J. Scattergood, "The Authorship of 'The Boke of Cupide'"; and Scattergood's edition of *The Works of Sir John Clanvowe*, 14.

113. Clanvowe, *Boke of Cupide*, ll. 281–5.

CHAPTER 3: CONVEYING HERESY: TEXTS, TIDINGS AND THE FORMATION OF A LOLLARD–HUSSITE FELLOWSHIP

1. From a letter from Jan Hus to Richard Wyche (1411). Printed in Novotný, *M. Jana Husi korespondence*, 85.

2. Goll, *Chronicon Universitatis Pragensis*, 571: "Et sic ibidem pluribus combustis libris, melioribus, ut creditur, reservatis, membranas et registra ab antiquo reservata igni subiecerunt psallentes et laudantes clamore valido Te deum laudamus pulsatisque campanis quasi pro mortuis, sperantes se iam habere omnium tribulacionum finem, cum tamen primo inicium, deo iusto iudice permittente, sumpserunt."

3. For discussion of the defense, see Herold, *Pražská univerzita a Wyclif*, 158–62 (with emphasis on Prokop of Plzeň's defense of *De ideis*); and (for a more general discussion of the entire defense) Novotný, *M. Jan Hus. Život a učení*, 1.1.418–29. The announcement of the disputation is in Goll, *Chronicon Universitatis Pragensis*, 572, although the date on which the announcement was made is not given.

4. Prague, Archiv Univerzity Karlovy 1/69. The request appears in the following context: "Anno Domini millesimo quadringestesimo decimo quintadecima die mensis Iunii hora decima septima in rectoratu magistri Iohannis Andree, in medicina doctoris, facta plena convocacione tocius universitatis sub pena presititi iuramenti conclusum est, quod universitas nullo modo consentit archiepiscopo Pragensi Sbinconi cum suis prelatis in conbustionem librorum magistri Iohannis Wykleff. Sed quod tota universitas visitet dominum Regem ipsumque petat ut talem impediat combustionem ne exinde confusio toti Regno, Domino Regi et universitati inferatur." This portion of the document is also printed by Höfler, *Geschichtschreiber*, ii.187; and Palacký, *Documenta Mag. Joannis Hus*, 734.

5. Goll, *Chronicon Universitatis Pragensis*, 571: "Sed ad instanciam domini Wenceslai, Romanorum et Bohemie regis, distulit suam vesanam sentenciam usque ad adventum domini Jodoci, antiqui Moravie marchionis. Et marchione nondum veniente prefatus archiepiscopus XVI die mensis Julii repositos libros Wicleff in medio archiepiscopalis curie in presencia Pragensis capituli, prelatorum ac multitudine cleri cremari precepit."

6. Šimek and Kaňák, *Staré letopisy české*, 42: "O to byla veliká bauřka a ruoznice. Někteří pravili, že jest mnoho jiných kněh spáleno nežli Viglefových, a proto se lidé búřili v ty časy, a najviece králi dvořané, na kanovníky a na kněží, a s nimi obecně všickni lidé v Praze, neb jedni drželi s kanovníky, a druzí s mistrem Husí, takže mezi sebú písně hančivé skládali jedni o druhých. A od té chvíle veliká

nechut mezi lidmi vzrostla." Cf. the entry in Goll, *Chronicon Universitatis Pragensis*, 572: "propter predictam combustionem et Magistri Johannis Hus et ceterorum excommunicacionem schisma magnum est factum in populo. Quidam enim gravissime receperunt excommunicacionem archiepiscopi pretactam, ita quod rumor factus fuit post hoc in ecclesia Pragensi. In die Marie Magdalene officiantes sub infula cum ceteris fere XL officiantibus ab altaribus divinis recesserunt. Et eodem die in ecclesia sancti Stephani in Nova civitate sex evaginatis gladiis predicatorem blasphemantem interficere voluerunt. Hic timor prostravit omnes plebanos, ut per amplius ab excommunicacione in lege dei non fundata cessaverunt."

7. Old Czech text in Daňhelka, *Husitské písně*, 131–2. Similar versions of these verses turn up often in manuscripts from this period. Archbishop Zbyněk seems to have been called mockingly "abeceda," a designation which suggests that the archbishop "didn't know what was written" in Wyclif's books because he couldn't even read them (i.e., he only knew his "ABCs"). See Nejedlý, *Počátky husitského zpěvu*, 419–20 and nn.

8. For discussion, see, for example, Šmahel, "Wyclif's Fortune in Hussite Bohemia," passim.

9. The letter is printed in Höfler, *Geschichtschreiber*, ii.170–1.

10. Studies of the 1410 correspondence include: Hudson, "Which Wyche? The Framing of the Lollard Heretic and/or Saint"; Hudson, "From Oxford to Prague: The Writings of John Wyclif and his English Followers in Bohemia"; Hudson, "William Taylor's 1406 Sermon: A Postscript"; Betts, "English and Czech Influences on the Hussite Movement," esp. 141–2; Waugh, "Sir John Oldcastle," esp. 441–4; and Poole, "On the Intercourse between English and Bohemian Wycliffites in the Early Years of the Fifteenth Century."

11. See Poole, "On the Intercourse," 309. Poole cites Johann Loserth's speculation that Oldcastle's letter demonstrates his familiarity with the unrest in Prague following the Archbishop of Prague's command to burn Wyclif's books. Poole is skeptical that news could travel to England so quickly and thinks that the letter does not necessarily refer to anything later than the excommunication of Zdislav of Zvířetice (the alternate addressee of Oldcastle's letter) on July 18. However, the letters are much too general for this kind of speculation to bear much fruit. Waugh ("Sir John Oldcastle," 443) reads the letters by Wyche and Oldcastle as congratulating their recipients for their retaliation against the measures taken by the archbishop to suppress heresy in Prague. This is about as specific as we can get.

12. For a helpful discussion of Wyche's rhetoric, see von Nolcken, "Richard Wyche, a Certain Knight, and the Beginning of the End."

13. Novotný suggests that the Anglo-Bohemian correspondence that year may even have been part of an attempt to replace lost Wycliffite texts. See *M. Jan Hus*, 1.1.459 and Novotný's n. 3. For documents pertaining to the controversy over Wyclif's books which erupted in Prague, see Palacký, *Documenta Mag. Joannis Hus*, 374–415.

14. Latin text from Novotný, *M. Jana Husi korespondence*, 76.
15. *Ibid.*, 73.
16. Hudson, "Lollard Sect Vocabulary."
17. Loserth, "Über die Beziehungen zwischen," 268. See below for discussion of Oldcastle's letter to Václav.
18. Novotný, *M. Jana Husi korespondence*, 78: "Et omnes fideles legis dominice amatores ex intimis meis precordiis nunc saluto, et specialiter vestrum in ewangelio coadiutorem Jacobellum."
19. Höfler, *Geschichtschreiber*, II.96–100.
20. Goll, *Chronicon Universitatis Pragensis*, 571–2.
21. The documents appear in Palacký, *Documenta Mag. Joannis Hus*, 580–90 and 590–5, respectively.
22. Sedlák prints Folkhyrde's letters (Latin and Czech) in *M. Jan Hus*, 182*–96*. Also printed (Latin only) in Baxter, *Copiale prioratus Sanctiandree*, 230–6.
23. Finke, *Acta Concilii Constanciensis*, IV.627–8. Cf. Jean d'Achery's sermon at Constance, given February 23, 1415: "Nam facultas theologie in universitate Parysiensi super huiusmodi errores seminatos potissime in regnis Boemie et Scotie . . . requisita dare deliberacionem suam." See ibid., II.399–400.
24. Gerson, *Oeuvres complètes*, III.340. Thanks to Daniel Hobbins for bringing this reference to my attention.
25. Bower, *Scotichronicon*, VIII.277/7.
26. Vyšný, "A Hussite in Scotland," 3. For records of Kravař at Paris, see Denifle and Chatelain, *Liber procuratorum nationis Anglicanae*, cols. 190, 196 and 197.
27. For discussion, see Betts, "The University of Prague: 1348," 8. See also Betts, "The Influence of Realist Philosophy," 48–9.
28. Discussed in Šmahel, *Die hussitische Revolution*, I.551; II.733 (also in his earlier Czech version, *Husitská revoluce*, II.45, 189). See also Walsh, "Die Rezeption der Schriften des Richard FitzRalph."
29. For the possibility that Raňkův taught at Oxford, see Šmahel, "Wyclif's Fortune," 469 and his n. 6; for discussion of Raňkův's scholarship for Czech students, see *ibid.*, 468–9 and his n. 5, and Šmahel's *Die hussitische Revolution*, II.789 (*Husitská revoluce*, II.215); see also Kaminsky, *History of the Hussite Revolution*, 24.
30. The manuscript containing their copies is now ÖNB 1294. Their 1406–7 itinerary is discussed in the previous chapter.
31. Aeneas Silvius Piccolomini, *Historia Bohemica*, I.222–4: "vir quidam genere nobilis ex domo, quam Putridi Piscis vocant, apud Oxoniam Anglia civitatem litteris instructus cum Iohannis Vicleffi libros offendisset, quibus 'De realibus universalibus' titulus inscribitur, magnopere illis oblectatus exemplaria secum attulit. Inter que 'De civili dominio,' 'De ecclesia,' 'De diversis questionibus,' contra clerum pleraque volumina veluti pretiosum thesaurum patrie sue intulit, imbutus iam ipse Vicleffistarum veneno et ad nocendum paratus. Nam quod erat familie sue cognomen Putridum Piscem, id est fetidum virus, in cives suos evomuit. Commodavit autem scripta, que attulerat, iis potissime, qui Theutonicorum odio tenebantur, Inter quos Iohannes eminuit, obscure loco natus, ex villa Hus, quod anserem significat, cognomentum mutuatus."

32. For discussion, see Hudson, "From Oxford to Prague," 644; and Šmahel, "Wyclif's Fortune," 469–70.
33. The tract is edited in Sedlák, *Studie a texty*, 11.44–108, with reference to Wyclif on 105.
34. For discussion, see Harvey, "Adam Easton and the Condemnation of John Wyclif, 1377."
35. *Ibid.*, 322–3.
36. Kaminsky, *History of the Hussite Revolution*, 24; Šmahel, "Wyclif's Fortune," 470–1.
37. Jerome made this claim much later during his trial at the Council of Constance in 1416. See von der Hardt, *Magnum oecumenicum Constantiense Concilium*, IV, cols. 634–5 and 651. For speculation on the possibility that Jerome made a second trip to England, see Šmahel, "Leben und Werk des Magisters Hieronymus von Prag," 89 and his n. 28; and Novotný, *M. Jan Hus*, 1.2.310 and his n. 1. The possibility of a second trip has not gained much support.
38. For the agreement, which I quote and discuss in Chapter 1, see Rymer, *Foedera*, VII.291.
39. It is difficult to say whether Ralph Mungyn's later opposition to the Hussite Wars developed as a result of personal communication with the Hussites. Mungyn may have known Peter Payne while Payne was still in England, but there is no evidence to suggest that their acquaintance continued after Payne's departure. Mungyn's pacifist position more likely arose in response to the increased discussion of English involvement in the Hussite Wars. The trial in which he was accused of defending the Bohemians occurred in late November and early December 1428, precisely when Cardinal Henry Beaufort – papal legate in charge of crusading efforts during the fourth crusade against the Hussites – was soliciting English support for a renewed attack on Bohemian soil. For references to Mungyn's opposition to fighting the Bohemians, see *Register of Henry Chichele*, III.197–205 passim. Mungyn was also associated with Nicholas Hoper, one of Oldcastle's former servants (*ibid.*, 199).
40. Payne's Bohemian career is most fully discussed in Cook, "Peter Payne, Theologian and Diplomat of the Hussite Reformation." See also more recently Šmahel, "Magister Peter Payne: Curriculum vitae eines englischen Nonkonformisten."
41. Hus' crisis concerning Wyclif during his trial at Constance will be discussed at length in the next chapter.
42. Johannes Cochlaeus, whose *Historia Hussitarum* (Mainz, 1549) was one of Foxe's other sources for information on the Bohemians, and who himself draws on Aeneas Silvius' account of the Bohemian student, seems not to be Foxe's direct source for this particular episode. Foxe's account more closely follows that in Aeneas' *Historia Bohemica* (which was published twice in the sixteenth century as part of his *Opera omnia* [Basel, 1551 and 1571]), mentioning details that do not appear in Cochlaeus, such as a longer list of Wyclif's books which the student carried. Cf. *Aeneae Sylvii Piccolominei Senensis . . . opera quae extant omnia*, 102–3.

43. Foxe writes: "There chaunced at that time a certayne student of the country of Bohemia to be at Oxford, one of a welthy house and also of a noble stocke. Who returning home from the vniuersitie of Oxford, to the vniuersitie of Prage: caryed with him certayne bookes of Wickliffe, *De realibus Vniuersalibus, De ciuili iure, & Diuino: De ecclesia, De questionibus varijs contra clerum &c.* . . . Iohn Hus hauing familiaritie wyth this yong man, in reading and perusing these bookes of Wickliffe, tooke such pleasure and fruit in reading therof, that not onely he began to defend this author openly in the schooles, but also in his sermons." See *Actes and monuments* (1583), 464.

44. Foxe may also have suspected that he was dealing with a calque, but, not knowing what it was based on, thought it best to leave out the reference altogether. Matthias Flacius, Foxe's source for Hus' reference to the student during Hus' trial at Constance, does not mention the student's name (which was again the source of humor), and so even if Foxe deduced that the two references (taken from Aeneas and Flacius) were to the same person, he would never have seen the student's actual name, Faulfiš, printed in any of his sources.

45. *Actes and monuments* (1583), 464.

46. *Česká nedělní postila*, 148.

47. Palacký, *Documenta Mag. Joannis Hus*, 313.

48. The testimonial is edited by Höfler in *Concilia Pragensia*, 53; and by Wilkins, *Concilia*, III.302. I discuss the history of this document fully in the next chapter.

49. Jerome's *recommendatio* is printed in Höfler, *Geschichtschreiber*, II.112–28 (falsely attributed to Hus). The record of Jerome's Vienna trial is edited by Kličman, *Processus iudiciarius contra Jeronimum de Praga*. Jerome's use of the Oxford testimonial is mentioned passim, esp. 15.

50. Von der Hardt, *Magnum oecumenicum Constantiense Concilium*, IV, cols. 644–5.

51. Palacký, *Documenta Mag. Joannis Hus*, 313. The stone was probably brought to Prague after the 1406–7 trip to England.

52. Hus certainly does not reply in 1410 (as Palacký claims). Spinka (*Letters of John Hus*, 47 n. 13) argues that Hus refers to his own excommunication, which was published in Prague on March 15, 1411. I would argue that there is at least evidence that Hus received the letter in 1411 rather than 1410 because he says (Novotný, *M. Jana Husi korespondence*, 85): "Litere portate sunt nobis primo in 2ª dominica ieiunii, quia Symon fuit in Vngaria cum eis." For Hudson's discussion of the two versions of Hus' reply, see "Which Wyche?," 233–4.

53. There is nothing in the manuscripts (e.g., abbreviations, marginalia) that would call the following reading into question.

54. Palacký, *Documenta Mag. Joannis Hus*, 14.

55. "Tantis laboribus" could refer either to the troubles Wyche took in the process of transcribing, or even the troublesome circumstances he was experiencing at the time of transcription. In Workman and Pope's translation (*Letters of John Hus*, 38), "exempla" is translated in the ablative singular ("by the example"), which the Latin text clearly does not sustain.

56. *exemplum* often signifies a moral example. However, "copy" and "transcript" are also attested. See the *Mittellateinisches Wörterbuch bis zum ausgehenden 13. Jahrhundert*, s.v. "exemplum." It must be noted, however, that Bohemian writers tended more often to use *exemplum* to signify a document or specimen of some kind. Unfortunately, considering the ambiguity of the references I am describing, the possible definitions range so widely as to yield little help. See *Latinitatis medii aevi lexicon Bohemorum*, s.v. "exemplum" (there is no entry for "exemplarium"). Possible definitions include (listing only the most relevant): "specimen," "exemplar, charta, quae describendo, transcribendo exstitit," "verba et litterae, sententia," "imitatio," "quod ad imitandum proponitur, exemplar," "documentum (quo praemonentur aut deterrentur homines)," and "testimonium." Niermeyer (who lists "exemplarium" and "exemplum" together) explains that in the context of the university the terms referred specifically to an official copy. See *Mediae Latinitatis lexicon minus*, s.v. "exemplar, exemplarium, exemplum."

57. Novotný, *M. Jana Husi korespondence*, 85.

58. Hudson, "Which Wyche?," 233.

59. See, for example, the *Mittellateinisches Wörterbuch bis zum ausgehenden 13. Jahrhundert*, s.v. "exemplar, exemplarium."

60. I translate "exemplaria" as "transcripts," rather than "manuscripts," since the term more accurately designates a specific kind of manuscript, namely one that is a copy of an exemplar, or model.

61. Hudson, "From Oxford to Prague," 643–4.

62. There is evidence, however, that Folkhyrde received permission from Henry IV to travel to London, granted on August 16, 1405. See Bain, *Calendar of Documents*, IV.144, no. 696: "The K. gives leave to Quintin Folkard of Scotland, presently in England, to come to London on his affairs for a month. Nottingham Castle." "On 11th September he has leave to go to Scotland with three servants, till Christmas and return, and to sell some of his own animals in England for his necessary expenses. Beverly." If Folkhyrde did return to London after Christmas, his stay almost certainly lasted into 1406, probably the year Faulfiš and Kněhnice arrived in England. This information does not, of course, explain how a man selling livestock (though he was also a preacher and *armiger*, at least in 1410) would have come into contact with Bohemian students at Oxford, or others like Richard Wyche, but it does place him on the scene in 1406. It should be noted that Wyche was probably in prison at Durham from 1406–7, a detail that reduces the chances of his having met Folkhyrde (let alone Faulfiš and Kněhnice) at that time. For further discussion of Folkhyrde, see Sanderson, *Ayrshire and the Reformation*, 37–8 and notes.

63. Hudson, "Which Wyche?," 236. These documents are found in PNK III.G.11.

64. Hudson, "William Taylor's 1406 Sermon," 104.

65. Sedlák, *M. Jan Hus*, 248*. Sedlák prints selections from Páleč's tract against Hus' *De ecclesia* in *ibid.*, 202*–304*. For further discussion, see Sedlák, "Pálčův spis proti Husovu traktátu 'De ecclesia'," 508–9.

66. Folkhyrde's letters are addressed as follows (from letters 1–4, respectively): "Quintinus universitati christianorum"; "Quintinus episcopo Glacovensi cum sui complicibus totoque clero regni Scocie"; "Quintinus Folkhyrde omnibus secularibus dominis et communitati"; and "Quintinus Folkhyrde suo curato et omnibus et singulis aliis." See Sedlák, *M. Jan Hus*, 182*, 184*, 186*, 187*.

67. The Czech translation of Wyche's letter is edited in Novotný, *M. Jana Husi korespondence*, 79–81. Sedlák edits the Czech translations of Folkhyrde's letters in *M. Jan Hus*, 189*-196*.

68. Novotný, *M. Jana Husi korespondence*, 83. Hus does not specifically say whether the sermon was delivered at Bethlehem Chapel (the most likely venue). If so, the reported number of people in attendance is certainly an exaggeration.

69. *Ibid.*, 84.

70. The text is edited by Svoboda, *Mistra Jakoubka ze Stříbra překlad Viklefova Dialogu*. Svoboda argues (xxxvii) that the translation was made sometime between 1410 and 1411.

71. Šmahel, "Wyclif's Fortune," 479; Svoboda, *Mistra Jakoubka ze Stříbra překlad*, xxviiff.

72. The text is discussed and compared with Wyclif's writings in Sedlák, *Studie a texty*, II.415–28.

73. Svoboda, *Mistra Jakoubka ze Stříbra překlad*, xxi.

74. Sedlák, *M. Jan Hus*, 248*.

75. The heading which accompanies Folkhyrde's letters is printed in *ibid.*, 182*: "Est quidam armiger nomine Quintinus Folkhyrde, qui insurgit in causa dei manu forti equitando per patrias et palam publicando in materna lingua ista que sequuntur in epistolis, ea per cartulas et cedulas dividendo et cuilibet manum extendenti porrigendo."

76. *Ibid.*, 189*: "Bieše jeden rytieř řádu a snad ještě jest, jménem Quintinus, Folkhyerde přiemím, jenž sě vykládá pastýř lida."

77. For Kněhnice, see Tříška, *Životopisný slovník*, s.v. "Georgius de Knienicz." Faulfiš's loan is discussed below.

78. Novotný, *M. Jana Husi korespondence*, 85 n. 17; Hudson, "Which Wyche?," 233–4.

79. Kaminsky, *History of the Hussite Revolution*, 95. Beyond the more precise dates when Šimon was certainly in Bohemia, PNK VIII.F.1, a manuscript otherwise filled with Wyclif's texts, contains notes about events in 1410–11 and a gloss by a student who claims to have determined under Šimon of Tišnov (fol. 114ʳ). Whether this student made his determination during this same time span, however, is impossible to say. Cf. Odložilík, "Z počátků husitství na Moravě," 20 n. 2.

80. Palacký, *Documenta Mag. Joannis Hus*, 434.

81. Šimon of Tišnov's possible connections with ÖNB 1294 (the manuscript containing Faulfiš and Kněhnice's copies of Wyclif's texts) are discussed by Loserth in *Johannis Wyclif tractatus de ecclesia*, xviii–xix. For Šimon's defense of Wyclif's *De ecclesia* in his later dispute with Pavel of Prague, see Odložilík, "Z počátků husitství na Moravě," passim.

82. For discussion, see Hudson, "A Lollard Compilation," 38–41.
83. That the name (or *alias*) may have been fairly common in Bohemia is suggested elsewhere. Another "Engliss," though not connected to Wycliffism, appears in documents from 1410 and earlier as "cubicularius" and "familiaris" of King Václav. See *Archiv český*, xxxv.55, 89, and 470.
84. It is also possible that "de aliis" refers to other *people*, rather than other things.
85. Bartoš ("Husův přítel z Českých Budějovic," 44) suggests that Faulfiš was in England in March 1411, basing his argument on Hus' indication in his letter to Wyche that others will be writing to Nicholas. I am not convinced. If, as I suggest here, Faulfiš discussed Arundel's *Constitutions* with a cook sometime in or just after 1409, then he must have come back to Bohemia to tell Hus about it (Hus clearly indicates that Faulfiš held the conversation with him in person). And if, as I discuss below, Faulfiš died while making a third trip to (or from) England, then clearly he could not have mentioned his conversation with the cook to Hus after that journey.
86. The *Postilla* was written in 1413, during the period of Hus' exile from Prague, and was completed on October 27 of that year.
87. I have chosen not to use Deanesly's English translation (in *Lollard Bible*, 400) because it is two steps removed from the Czech and is not entirely accurate (Deanesly translates from Palacký's Latin translation of the original Czech). For Palacký's Latin translation, see *Documenta Mag. Joannis Hus*, 729. Also printed (from Palacký) in Loserth's edition of Wyclif's *De ecclesia*, xviii n. 1. Neither Deanesly nor Palacký was familiar with Mníšek's version, printed below. The Czech text is as follows (from Hus, *Česká nedělní postila*, 148): "I slyšal sem od věrného dobré paměti, od Nikoláše, jenž slúl Faulfiš, že, když jest byl v Englantu, poznal jest jednoho kuchaře, s nímž jest stál na ztravě; že když biskup tázal ho, proč by četl písmo englicky proti jeho zápovědi, a on bránil sě písmem, tehdy řekl jemu biskup: Vieš-li, s kým mluvíš? Odpověděl, že s biskupem člověkem. A biskup die jemu: I smieš ty, biedný laiče, se mnú z písma mluviti? A on jemu odpovědě: Já viem, že ty nejsi věččí než Kristus, a mám za to v naději, že já nejsem horší než ďábel. A poňavadž milostivý Kristus tíše jest slyšal písmo od ďábla, i proč by ty neslyšal, jsa menší než Kristus, ote mne člověka? A biskup, rozhněvav sě, nechtěl s ním mluviti, tak že kuchař přemohl písmem biskupa jako Kristus ďábla."
88. Palacký translates "proti jeho zápovědi" as "contra mandatum," which Deanesly renders, "contrary to the edict." The sense is clear in any of these translations.
89. Fol. 86^{r-v}. Translated from the transcription in Hus, *Leccionarium bipartitum, pars hiemalis*, 484: "In Anglia factum est, quod defendebant laycis legere Scripturas in ydyomate eorum. Contigit, quod quidam cocus, purus laycus, studebat vulgariter Scripturam et eam sepius legebat. Quem cum vidisset episcopus legentem, increpavit eum: 'Cur hoc legis?' Qui respondit: 'Tamen lex data est adiscendi tam secularibus quam spiritualibus et Scriptura dicit: "Omnis spiritus laudet Dominum."' Cui episcopus: 'O tu vilis etc., ne Scriptura te vis defendere?' Qui respondit: 'Credo, quod non es melior Cristo nec ego, ut spero, sum peior dyabolo. Ex quo? Cristus ex Scriptura

respondebat dyabolo et econtra dyabolus per Scripturam cum eo circuibat. Cur igitur prohibes me loqui ex Scriptura?'" Vidmanová ("Husův přívrženec Mikuláš Mníšek," 63) suggests that Mníšek may have been the "Nicolaus" mentioned by Hus in his reply to Richard Wyche. Considering the significant amount of evidence which places Mikuláš Faulfiš in England on other occasions (including Hus' reference, in his own version of the anecdote about the cook, to "Nicolaus, who was known as Faulfiš"), I find the possibility to be very unlikely. I thank Pavel Soukup for bringing this reference to my attention.

90. For discussion of Walter Brut's literacy, see Hudson, *"Laicus litteratus*: The Paradox of Lollardy,"* 222–36; and Minnis, "Making Bodies: Confection and Conception in Walter Brut's Vernacular Theology," Chapter 4 of his *Translations of Authority*.

91. Deanesly, *Lollard Bible*, 400.

92. The dating of the *Constitutions* is discussed in Cheney, *Medieval Texts and Studies*, 172 n. 7.

93. Record in *Archiv český*, xxxvi.440. Cf. Pletzer, "Českobudějovická rodina Faulfišů," 53.

94. I discuss this development in the next chapter.

95. Palacký, *Documenta Mag. Joannis Hus*, 313.

96. The record of the dispute is in *Archiv český*, xxxvi.440. For discussion, see Hudson, "Which Wyche?," 234 and nn.

97. *Actes and monuments* (1583), 620 (emphasis added).

98. Matthias Flacius, *Iohannis Hus et Hieronymi Pragensis historia et monumenta* (Nuremberg, 1558), i.xxvʳ. I thank Phillip Haberkern for directing my attention to this text.

99. The letter is printed in Johann Loserth, "Über die Beziehungen," 268–9. The manuscript is Herrnhut, Universitätsbibliothek MS 1.61. It was an audacious move for Oldcastle to write directly to the Bohemian king (his daring is of course attested elsewhere, as I discuss in Chapter 4), but he shows some deference in signing the letter "per vestrum humilem servitorem Johannem Oldecastellum militem, dominum de Cobham."

100. Loserth, "Über die Beziehungen," 268: "O quam suave, quod Wenceslaus Romanorum et Boemie Rex exemplum et speculum primicieque ceterorum regum zyzaniam, falsos sacerdotes, in oreum congregatam sagaciter et studiose a tritico segregavit et triticum, veros Christi sacerdotes, in statu evangelice paupertatis corroboravit."

101. For this theory, see *ibid.* and Novotný, *M. Jana Husi korespondence*, 169.

102. *M. Jana Husi korespondence*, 169.

103. Waugh, "Sir John Oldcastle," 444 n. 61; Sedlák, *M. Jan Hus*, 201 n. 4.

104. Loserth, "Über die Beziehungen," 268.

105. Novotný, *M. Jana Husi korespondence*, 85.

106. Kaminsky, *History of the Hussite Revolution*, 73–4.

107. Netter, *Doctrinale*, i, col. 623: "Dogma Wiclevisticum, praecipuus ejus discipulus Joannes Hus a Joanne veteris Castri sibi demandari ab Anglia in Bohemiam petiit."

108. Waugh, "Sir John Oldcastle," 444.
109. *A brefe chronicle*, 8^r. See also Bale, *The laboryouse journey*, sig. F.iii.^{v}: "That noble and valyaunt captayne syr Iohan Oldecastell, called also the Lorde Cobham, perceyuynge the outrage of the Romyshe popes clergye in hys tyme agaynste the good doctryne of Iohan Wicleue, caused all hys workes to be coppyed oute by moste fayre wryters, at his owne great cost and charge, and so conuayed them into the lande of Beme, that they myghte be there preserued from destruccyon."
110. Though, of course, Pavel Kravař traveled to St. Andrews in 1433, as I discuss above.
111. I discuss the 1416 episode in greater detail in Chapter 4.
112. For discussion of the idea of the "nation" in Bohemia during this period, see Šmahel, *Idea národa v husitských Čechách*. See also Šmahel's earlier work in English, "The Idea of the 'Nation' in Hussite Bohemia. "

CHAPTER 4: "AD REGNA ET LOCA EXTRANEA": DIPLOMACY AGAINST HERESY, 1411–1416

1. From a 1411 letter by Thomas Arundel, Archbishop of Canterbury, now in PNK MS VIII.G.13, fol. 118^v. The letter is edited (with the wrong folio listed) by Höfler, *Geschichtschreiber*, II.193.
2. Sigismund was elected King of the Romans on September 10, 1410, though he was challenged by his cousin Jošt, the Margrave of Moravia. Jošt died on January 18, 1411, and Sigismund was elected once again on July 21 of that year. He was not crowned Holy Roman Emperor until 1433, though in many documents before that time (in several English chronicles, for example) he is designated "Emperor."
3. For the location of the meeting (recorded under July 14, 1411) see Böhmer, *Die Urkunden Kaiser Sigmunds*, I.6 (no. 62). Much of my outline of the negotiations with Sigismund is a synopsis of C. M. D. Crowder's discussion in "Henry V, Sigismund, and the Council of Constance," esp. 94–8 and the notes therein. Crowder (96–8 and nn.) also provides an excellent outline of previous renderings of the 1411 embassy. He does not, however, address the embassy's activities en route in 1411, or subsequent embassies' involvement with issues of heresy. For a more recent summary of Sigismund's relations with the English throughout his reign, see Bárány, "Anglo-Luxembourg Relations during the Reign of Emperor Sigismund."
4. Rymer, *Foedera*, VII.674–5.
5. Crowder, "Henry V, Sigismund, and the Council of Constance," 96 and his n. 16. Mirot and Deprez, *Les Ambassades anglaises*, 71 (nos. 572 and 573) list payments for them for the periods of April 12(?)–October 31 (von Clux) and April 13–October 31 (Stokes).
6. Crowder, "Henry V, Sigismund, and the Council of Constance," n. 21. The date of departure on April 14 for Hartung is according to Crowder.
7. *Ibid.*, 96, 97 and his nn. 14 and 21. See also my n. 104 (below).

8. Some English knights stayed on at Ofen after Stokes and von Clux had returned to England, as is evident from their presence at the jousts there in May the next year. See Wylie, *History of England under Henry the Fourth*, III.403 n. 1.

9. Jan Hus, *Contra Iohannem Stokes*, 59–60 (emphasis added).

10. Fol. 118^v. See n. 1 (above).

11. The testimonial circulated widely in fifteenth-century Bohemia and is still extant in a number of Bohemian manuscripts, including PNK XI.E.3, fol. II^r (following the most recent foliation); PKMK D.50, fol. 23^{r-v}; and PNK MS Cim D.79 (formerly Stará Boleslav, Kapitulní knihovna C.132), fols. 153^r-154^r. I have recently discovered another copy of the letter in ÖNB 4483, which is not included in the modern foliation. The testimonial is edited by Höfler (from PNK XI.E.3, though with some errors of transcription) in *Concilia Pragensia*, 53; and by David Wilkins (from London, British Library Cotton Faustina C.vii) in *Concilia*, III.302. The date when the document reached Prague is usually said to be 1407. For one exception, see Novotný, *M. Jan Hus*, 1.1.313. Novotný mentions that it could have come to Prague as late as 1408, recalling that Jiří of Kněhnice, who together with Mikuláš Faulfiš carried the letter from England, next appears in a reference stating that he took his exams for the degree of bachelor in Prague in 1408. Novotný mistakenly gives his name as "Mikuláš z Kněhnic," but must mean Jiří. Novotný's reference to Jiří is corroborated by Tříška, *Životopisný slovník*, 118.

12. Höfler, *Concilia Pragensia*, 53.

13. *Loci e libro veritatum*, 20: "Et iste Petrus haereticus fuit magister arcium Oxoniae valde subdolus et furatus fuit sigillum commune Universitatis, sub quo scripsit haereticis Pragensibus quod Oxonia et tota Anglia fuit fidei Pragensium, exceptis falsis fratribus mendicantibus. Haec scripsit ille falsus haereticus qui vocabatur Oxoniae Petrus Clerk."

14. Harvey, "Diffusion of the *Doctrinale*," 282–3. For Netter's discussion of the Oxford testimony, see Netter, *Doctrinale*, II, cols. 18–19. As I mention below, Gascoigne also had a copy of Constance *Acta* available to him, from which he could also have learned of the testimony. Gascoigne's claim (*Loci e libro*, 20) that the letter stated "quod Oxonia et tota Anglia fuit fidei Pragensium, exceptis falsis fratribus mendicantibus" is not found in Netter, nor does the statement appear in the extant copies of the testimony.

15. Netter probably wrote the *Doctrinale* throughout the 1420s. Gascoigne compiled his *Dictionarium theologicum* throughout much of his career, but his work almost certainly post-dates Netter.

16. Emden, *An Oxford Hall*, 140–3.

17. Cf. Catto, "Wyclif and Wycliffism," esp. 241–53.

18. Palacký, *Documenta Mag. Joannis Hus*, 313. The episode is discussed in detail below.

19. *Ibid.*, 154 and 161, respectively. Hus' reply to a later accusation during his trial at Constance suggests that he may have made this statement as early as 1403. Hus, accused during his trial of having once said: "Utinam anima mea esset ibi, ubi

est anima Joannis Wiclef." replied "quod verum est, quod ante annos XII, antequam adhuc libri ipsius theologicales fuissent in Bohemia, et libri in artibus sibi valde bene placebant, et non constabat sibi, nisi de bona ejus vita, dixit: Nescio, ubi est anima ipsius Joan. W.; spero, quod sit salvatus et timeo, ne sit damnatus; vellem tamen in spe, quod anima mea esset ibi, ubi est anima Joannis W." See *ibid.*, 280. Cf. von der Hardt, *Magnum oecumenicum Constantiense Concilium*, iv, cols. 413–14, where several episodes during which Hus allegedly gave evidence for Wyclif's innocence have been conflated.

20. *Super IV. Sententiarum*, 621: "Hec propter illos disserui, qui iudicio temerario Magistrum Johannem Wiclef certitudinaliter asserunt et predicant esse dampnatum eternaliter in inferno. Ego autem a temerario volens declinare iudicio, spero, quod sit de numero salvandorum. Et si est in celo, laudetur gloriosus Dominus, qui eum ibi constituit; si in purgatorio, liberet eum misericors Dominus cicius; si in inferno, maneat in eterno supplicio ex Dei iusto iudicio."
21. *Contra Iohannem Stokes*, 62–6.
22. The text is edited by Höfler (who incorrectly ascribes it to Hus) in *Geschichtschreiber*, ii.112–28.
23. The record of the proceedings against Jerome is edited in Klicman, *Processus iudiciarius contra Jeronimum*. Jerome's use of the Oxford testimonial is mentioned passim.
24. Von der Hardt, *Magnum oecumenicum Constantiense Concilium*, iv, cols. 644–5.
25. *Documentary Culture and the Making of Medieval English Literature*, 13.
26. *Making of Medieval Forgeries*, 4.
27. *Ibid.*, 13.
28. The testimony is not included in the modern foliation, but appears on a half sheet which has been bound between fols. 174^v and 175^r. It is, however, listed in the table of contents, numbered d 37, entitled "Bulla pro Vyclef."
29. Additional evidence of the complications caused by the testimonial can be found in a note to a copy of the letter in PNK XI.E.3, where the annotator has received conflicting reports about Wyclif, writing: "Universitas Parisiensis valde eum vituperat in una litera Conrado missa." The identity of "Conrad" is not clear.
30. Klicman, *Processus iudiciarius contra Jeronimum*, 5: "Item in die Cene [March 20, 1410] predicando coram rege Ungarie, deducendo thema hoc: 'Mandatum novum do vobis', multa dixit in diminucionem status clericalis et libertatis eiusdem, imo et contra emunitatem, quod tandem rex motus eum ad verba posuit et valde indignanter sermonem illum accepit."
31. Klicman, *Processus iudiciarius contra Jeronimum*, 21. Berthold's business at Oxford in 1410 is unclear, though he is known to have been a student at Oxford several years before. See Rennhofer, *Die Augustiner-Eremiten in Wien*, 105–6, 267; Aschbach, *Geschichte der Wiener Universität*, 1.441; Catto, "Wyclif and Wycliffism," 198; and Trapp, "Unchristened Nominalism," passim.
32. The reference to "the parish church of Wyclif" is difficult to interpret. Does this mean "Wyclif's parish church" (i.e., Lutterworth)? Or could Berthold perhaps have regarded Wyclif's surname as a toponym (there is, after all, a

hamlet called Wyckliffe in North Yorkshire)? For the latter possibility, we do have other Central European examples, as in the so-called "Veršované letopisy" ("Verse Chronicle"): "V Englantě jedno město Viklef slovíše, / v němž ten Jan Viklef farářem bíše [In England was a certain city called 'Wyclif,' / in which this John Wyclif was a priest]." Old Czech text printed in Svejkovský, *Veršované skladby doby husitské*, 156.

33. Klicman, *Processus iudiciarius contra Jeronimum*, vi, 5.
34. *Ibid.*, viii–x.
35. For Arundel's itinerary, see Salter, *Snappe's Formulary*, 102.
36. "nec fuerat . . . per nostros prelatos post ejus humationem traditus incendiis." Höfler, *Concilia Pragensia*, 53; Wilkins, *Concilia*, iii.302.
37. Palacký, *Documenta Mag. Joannis Hus*, 313. The stone was likely brought to Prague along with the testimonial letter. Páleč was probably aware of the irony of such worship (if indeed it did take place): this kind of veneration was distinctly opposed to Wyclif's tenets, but parallels are found elsewhere. Many of Wyclif's later followers revered him like a saint, and there were even claims of miraculous occurrences at the site of his bones' eventual cremation. Similar instances were likewise reported of the site where Richard Wyche was executed (†1440). See also von Nolcken, "Another Kind of Saint," 429–43.
38. Netter, *Doctrinale*, ii, cols. 25–6: "Haec sancta Synodus declarat, definit, et sententiat eundem Joannem Wicleffum fuisse notorie haereticum pertinacem, ac in haeresi decessisse, anathematizando ipsum pariter, et ejus memoriam condemnando. Decernitque, et ordinat, corpus ejus et ossa, si ab aliis fidelium corporibus discerni possunt, exhumari, et procul ab Ecclesiastica sepultura jactari, secundum canonicas, et legitimas sanctiones." The caveat about distinguishing Wyclif's bones from those surrounding them is a possible indication that his body was known to have been disturbed for one reason or another. This is not necessarily the case, however, as churchyards could be at that time relatively impermanent or highly mutable resting places. Charnel houses and pits, for example, were regularly used, particularly in populated areas (which Lutterworth was not) to place the bones which had been removed to make way for fresh burials. Graves were commonly disturbed by animals, and grave boundaries themselves were often indeterminate, the bodies therein frequently upset by the digging of new graves. See Daniel, *Death and Burial in Medieval England*, esp. 123.
39. Palacký, *Documenta Mag. Joannis Hus*, 569. The document is dated from Constance, July 26, 1415.
40. *Contra Iohannem Stokes*, 64.
41. Von der Hardt, *Magnum oecumenicum Constantiense Concilium*, iv, col. 413; cf. Mladoňovice's account in Palacký, *Documenta Mag. Joannis Hus*, 279–80.
42. *Johannis Wiclif trialogus*, 339, 374, 376, 377, 445, 447; see also Aston, "Wycliffe and the Vernacular," 28, 69. Cf. Netter, *Doctrinale*, ii, cols. 22–3.
43. Cf. Dahmus, *The Prosecution of John Wyclyf*, 151–2.

44. Catto, "Wyclif and Wycliffism," 251.
45. For discussion of the committee's work, see Hudson, "Notes of an Early Fifteenth-Century Research Assistant," 685–97.
46. The letter which accompanied the list is printed in Salter, *Snappe's Formulary*, 128–30.
47. *Loci e libro veritatum*, 116.
48. *Doctrinale*, II, cols. 19–20.
49. Arundel's letter to John XXIII must have been written after March 17, 1411, when the list of errors was initially submitted to convocation. He may have written it before departing on his visitation just a few days after the provincial synod, but we also know that he actively dispatched letters even as he traveled. His letters to Oxford and Prague were written, for example, when he was visiting the diocese of Norwich (Salter, *Snappe's Formulary*, 102). Arundel was in Norwich diocese in April and into May. I have not been able to make sense of the locations from which he addressed the letters ("Girnkner" and "Korkewe"). Perhaps his letter to John XXIII was written nearer to May 8, when he wrote these other letters concerning related issues.
50. Salter, *Snappe's Formulary*, 133–5.
51. The letter appears in London, British Library MS Cotton Faustina C.vii, and is printed in Salter, *Snappe's Formulary*, 133–5 (with the request for exhumation on 135).
52. *Ibid.*, 129: "et quia per vos, si placet, ulterius beatissimo patri nostro summo pontifici has iterum cupimus intimari."
53. Netter, *Doctrinale*, II, cols. 18–19: Netter laments how "per quam abducunt fideles doctrinis suis variis, et peregrinis haeretici Wiclevistae, affirmantes voce valida, quod doctrina sua sit laudata in remotis partibus, et in Studiis generalibus Parisiis, Oxoniae, Bononiae, et per fines Hispaniae, Angliae, et Franciae comprobata: unde, ut fertur, literas approbatorias furtive signari fecerunt sigillo Universitatis Oxoniae, quas apud Pragenses pro grandi authoritate monstrarunt."
54. Palacký, *Documenta Mag. Joannis Hus*, 313. See below for a detailed discussion.
55. See n. 11 (above).
56. *Actes and monuments* (1583), 448, where Foxe lists his source in the margin; Matthias Flacius, *Iohannis Hus et Hieronymi Pragensis historia et monumenta*, II.366ᵛ.
57. Hus' challenge to debate Stokes is printed with Stokes' refusal in Novotný, *M. Jana Husi korespondence*, 102–4. Hus' defense of Wyclif is printed in *Contra Iohannem Stokes*, 57–70. Hus indicates Stokes' absence at the end of his defense (70): "Hec breviter contra assercionem domini Stokes, qui benigne et honorifice per magistros reverendos et quamplures dominos sub firmissima assecuracione ad actum vocatus – ex qua causa nescio – noluit huc venire etc." It should be noted that the modern editor of Hus' position against Stokes confuses John Stokes with the earlier Cistercian Peter Stokes.
58. Novotný, *M. Jana Husi korespondence*, 103.
59. *Ibid.*, 103–4.

60. In a puzzling passage of Hus' *Contra Iohannem Stokes*, Hus argues against the alleged charge by Stokes "cum suo comite milite Hartung Glux" that Wyclif "non fuit Anglicus, sed Theutonicus." Hus postulates the intent of their allegation as follows: "isto antecedente supposito per eos ut vero Wigleff est hereticus et Wigleff est Theutonicus, tota heresis est Theutonicis fontaliter ascribenda. Patet consequencia ex illo, quia per eos fons et origo tocius heresis est Theutonicus Iohannes Wigleff." He then produces several arguments to refute the charge. The claim could be a sign that Stokes and von Clux were aware of the bitter rivalry between German- and Czech-speaking Bohemians in Prague. Just two years earlier, this rivalry had resulted in the exodus of German masters and students from the university, who left to establish a new university in Leipzig. There are signs, too, that Hus and his friends considered it important that Wyclif was *not* a German, not least because his realist doctrines could be combined with native Bohemian reformist positions in opposition to the staunchly nominalist Germans at the university in Prague. The potential for Wyclif's positions to be used against the Germans is most clearly expressed in a gloss to one of Wyclif's philosophical texts which Hus copied in 1398 (though Hus was not the glossator): "Haha, Germans, haha, out out!" For discussion, see Šmahel, "Wyclif's Fortune," 470–1. A few years later in 1403, however, after Johann Hübner's attempts to condemn forty-five articles drawn from Wyclif's texts in Prague, the following passage appears in a letter which was written to Hübner (perhaps by Hus) in defense of the offending articles : "Et quid, mi domine magister, si foret hereticus, dato et non concesso, non foret fortassis mirum, cum supposita ydyomatis vestri ut frequenter sunt heretica ex communi fama: Teotunicus hereticus, Boemus fur naturaliter. Et cum ipse Vicleph sit Anglicus, qui ex ydyomate saxonico ex cronicis ortum traxerunt, concludatis." The letter is printed by Sedlák (from whom I cite here), *M. Jan Hus*, 94*–98*; and Novotný, *M. Jana Husi korespondence*, 11–15. Compare the inscription in Brno, Moravská zemská knihovna 109, fol. 137^r (sixteenth century): "Arianus hereticus turbavit Itallos, Vikleff Germanos, Lutter Misnenses, Hus Boemos."
61. Novotný, *M. Jana Husi korespondence*, 104.
62. Hudson, "Notes of an Early Fifteenth-Century Research Assistant," 696; Catto, "Wyclif and Wycliffism," 248.
63. *Contra Iohannem Stokes*, 66.
64. This may be a reference to the use of parchment as opposed to paper (paper was much more common in Bohemia in the early fifteenth century).
65. Cf. Catto, "Wyclif and Wycliffism," 242. The charge against the university concerning the testimonial letter is found in Wilkins, *Concilia*, III.336.
66. *Ibid.*
67. For Mladoňovice's *Relatio*, see Palacký, *Documenta Mag. Joannis Hus*, 235–324. References like these to the English are found passim. John Stokes was also present at Constance during Hus' trial; see *ibid.*, 277, 308.
68. For example, *ibid.*, 313, where the "Anglici" are said to present incriminating documents on the floor of the council, or to interrogate Hus as a collective body.

69. *Ibid.*
70. *Ibid.*
71. By the time of the Council of Constance, the list of 267 errors seems to have been reduced slightly. For discussion of the compilation and subsequent history of the list, see Hudson, "Notes of an Early Fifteenth-Century Research Assistant."
72. Note, for example, the following passage from that earlier letter (Salter, *Snappe's Formulary*, 129): "Doctor quidem nouellus dictus Iohannes Wyclyffe, non electus sed infectus agricola vitis Cristi, iam infra paucos annos pulcherrimum agrum vestrum Cantuariensis prouincie tot variis seminauit zizaniis totque pestiferis plantauit erroribus, tot denique sue secte procreauit heredes, quod sicut probabiliter credimus absque mordacibus sarculis et censuris asperrimis explantari vix poterunt aut euelli. . . . Nos tamen ista mala cura vigili ponderantes, uestre prudentissime paternitatis auctoritate suffulti, vestrisque salutaribus et votivis suadelis et monitis pro viribus obsequentes, per duodecim electissimos viros, magistros et doctores, multos libros et libellos aliosque tractatus et opuscula multa prelibati Iohannis longa deliberacione perspeximus, et multas conclusiones in eis, et que nobis videntur erronee et heretice et sanctorum patrum determinationi contrarie, studiose signauimus, signatas excerpsimus, excerptas morose digessimus, et digestas censuimus sacre doctrine contrarias, et per consequens reas igne. Sed cum apud plurimos nostra satis parva censeatur auctoritas, easdem conclusiones, simul et in unum redactas vestro, pater inclyte, vestrorumque confratrum maturiori examini denuo recensendas offerimus."
73. It should be noted that Arundel died in February 1414, before the Council of Constance began.
74. Palacký, *Documenta Mag. Joannis Hus*, 278.
75. *Ibid.*, 299–300. Hus later tried to explain himself to Sigismund (*ibid.*, 310): "Et etiam rogo, quod solum mihi detur audientia ad tantum, quod possim meam intentionem declarare in certis punctis et articulis mihi objectis, et specialiter de papa, capitibus et membris ecclesiae, in quibus mecum aequivocant, quod meam intentionem concipiant; quia ego concedo et dico, quod papa, episcopi, praelati [etc.] si sint praesciti et in peccatis mortalibus, non sunt vere tales quoad merita, nec digne coram deo pro tunc, sunt tamen quoad officia tales, scil. papae, episcopi, praelati [etc.], cum, ut dixi, sint indigni ministri sacramentorum."
76. Most of the major chronicles, and many of the minor ones, report the visit. See, for example, the account edited by Kingsford, "An Historical Collection of the Fifteenth Century"; as well as Kingsford's "A Legend of Sigismund's Visit to England."
77. He also intended to negotiate for peace between the English and French, though his efforts of course failed.
78. For discussion of Lucas and his ties to Lollardy, see Jurkowski, "Lawyers and Lollardy," 164–6.
79. London, National Archives, KB 27/624, rot. 9 rex: "Thomas Lucas magister in artibus de Andover in comite Suthampton [Hampshire] Gentilman

quartodecimo die Augusti Anno regni domini Regis nunc quarto apud villam Westm. proditorie imaginavit ad deponendum, destruendum, ac interficiendum dictum dominum Henricum Regem simul cum aliis per imaginacionem diversarum billarum necnon cuiusdam littere Sigismundo Regi Romanorum iam tarde porrecto in discontinencia diversos articulos, videlicet quod non liceat aliquibus religiosis habere nec gaudere possessionibus temporalibus, ac eciam in hac predicta contenta fuit quod Ricardus nuper Rex Anglie fuit et est vivens in partibus Scocie in villa de Edyngburgh, et quod ipse est Rex Anglie modo vivens; et dictas billas in diversis locis regni Anglie, videlicet Cantuarie in comite Kant., ac Londonie in diversis stratis dictarum billarum proiecit; ac dictus Thomas false et proditorie procuravit diversos homines, videlicet Ricardum Benet 'Wolman,' Johannem Whitlok et alios ignotos ad deponendum, destruendum, et interficiendum dictum Henricum Regem Anglie nunc; et idem Thomas cum tota voluntate sua ipsum Henricum Regem Anglie tunc ibidem proditorie deposuisse, destruisse, necnon interfecisse volluisset; ac eciam idem Thomas fuit et est consenciens, agens, concilians, et sonens omnibus operibus Johannis Oldcastell, tam in oppinionibus lollardrie quam in omnibus aliis suis maleficis proditorie per dictum Johannem Oldcastell versus dictum dominum Regem."

80. Woolman and Bekeryng were sentenced on September 29, 1416. Benedict Woolman is no doubt the "Richard Benet" mentioned in Lucas' trial (cited above, n. 79). Cf. Thomson, *Later Lollards*, 16.

81. The trial record is printed in Riley (whose translation I cite here), *Memorials of London and London Life*, 638–41.

82. Crowder, "Henry V, Sigismund, and the Council of Constance," 98.

83. Böhmer, *Die Urkunden Kaiser Sigmunds*, II.436 (no. 12260); Finke, *Acta Concilii Constanciensis*, I.377–9. Receipts of payment for Sydenham and Hungerford are printed in Mirot and Deprez, *Les Ambassades anglaises*, 2–3. Cf. *ibid.*, 73 (nos. 584 and 586).

84. Rymer, *Foedera*, IX.155–6.

85. Böhmer, *Die Urkunden Kaiser Sigmunds*, II.435–6 (no. 12254); Finke, *Acta Concilii Constanciensis*, I.376. Contrary to what Böhmer and Finke indicate, however, Sigismund's letter must have been written earlier than the end of July. Henry's letter commissioning Hungerford and the others to meet with Sigismund is dated July 23. He shows signs in that letter that Hartung has recently returned with news from Sigismund. The timing would require that Hartung must have departed from the meeting with Sigismund in Germany by early July at the latest.

86. Finke, *Acta Concilii Constanciensis*, I.374.

87. Chaplais, *English Diplomatic Practice in the Middle Ages*, 157–8.

88. The suggestion was also made by Crowder, "Henry V, Sigismund, and the Council of Constance," 100.

89. This copy of the document is edited, with several irregularities, by Stülz, "Sitzung vom 12. Juni 1850," 64–7. Unfortunately, the book in which the text was found, whether it was a manuscript or early print, is not identified in

Stülz' edition. I provide an edition of the Třeboň copy in Appendix B, as well as a slightly adjusted edition of the second copy of the text derived from Stülz. The two copies are very similar, though the copy in Stülz is more detailed. Nonetheless, the Třeboň copy is far less confused when it comes to English names, and so I use it here where Stülz is unclear. See Appendix B for further discussion.

90. Beverly is called "Boborle" in Stülz' version, but the Třeboň copy, which is much clearer with names, calls him "Beuerle." The spelling of names, of course, was easily corrupted in the process of copying medieval texts. This is clearly the Beverly who was drawn and hanged according to one of the English accounts, where he is also called "syr" and "a preest." See Kingsford, *English Historical Literature*, 293. The "nouitates de Anglia" texts introduce Beverly as one of many priests ("inter quos plures clerici Wicleuiste erant et vnus precipuus ... nomine ... Bouorle"), and he is said to have been executed with several other "prespiteri." Elsewhere, too, names evidently confused the scribe of Stülz' version, as Oldcastle is on several occasions called "the Baron of Eckhaym (or Elckhaim)" – meaning "Eltham," also the place where Henry was staying when he learned of the plot. At other points, however, Oldcastle is the "Baron of Kobha [Cobham]," though in one instance the reference is struck out, replaced by some variant of "Eltham."

91. See, for example, references to Acton in three of the chronicle accounts edited by Kingsford, *English Historical Literature*, 284–5, 292–3 and 324–5.

92. *Chronica maiora of Thomas Walsingham*, 390–5; Taylor and Roskell, *Gesta Henrici Quinti*, 3–11. My purpose here is not to discuss the veracity of the account's claims. The pro-Lancastrian bent of the accounts in Walsingham and the *Gesta* has been discussed at length elsewhere. See, for example, Strohm, *England's Empty Throne*, esp. 63–100 and the notes provided therein.

93. As further evidence that the English began to share their resources for fighting heresy with those interested in combating Wycliffism in Bohemia, William Woodford's *De causis condemnationis XVIII articulorum damnatorum Iohannis Wyclif* survives in four Bohemian copies: PKMK D.51, fols. 1^r–22^r, 26^v–53^v; PKMK D.62, fols. 48^r–119^r; PNK IV.G.14, fols. 1^r–107^r; and Prague, Národní muzeum XVI.C.4, fols. 96^r–134^v (*pace* Sharpe [*Handlist*, 820], who lists this last under the National Library). The copy in PKMK D.62 is from 1418, and was probably copied at Constance. The others also appear to be fifteenth-century copies.

94. The evidence is inconclusive. For a recent discussion, see Röhrkasten, "Thomas Netter: Carmelite and Diplomat," esp. 124–8.

95. *Oxford Dictionary of National Biography*, s.v. "Netter [Walden], Thomas" (contributed by Anne Hudson).

96. *Eberhart Windeckes Denkwürdigkeiten*, 38.

97. Taylor and Roskell, *Gesta Henrici Quinti*, 129–31; Kingsford, *First English Life of King Henry the Fifth*, 67.

98. Harvey, "The Diffusion of the *Doctrinale*," 282, 289–90; Carlson, "Whethamstede on Lollardy," 25.

99. Harvey, "John Whethamstede," 109.

100. Crowder, "Constance Acta in English Libraries," 481, 493; Harvey, "John Whethamstede," 111.
101. Wright, "Continuity in XV Century English Humanism," 372.
102. *Ibid.*, 375.
103. The suggestion is made by Seymour, *Selections from Hoccleve*, 129. "The Remonstrance against Oldcastle" is printed in *ibid.*, 61–74, with the characterization of Henry (quoted above) at l. 499.
104. Hoccleve's Formulary, now London, British Library Add. ms 24062, contains the second set of instructions for the Stokes–von Clux embassy of 1411. The text is edited (from fols. 146^v–147^r) by Pierre Chaplais, *English Medieval Diplomatic Practice*, 1.97–8 (no. 64). The manuscript also contains a letter congratulating Sigismund on his election as King of the Romans (fol. 148^r). Prophete's Formulary, London, British Library Harley 431, contains the commission for Stokes and von Clux (fol. 101^r); their instructions (fols. 101^v–102^r); letters of credence (fol. 102^{r-v}); and a letter from Henry V's brother, Thomas, Duke of Clarence, probably carried to Sigismund by Hungerford and the other ambassadors after Hartung's return in summer 1414 (fol. 113^r). Documents such as these were preserved in the formularies which contain them for a number of reasons, one of them being that they were considered to be models for specific kinds of correspondence (e.g., letters of credence, etc.). The number of them which were preserved in the formularies does not necessarily represent the sum total of documents pertaining to the embassies which were produced at the Privy Seal.
105. Netter, *Doctrinale*, ii, col. 18.

CHAPTER 5: THE AFTERMATH: BOHEMIA IN ENGLISH RELIGIOUS POLEMIC BEFORE FOXE

1. From Andrew Boorde, *Fyrst boke of the introduction of knowledge* (London, 1542?), ch. 13.
2. For an excellent discussion concerning the difficulty of defining (and dating) "the Reformation" in England, see Haigh, *English Reformations*, esp. 12–21. I use the dates of the Henrician political Reformation because legislation was passed during this period which helped put an end to the strand of polemic which I discuss in this chapter.
3. This was especially true before the Hussite connections with the Waldensians became more pronounced.
4. See below, n. 9.
5. For discussion of these rebellions, see Aston, "Lollardy and Sedition."
6. It is difficult to give exact dates for Netter's composition of the three volumes of his *Doctrinale*. Most of the work must have been completed during the decade prior to Netter's death (1430), though it is uncertain when he began writing. For more on the dating of the *Doctrinale* see Hudson, *Premature Reformation*, 51; and Aston, "William White's Lollard Followers," 76–7 and nn.
7. For discussion, see Harvey, "The Diffusion of the *Doctrinale*," 281.

8. In fact, Netter's intention was never solely to attack the English Lollards. His original title (not printed in Blanciotti's edition) seems to have referred to Wycliffites and Hussites. See Aston, "William White's Lollard Followers," 76–7 and accompanying notes. Thomas Gascoigne indicates the scope of Netter's attack in his *Dictionarium theologicum*: "Ipse enim doctor Walden . . . scripsit contra Wyclyf et Hus et Ieronimum de Praga tria volumina, vocata ab ipso doctrinale antiquitatum ecclesiae." See *Loci e libro veritatum*, 2.

9. Netter's incomplete knowledge of the heretical correspondence is exemplified by his suspicion that Sir John Oldcastle had busied himself in obtaining many of Wyclif's books at the request of Jan Hus. See *Doctrinale*, I, col. 623: "Dogma Wiclevisticum praecipuus ejus discipulus Joannes Hus a Joanne veteris Castri sibi demandari ab Anglia in Bohemiam petiit."

10. *Doctrinale*, II, col. 26.

11. *Ibid.*, I, col. 355.

12. *Ibid.*, III, col. 146.

13. *Ibid.*, col. 199.

14. *Ibid.*, col. 568. Netter's references to "the ransacking of holy sites," "the burning of monasteries," and "terrible slaughters" are not unusual in accounts of Bohemia, but I have found no precedent for his references to more specific forms of torture.

15. The papal letters acknowledging the first two volumes of Netter's *Doctrinale* are dated April 1, 1426 (vol. 1) and August 8, 1427 (vol. 2). For discussion of the dedication, see Aston, "William White's Lollard Followers," 76–7 and nn.

16. See *ibid.* for discussion.

17. The Latin text of the complete letter is printed in Gratius Ortwinus, *Fasciculus rerum expetendarum et fugiendarum*, II.616–17.

18. The English reaction can be gauged in part by the response the Privy Council gave to Cardinal Henry Beaufort (the papal legate responsible for crusade initiatives against the Hussites) in December 1428, granting only part of what Beaufort had petitioned for in his request for aid in the crusade against the Hussites. See Fudge, *The Crusade Against Heretics in Bohemia*, 251–3 (for Beaufort's petition) and 253–5 (response from the Privy Council). The St. Albans Chronicler gives a somewhat different impression of the English response to the papal request. He mentions the convocation during which the pope asked the English clergy for a tenth (integram decimam) "in destructione haereticorum Boemiae." See *Chronica monasterii S. Albani a Johanne Amundesham*, 1.24. The account does not mention whether or not the pope got what he requested, giving only the vague statement that "statuta et ordinationes edita sunt contra Lollardos in hac Convocatione, qui tam Boemiae quam in pluribus partibus Angliae nimium saevire et rebellare contra Christianam fidem dolose elaboravere et laborant" (1.32). These "statuta et ordinationes" probably include the permission given to Cardinal Beaufort to proclaim the cross and raise a volunteer army (funded by Rome) throughout England. In any case, there is no explicit indication in this account that the English were sluggish in their response.

19. The Lollard rising in 1431 may have reminded them of the chastisement that Martin V had given them three years earlier. This rising was crushed with disproportionate force, perhaps with the intention that the English response would be noticed abroad. The response also demonstrated that the English were aware of their tarnished reputation.

20. The royal procuration "De tractando super reductione Boemorum," issued December 1, 1432, is printed in Rymer, *Foedera*, x.529–30. For further discussion of English involvement at the Council, see Schofield, "The First English Delegation to the Council of Basel." Even as the English were showing signs that they would add their support to the conciliar cause, however, they remained hesitant. Before Henry made his decision to send his ambassadors, he had faced substantial pressure by many of the European princes who supported the council. His correspondence with the council, as well as with the pope, indicates that this pressure had affected his decision. Henry was also dissatisfied with the news from Basle telling him that, instead of voting by "nations," as had been the practice at Constance, decisions at this council would be made by "deputations" consisting of international groupings. Largely as a result of this new system of voting, the English refused to become fully incorporated members of the council; they would never be completely on board with policies that could in any way compromise what they perceived to be their domestic interests.

21. His work seems to have had its greatest readership in Carmelite and conciliar circles. However, Thomas Gascoigne (discussed below) was familiar with Netter's work, as well as with the fact that Netter had written against Wyclif, Hus, and Jerome of Prague (see above, n. 8). For discussion, see Harvey, "Diffusion of the *Doctrinale*."

22. *Repressor*, 1.85.

23. *Ibid.*, 85–6. The stance that individualized interpretation easily gives way to communal strife was often put forth during the debate on vernacular translation at Oxford (1401) and in the years leading up to and following Arundel's *Constitutions* (implemented 1409), the legislation that sought to curtail vernacular translation in England. For discussion of religious politics during this period, see Watson, "Censorship and Cultural Change," esp. 840–47; and Hudson, "The Debate on Bible Translation." It should be noted, of course, that Pecock is not discussing translation, but interpretation. Nonetheless, he applies many of the arguments that had been used in the past against translation. With his bestial imagery, too, Pecock draws upon an established polemical motif in England, one in which humans behave like brutes in the absence of a strict, well-run social hierarchy. Chroniclers recounting the 1381 Peasants' Revolt, as well as John Gower, who treated the same event in his poem *Vox clamantis*, provide some of the most notable examples of this motif. Cardinal Wolsey's account (discussed below) specifically depicts the Bohemians acting like beasts.

24. *Repressor*, 1.86.

25. *Ibid.* When Pecock refers to the destruction of the "vniuersite of Prage," he is likely making an oblique reference to the exodus of German faculty and students from Charles University in 1409, which occurred after Jan Hus and others convinced Václav IV to pass the decree of Kutná Hora (January 18, 1409), thereby giving more votes to the *nacio Bohemorum* at the university. This event indeed resulted in what could be considered the "wepeable destruccioun" of most of the university faculties. Hus' actual role in this process is uncertain. For discussion, see Šmahel, "The Kuttenberg Decree."

26. *Repressor*, 1.86.

27. *Ibid.* Pecock's statement here sounds very similar to a comment expressed by Pope Martin V in his 1428 letter to the English Church hierarchy (discussed above).

28. *Loci e libro veritatum*, 5.

29. *Ibid.* Gascoigne's sources of information about Bohemia include Netter's *Doctrinale* (see above, n. 8), and copies of the *Acta* from the Councils of Constance and Basle, which he claims to have seen (see, for example, *Loci e libro veritatum*, 115 and 116).

30. At another point (*ibid.*, 9–10), Gascoigne also blames the queen of Bohemia for defending Hus and his followers, as well as Peter Payne. In fact, there was plenty of blame to go around, and not everyone who cited the Bohemian situation did so in the context of religious polemic. Surely, political ineptitude must have had something to do with the revolution in Bohemia, suggests John Fortescue, political theorist and likely tutor to Prince Edward. Indeed, Fortescue gives no indication that heresy (let alone an Anglo-Bohemian heretical alliance) had anything to do with the destruction in Bohemia. As far as he was concerned, the revolution was the result of poor governance. In his *Difference between an Absolute and Limited Monarchy* (*c.*1471, known commonly as *The Governance of England*), he embeds his reference to Bohemia in an argument against the idea that a king can prevent uprisings among the commoners by keeping them poor. "It seems," he argues, "that poverty has been the whole cause of all such risings. The poor man has been stirred thereto by occasion of his poverty, in order to get goods, and the rich men have gone with them, because they did not want to be made poor by losing their goods. What then would happen, if all the commons were poor? Truly it is likely that this land then should be like the realm of Bohemia, where the commons, because of poverty, rose upon the nobles, and made all their goods to be in common." See *On the Laws and Governance of England*, 109.

31. For discussion of the Leipzig Disputation, and especially the dispute over Luther's debt to Hus, see Hendrix, "'We Are All Hussites'?"

32. Luther wrote this in a letter to Georg Spalatin, dated February 14, 1520. The relevant passage is as follows: "Ego imprudens hucusque omnia Iohannis Huss et docui et tenui. Docuit eadem imprudentia et Iohannes Staupitz. Breviter: sumus omnes Hussitae ignorantes. Denique Paulus et Augustinus ad verbum sunt Hussitae. Vide monstra, quaeso, in quae venimus sine duce et doctore

Bohemico. Ego prae stupore nescio, quid cogitem, videns tam terribilia Dei iudicia in hominibus, quod veritas euangelica apertissima iam publice plus centum annis exusta, pro damnata habetur, nec licet hoc confiteri." From *D. Martin Luthers Werke*, II.42.

33. The English translation (from which I quote in this chapter) is in Henry VIII, *Assertion of the Seven Sacraments*, in *Miscellaneous Writings of Henry the Eighth*. This is the treatise which, after it was presented to Pope Leo X, helped earn Henry his title "fidei Defensor."

34. *Ibid.*, 55.

35. *Ibid.*

36. *Dialogue*, II.361.

37. *Assertion*, 28.

38. *Ibid.*

39. *Ibid.* Clark elaborates on Luther's relationship with Hus as follows: "tracing the steps of the Hussites [Luther] has added so much poison to them, that now the enemy appears more formidable; by how much more he equalizes all arch-heretics in his doctrine, & surpasses them in his malicious and wicked intentions: indeed the danger is also so much the greater, as 'tis easier to add worse proceedings to bad beginnings than to begin ill; and to increase inventions than to invent."

40. *A dyaloge describing the originall grou[n]d of these Lutheran faccyons* (London, 1531), sig. E^v.

41. *Dialogue*, I.192.

42. More often relies on argument by analogy in the *Dialogue*. On another occasion he mentions that Wyclif, whose teachings were brought to Bohemia and taught by Hus and others, "was the occasyon of the vtter subuersyon of that hole realme bothe in fayth & good lyuyng with the losse also of many a thousand lyues." Then More gives the following analogy: "And as he [Wyclif] began agayn the olde heresyes of those auncyent heretykes whom & whos errours the chyrch of cryst had condempned & subdued many dyuers agys afore so doth luther agayn begyn to set vp his" (1.315).

43. See especially *Ep.* 950. (*Correspondence of Erasmus, Letters 842 to 992*, 321–3.)

44. *Ibid.* 323.

45. *Ibid.*

46. For discussion of Erasmus' correspondence with the Bohemians, see Allen, "Erasmus and the Bohemian Brethren."

47. *Life and Death of Cardinal Wolsey*, 179–80.

48. See, for example, the poem by Andrew Boorde in the epigraph to this chapter, from his *Fyrst boke of the introduction of knowledge* (1542?). Boorde also tells of fantastical beasts which are said to be found in Bohemia. No doubt he relied on hearsay for his account; Bohemia's reputation had developed for a long time, and references to fantastical creatures dwelling there became a commonplace. It should also be noted that Boorde dedicated his *Boke* to "the right honorable and gracios lady Mary doughter of our souerayne lord kyng Henry the eyght."

AFTERWORD

1. Sebald, *Austerlitz*, 100.

APPENDIX A: THREE VERSE EULOGIES
OF ANNE OF BOHEMIA: AN EDITION

1. See n. to l. 1 in the Textual and explanatory notes.
2. Alternatively, "pinguia mense" could be a poetic periphrasis for "feasts," rendering the phrase: "Are your feasts splendid?"

Bibliography

PRIMARY SOURCES

Amundesham, Johannes. *Chronica monasterii S. Albani a Johanne Amundesham.* Edited by H. T. Riley. 2 vols. London, 1870–1.

Archiv český. Vols. XXXV–XXXVI, edited by Gustav Friedrich. Prague, Domestikální fond český, 1935, 1941.

Arnold, T., ed. *Select English Works of John Wyclif.* 3 vols. Oxford, 1869–71.

Bain, Joseph, ed. *Calendar of Documents Relating to Scotland.* 4 vols. Edinburgh, 1881–8.

Bale, John. *A brefe chronicle.* Antwerp, 1544; see STC (2nd edn.) 1276.

Examination and Death of Lord Cobham. In *Select Works of John Bale,* edited by Henry Christmas, 5–59. Cambridge, 1849.

The laboryouse journey. London, 1549; see STC (2nd edn.) 15445.

Scriptorum illustrium Maioris Brytanniae catalogus. 2 vols. Basle, 1557, 1559. Reprint, Farnborough: Gregg International, 1971.

Barlow, William. *A dyaloge describing the originall grou[n]d of these Lutheran faccyons.* London, 1531; see STC (2nd edn.) 1461.

Bartoš, František M. *Tetragonus Aristotelis: konciliaristický projev s počátku velikého církevního rozkolu. Historický archiv* 41 (1916), 12–42.

Baxter, James H., ed. *Copiale prioratus Sanctiandree.* London: Oxford University Press, 1930.

Bloomfield, Morton W. *Incipits of Latin Works on the Virtues and Vices, 1100–1500 A.D.* Cambridge, MA: Medieval Academy of America, 1979.

Böhmer, J. F., ed. *Die Urkunden Kaiser Sigmunds (1410–1437).* 2 vols. Regesta Imperii 11. Hildesheim: Georg Olms, 1968.

Boorde, Andrew. *Fyrst boke of the introduction of knowledge.* London, 1542?; see STC (2nd edn.) 3385.

Bower, Walter. *Scotichronicon.* Edited by D. E. R. Watt. 8 vols. Aberdeen University Press, 1987.

Bühler, Curt F. "A Lollard Tract: On Translating the Bible into English." *Medium Aevum* 7 (1938): 167–83.

Calendar of Close Rolls, Richard II. Vol. III, *1385–1389,* edited by H. C. Maxwell Lyte. London: H. M. Stationery Office, 1921.

Calendar of Entries in the Papal Registers Relating to Great Britain and Ireland. Vol. IV, *Papal Letters, A.D. 1362–1404*, edited by W. H. Bliss, and J. A. Twemlow. London: H. M. Stationery Office, 1902.

Cavendish, George. *The Life and Death of Cardinal Wolsey.* Edited by Richard S. Sylvester. EETS 243. London: Oxford University Press, 1959.

Chaucer, Geoffrey. *The Legend of Good Women.* In *The Riverside Chaucer*, edited by Larry D. Benson, 587–630. Boston: Houghton Mifflin, 1987.

Chichele, Henry. *The Register of Henry Chichele.* Edited by E. F. Jacob. 4 vols. Oxford: Clarendon, 1938–47.

Chitty, Herbert and E. F. Jacob. "Some Winchester College Muniments." *English Historical Review* 49 (1934): 1–13.

Clanvowe, John. *The Boke of Cupide.* In *The Works of Sir John Clanvowe*, edited by V. J. Scattergood, 35–53.

The Two Ways. In *The Works of Sir John Clanvowe*, edited by V. J. Scattergood, 57–80.

The Works of Sir John Clanvowe. Edited by V. J. Scattergood. Cambridge: D. S. Brewer, 1975.

Cochlaeus, Johannes. *Historia Hussitarum.* Mainz, 1549.

A compendious olde treatyse, shewynge howe that we ought to haue ye scripture in Englysshe. Antwerp, 1530; see STC (2nd edn.) 3021.

Crowley, Robert. *The true copye of a prolog.* London, 1550; see STC (2nd edn.) 25588.

Daňhelka, Jiří, ed. *Husitské písně.* Prague: Československý spisovatel, 1952.

Denifle, Henricus and Aemilius Chatelain, eds. *Liber procuratorum nationis Anglicanae (Alemanniae) 1406–1466.* Auctarium chartularii Universitatis Parisiensis 2. Paris: H. Didier, 1937.

Dickinson, Francis Henry, ed. *Missale ad usum insignis et praeclarae ecclesiae Sarum.* London, 1861–83.

Dobrovský, Josef. *Korrespondence Josefa Dobrovského.* Edited by Adolf Patera. 4 vols. Prague: Česká akademie věd a umění, 1895–1913.

Dreves, Guido Maria and C. Blume, eds. *Analecta hymnica medii aevi.* 55 vols. Leipzig: O. R. Reisland, 1886–1926.

Duchesne, Louis, ed. *Le Liber pontificalis: texte, introduction et commentaire.* 3 vols. Paris: E. Thorin, 1955–57.

Eccles, Mark, ed. *The Macro Plays.* EETS 262. London: Oxford University Press, 1969.

Erasmus, Desiderius. *The Correspondence of Erasmus, Letters 842 to 992, 1518–1519*, translated by R. A. B. Mynors and D. F. S. Thomson. Collected Works of Erasmus 6. Toronto University Press, 1982.

Finke, Heinrich, ed. *Acta Concilii Constanciensis.* 4 vols. Münster: Regensbergsche Buchhandlung, 1896–1928.

Flacius, Matthias. *Iohannis Hus et Hieronymi Pragensis historia et monumenta.* 2 vols. Nuremberg, 1558.

Fortescue, John. *On the Laws and Governance of England.* Edited by Shelley Lockwood. Cambridge University Press, 1997.

Foxe, John. *Actes and monuments*. London, 1563; see STC (2nd edn.) 11222a.
    Actes and monuments. London, 1583; see STC (2nd edn.) 11225.
    Commentarii rerum in ecclesia gestarum. Strasbourg, 1554.
Fudge, Thomas A. *The Crusade Against Heretics in Bohemia, 1418–1437*. Aldershot: Ashgate, 2002.
Gascoigne, Thomas. *Loci e libro veritatum: Passages Selected from Gascoigne's Theological Dictionary*. Edited by J. E. T. Rogers. Oxford, 1881.
Gerson, Jean. *Jean Gerson, Oeuvres complètes*. Edited by Palémon Glorieux. 11 vols. in 10. Paris: Desclée, 1960–73.
Goll, Jaroslav, ed. *Chronicon Universitatis Pragensis*. Fontes rerum Bohemicarum 5, 567–88. Prague, 1893.
Gower, John. *The Complete Works of John Gower*. Edited by G. C. Macaulay. 4 vols. Oxford: Clarendon, 1899–1902.
Graham, Barry. *The Litoměřice Gradual of 1517: Lovosice, Státní Okresní Archiv Litoměřice IV C 1*. Prague: L. Marek, 1999.
Haydon, F. S., ed. *Eulogium (historiarum siue temporis)*. 3 vols. Rolls Series 9. London, 1858–63.
Henderson, William G., ed. *Missale ad usum insignis ecclesiae Eboracensis*. 2 vols. Durham, 1872–4.
    ed. *Missale ad usum percelebris ecclesiae Herfordensis*. Leeds, 1874.
Henry VIII. *Assertion of the Seven Sacraments*. In *Miscellaneous Writings of Henry the Eighth*, edited by Francis Macnamara, 25–154. London: Golden Cockerel, 1924.
Hilton, Walter. *The Scale of Perfection*. Edited by Thomas H. Bestul. Kalamazoo, MI: Medieval Institute, 2000.
    Walter Hilton's Mixed Life: Edited from Lambeth Palace MS 472. Edited by S. J. Ogilvie-Thomson. Salzburg: Institut für Anglistik und Amerikanistik, 1986.
Hoccleve, Thomas. *Selections from Hoccleve*. Edited by M. C. Seymour. Oxford: Clarendon, 1981.
Höfler, Konstantin, ed. *Concilia Pragensia, 1353–1413*. Prague, 1862. Reprint, Vienna: H. Geyer, 1972.
    ed. *Geschichtschreiber der husitischen Bewegung in Böhmen*. 3 vols. Vienna, 1856–66.
Horstmann, Carl, ed. *Nova legenda Anglie*. 2 vols. Oxford: Clarendon, 1901.
Hudson, Anne, ed. *Selections from English Wycliffite Writings*. University of Toronto Press, 1997.
    ed. *Two Revisions of Rolle's Psalter Commentary*. EETS. London: Oxford University Press, forthcoming.
Hus, Jan. *Česká nedělní postila*. Edited by Jiří Daňhelka. Magistri Iohannis Hus Opera Omnia 2. Prague: Academia, 1992.
    Contra Iohannem Stokes. In *Polemica*, edited by Jaroslav Eršil, 59–70.
    Defensio articulorum Wyclif. In *Polemica*, edited by Jaroslav Eršil, 143–232.
    Leccionarium bipartitum, pars hiemalis. Edited by Anežka Vidmanová-Schmidtová. Magistri Iohannis Hus Opera Omnia 9. Prague: Academia, 1988.

Polemica. Edited by Jaroslav Eršil. Magistri Iohannis Hus Opera Omnia 22. Prague, Academia, 1966.

Super IV. Sententiarum. Edited by Wenzel Flajšhans and Marie Komínková. Magistri Iohannis Hus Opera Omnia 2. Prague: Josef R. Vilímek, 1905.

James, Thomas. *An apologie for Iohn Wickliffe.* Oxford, 1608; see STC (2nd edn.) 14445.

Kingsford, C. L. *English Historical Literature in the Fifteenth Century.* Oxford: Clarendon, 1913.

"An Historical Collection of the Fifteenth Century." *English Historical Review* 29 (1914): 505–15.

"A Legend of Sigismund's Visit to England." *English Historical Review* 26 (1911): 750–1.

Kingsford, C. L. ed. *The First English Life of King Henry the Fifth.* Oxford: Clarendon, 1911.

Klicman, Ladislav, ed. *Processus iudiciarius contra Jeronimum de Praga habitus Viennae A. 1410–1412.* Prague, 1898.

Knighton, Henry. *Knighton's Chronicle, 1337–1396.* Edited by G. H. Martin. Oxford: Clarendon, 1995.

Luther, Martin. *D. Martin Luthers Werke, Kritische Gesamtausgabe. Briefwechsel.* 18 vols. Weimar: Hermann Böhlaus Nachfolger, 1930–85.

Maidstone, Richard. *Concordia: The Reconciliation of Richard II with London.* Translated by A. G. Rigg, edited by David R. Carlson. Kalamazoo, MI: Medieval Institute, 2003.

Matěj of Janov. *Regulae veteris et novi testamenti.* 4 vols. Edited by Vlastimil Kybal. Innsbruck: Wagner, 1908–13; *Matthiae de Janov, dicti Magister Parisiensis Regulae veteris et novi testamenti, liber V, De corpore Cristi.* Edited by Jana Nechutová. Munich: R. Oldenbourg, 1993.

Migne, Jacques-Paul, ed. *Patrologia Latina.* 221 vols. Paris, 1844–65.

Milton, John. *Of Reformation.* In *The Complete Prose Works of John Milton.* Vol. 1, edited by Don M. Wolfe, 517–617. New Haven: Yale University Press, 1953.

More, Thomas. *A Dialogue concerning Heresies.* Edited by Thomas M. C. Lawler, G. Marc'hadour and R. C. Marius. 2 vols. The Yale Edition of the Complete Works of St. Thomas More 6. New Haven: Yale University Press, 1981.

Nejedlý, Zdeněk. *Počátky husitského zpěvu.* Prague: Královská česká společnost náuk, 1907.

Netter, Thomas. *Doctrinale antiquitatum fidei Catholicae Ecclesiae.* Edited by B. Blanciotti. 3 vols. Venice, 1757–9. Reprint, Farnborough: Gregg International, 1967.

Novotný, Václav, ed. *M. Jana Husi korespondence a dokumenty.* Prague: Komise pro vydávání pramenů náboženského hnutí českého, 1920.

Ortwinus, Gratius. *Fasciculus rerum expetendarum et fugiendarum.* Edited by Edward Brown. 2 vols. London, 1690. Reprint, Tucson, AZ: Audax, 1967.

Palacký, František, ed. *Documenta Mag. Joannis Hus vitam, doctrinam, causam in Constantiensi concilio actam … illustrantia.* Prague, 1869.

Pecock, Reginald. *The Repressor of Over Much Blaming of the Clergy.* Edited by Churchill Babington. 2 vols. London, 1860. Reprint, Wiesbaden: Kraus, 1966.

Perroy, Edouard. *The Diplomatic Correspondence of Richard II.* London: Royal Historical Society, 1933.

Philippe de Mézières. *Philippe de Mézières' Campaign for the Feast of Mary's Presentation.* Edited by William E. Coleman. University of Toronto Press, 1981.

Piccolomini, Aeneas Silvius. *Aeneae Sylvii Piccolominei Senensis ... opera quae extant omnia.* Basel, 1551. Reprint, Frankfurt: Minerva, 1967.

Historia Bohemica. Edited by Joseph Hejnic, and Hans Rothe. 3 vols. Cologne: Böhau, 2005.

Rolle, Richard. *The Incendium amoris of Richard Rolle of Hampole.* Edited by Margaret Deanesly. Manchester University Press, 1915.

The Psalter or Psalms of David and Certain Canticles, with a Translation and Exposition in English by Richard Rolle of Hampole. Edited by H. R. Bramley. Oxford, 1884.

Rymer, Thomas, ed. *Foedera, conventiones, literae, et cujuscunque generis acta publica, inter reges Angliae, et alios quosuis imperatores, reges, ...* 20 vols. London, 1704–35.

Salter, H. E., ed. *Snappe's Formulary and Other Records.* Oxford: Clarendon, 1924.

Sanderson, William. *A compleat history of the lives and reigns of, Mary Queen of Scotland, and of her son and successor, James the Sixth, King of Scotland, and (after Queen Elizabeth) King of Great Britain, France, and Ireland, the First ...* London, 1656; see Wing s647.

Sedlák, Jan. *M. Jan Hus.* Prague: Dědictví sv. Prokopa, 1915.

Miscellanea Husitica Ioannis Sedlák. Prague: Univerzita Karlova, 1996.

Studie a texty k náboženským dějinám českým. 2 vols. Olomouc: Matice Cyrilmetodějská, 1914–15.

Shakespeare, William. *Much Ado about Nothing.* In *The Riverside Shakespeare* (2nd edn.), edited by G. Blakemore Evans and J. J. M. Tobin. Boston: Houghton Mifflin, 1997.

Shirley, W. W., ed. *Fasciculi zizaniorum Magistri Johannis Wyclif cum tritico.* London, 1858.

Šimek, František and Miloslav Kaňák, eds. *Staré letopisy české.* Prague: Státní nakladatelství krásné literatury, hudby a umění, 1959.

Spinka, Matthew. *The Letters of John Hus.* Manchester University Press, 1972.

Stow, George B., ed. *Historia vitae et regni Ricardi Secundi.* Philadelphia: University of Pennsylvania Press, 1977.

Stow, John. *A Survey of London by John Stow.* Edited by C. L. Kingsford. 2 vols. Oxford: Clarendon, 1908.

Stülz, Jodok. "Sitzung vom 12. Juni 1850." *Sitzungsberichte der Philosophisch-Historischen Classe* 5 (1850): 64–7.

Suso, Heinrich. *Heinrich Seuses Horologium sapientiae.* Edited by Pius Künzle. Universitätsverlag Freiburg Schweiz, 1977.

Svejkovský, František, ed. *Veršované skladby doby husitské*. Prague: Nakladatelství Československé akademie věd, 1963.

Svoboda, Milan, ed. *Mistra Jakoubka ze Stříbra překlad Viklefova Dialogu*. Prague: Česká akademie císaře Františka Josefa pro vědy, slovesnost a umění, 1909.

Szittya, Penn R. "'Sedens super flumina': A Fourteenth-Century Poem against the Friars." *Mediaeval Studies* 41 (1979): 30–43.

Tait, James, ed. *Chronica Johannis de Reading et Anonymi Cantuariensis, 1346–1367*. Manchester University Press, 1914.

Taylor, Frank and John S. Roskell, eds. *Gesta Henrici Quinti*. Oxford: Clarendon, 1975.

Thompson, E. F., ed. *Chronicon Angliae, ab Anno Domini 1328 usque ad annum 1388*. London, 1874.

Todd, James H., ed. *Three Treatises*. Dublin, 1851.

Tomassetti, Luigi, ed. *Bullarum, diplomatum et privilegiorum sanctorum Romanorum pontificum Taurinensis editio*. 25 vols. Turin, 1857–72; Naples, 1867–85.

Truhlář, Josef, ed. *Život Jana z Jenšteina, arcibiskupa pražského*. Fontes rerum Bohemicarum 1, 437–68. Prague, 1873.

Usk, Adam. *The Chronicle of Adam Usk 1377–1421*. Edited by Christopher Given-Wilson. Oxford: Clarendon, 1997.

Von der Hardt, Hermann, ed. *Magnum oecumenicum Constantiense Concilium*. 6 vols. Frankfurt and Leipzig, 1696–1700.

Walsingham, Thomas. *The Chronica maiora of Thomas Walsingham (1376–1422)*. Edited by David Preest, and James G. Clark. Woodbridge: Boydell, 2005.

The St. Albans Chronicle: The Chronica maiora of Thomas Walsingham, vol. 1, *1376–1394*. Edited by John Taylor, Wendy R. Childs and Leslie Watkiss. Oxford: Clarendon, 2003.

Wilkins, David, ed. *Concilia Magnae Britanniae et Hiberniae*. 4 vols. London, 1737.

Windecke, Eberhart. *Eberhart Windeckes Denkwürdigkeiten zur Geschichte des Zeitalters Kaiser Sigmunds*. Edited by Wilhelm Altmann. Berlin, 1893.

Winn, Herbert E., ed. *Wyclif: Select English Writings*. London: Oxford University Press, 1929.

Workman, Herbert B. and R. Martin Pope, eds. *The Letters of John Hus*. London: Hodder and Stoughton, 1904.

Wormald, Francis, ed. *English Benedictine Kalendars after A.D. 1100*. 2 vols. London: Henry Bradshaw Society, 1946.

Wright, Thomas. *Political Poems and Songs relating to English History*. 2 vols. London, 1861.

Wyclif, John. *De officio regis*. Edited by Alfred W. Pollard and Charles Sayle. London, 1887.

De triplici vinculo amoris. In *John Wiclif's Polemical Works in Latin*, vol. 1, edited by Rudolf Buddensieg. London, 1883.

Iohannis Wyclif sermones. Edited by Johann Loserth. 4 vols. London, 1886–9.

Johannis Wiclif trialogus cum supplemento trialogi. Edited by Gotthard Lechler. Oxford, 1869.

Johannis Wyclif tractatus de ecclesia. Edited by Johann Loserth. London, 1886.
Opera minora. Edited by Johann Loserth. London: Wyclif Society, 1913.

SECONDARY SOURCES

Allen, Hope Emily. "Some Fourteenth Century Borrowings from 'Ancren Riwle'." *Modern Language Review* 18 (1923): 1–8.
Writings Ascribed to Richard Rolle, Hermit of Hampole, and Materials for His Biography. London: Oxford University Press, 1927.
Allen, Percy S. "Erasmus and the Bohemian Brethren." In *The Age of Erasmus: Lectures Delivered in the Universities of Oxford and London*, 276–98. Oxford: Clarendon, 1914.
Andrews, Frances. *The Other Friars: Carmelite, Augustinian, Sack and Pied Friars in the Middle Ages.* Woodbridge: Boydell, 2006.
Armitage-Smith, Sydney. *John of Gaunt.* London: Archibald Constable, 1905.
Aschbach, Joseph. *Geschichte der Wiener Universität.* 3 vols. Vienna, 1865–88.
Aston, Margaret. "John Wycliffe's Reformation Reputation." In *Lollards and Reformers*, 243–72.
Lollards and Reformers: Images and Literacy in Late Medieval Religion. London: Hambledon, 1984.
"Lollardy and Sedition, 1381–1431." In *Lollards and Reformers*, 1–47.
"Lollardy and the Reformation: Survival or Revival?" In *Lollards and Reformers*, 219–42.
"William White's Lollard Followers." In *Lollards and Reformers*, 71–100.
"Wycliffe and the Vernacular." In *Faith and Fire: Popular and Unpopular Religion, 1350–1600*, 27–72. London: Hambledon, 1993.
Aston, Margaret and Colin Richmond, eds. *Lollardy and the Gentry in the Later Middle Ages.* New York: St. Martin's, 1997.
Bárány, Attila. "Anglo-Luxembourg Relations during the Reign of Emperor Sigismund." In *Sigismund von Luxembourg: Ein Kaiser in Europa: Tagungsband des internationalen historischen und kunsthistorischen Kongresses in Luxembourg, 8–10 Juni 2005*, 43–59. Mainz: Philipp von Zabern, 2006.
Bartoš, František M. "Husův přítel z Českých Budějovic." *Jihočeský sborník historický* 19 (1950): 43–4.
"Z dávných styků našich s Anglií." *Časopis Musea Království Českého* 93 (1919): 203–4.
Betts, R. R. "English and Czech Influences on the Hussite Movement." In *Essays in Czech History*, 132–59.
Essays in Czech History. London: Athlone, 1969.
"The Influence of Realist Philosophy on Jan Hus and His Predecessors in Bohemia." In *Essays in Czech History*, 42–62.
"The University of Prague: 1348." In *Essays in Czech History*, 1–12.
Biasiotto, Peter R. *History of the Development of Devotion to the Holy Name.* St. Bonaventure, NY: St. Bonaventure College and Seminary, 1943.
Bourdieu, Pierre. *The Logic of Practice.* Stanford University Press, 1990.

Bowers, John M. *The Politics of Pearl: Court Poetry in the Age of Richard II.* Cambridge: D. S. Brewer, 2001.

Brady, M. T. "Lollard Sources of 'The Pore Caitif.'" *Traditio* 44 (1988): 389–418.

"The Pore Caitif: An Introductory Study." *Traditio* 10 (1954): 529–48.

"Rolle and the Pattern of Tracts in 'The Pore Caitif.'" *Traditio* 39 (1983): 456–65.

"Rolle's 'Form of Living' and 'The Pore Caitif.'" *Traditio* 36 (1980): 426–35.

Brandenbarg, Ton. "Saint Anne: A Holy Grandmother and Her Children." In *Sanctity and Motherhood: Essays on Holy Mothers in the Middle Ages,* edited by Anneke B. Mulder-Bakker, 31–65. New York: Garland, 1995.

Carlson, David R. "Whethamstede on Lollardy: Latin Styles and the Vernacular Cultures of Early Fifteenth-Century England." *Journal of English and Germanic Philology* 102 (2003): 21–41.

Catto, J. I. "Sir William Beauchamp between Chivalry and Lollardy." In *The Ideals and Practice of Medieval Knighthood,* vol. III, *Papers from the Fourth Strawberry Hill Conference, 1988,* edited by Christopher Harper-Bill and Ruth Harvey, 39–48. Woodbridge: Boydell, 1990.

"Wyclif and Wycliffism at Oxford: 1356–1430." In *The History of the University of Oxford,* vol. II, *Later Medieval Oxford,* edited by J. I. Catto and Ralph Evans, 175–261. Oxford: Clarendon, 1992.

Chaplais, Pierre. *English Diplomatic Practice in the Middle Ages.* London: Hambledon, 2003.

English Medieval Diplomatic Practice Part I, Documents and Interpretation. 2 vols. London: H. M. Stationery Office, 1982.

Cheney, C. R. *Medieval Texts and Studies.* Oxford: Clarendon, 1973.

Cole, Andrew. *Literature and Heresy in the Age of Chaucer.* Cambridge University Press, 2008.

Cook, William R. "Peter Payne, Theologian and Diplomat of the Hussite Revolution." Unpublished PhD diss., Cornell University, 1971.

Copeland, Rita. *Pedagogy, Intellectuals, and Dissent in the Later Middle Ages: Lollardy and Ideas of Learning.* Cambridge University Press, 2001.

Crompton, J. "John Wyclif: A Study in Mythology." *Transactions of the Leicestershire Archaeological and Historical Society* 42 (1966–7): 6–34.

Crowder, C. M. D. "Constance Acta in English Libraries." In *Das Konzil von Konstanz,* edited by August Franzen and Wolfgang Müller, 477–517. Vienna: Herder, 1964.

"Henry V, Sigismund, and the Council of Constance, a Re-examination." In *Historical Studies,* vol. IV, edited by G. A. Hayes-McCoy, 93–110. London: Bowes and Bowes, 1963.

Dahmus, Joseph H. *The Prosecution of John Wyclyf.* New Haven: Yale University Press, 1952.

Daniel, Christopher. *Death and Burial in Medieval England, 1066–1550.* London: Routledge, 1997.

Deanesly, Margaret. *The Lollard Bible.* Cambridge University Press, 1920.

Dickens, A. G. *Reformation and Society in Sixteenth-Century Europe.* London: Harcourt, Brace and World, 1966.

Dictionary of Medieval Latin from British Sources. Edited by D. R. Howlett and R. E. Latham. Oxford University Press, 1975–.

Doyle, A. I. "Carthusian Participation in the Movement of Works of Richard Rolle between England and Other Parts of Europe in the 14th and 15th Centuries." *Analecta Cartusiana* 55 (1981): 109–20.

"The Shaping of the Vernon and Simeon Manuscripts." In *Chaucer and Middle English Studies in Honour of Rossell Hope Robbins,* edited by Beryl Rowland, 328–41. Kent State University Press, 1974.

Du Cange, Charles du Fresne, ed. *Glossarium ad scriptores mediae et infimae latinitatis.* Niort: Léopold Favre, 1883–7.

Emden, Alfred B. *An Oxford Hall in Medieval Times.* Oxford: Clarendon, 1927.

Everett, Dorothy. "The Middle English Prose Psalter of Richard Rolle of Hampole." *Modern Language Review.* Pts. 1 and 2 in 17 (1922): 217–27, 337–50; pt. 3 in 18 (1923): 381–93.

Ghosh, Kantik. "Wycliffism and Lollardy." In *The Cambridge History of Christianity.* Vol. 4, edited by Miri Rubin and Walter Simons, 433–45. Cambridge University Press, 2009.

The Wycliffite Heresy: Authority and the Interpretation of Texts. Cambridge University Press, 2002.

Gonnet, Giovanni. "L'Internationale Valdo-Hussite." *Heresis* 13–14 (1989): 235–53.

Green, Richard Firth. "An Epitaph for Richard, Duke of York." *Studies in Bibliography* 41 (1988): 219–25.

"Jack Philipot, John of Gaunt, and a Poem of 1380." *Speculum* 66 (1991): 330–41.

Gustavson, Kevin. "Richard Rolle's *English Psalter* and the Making of a Lollard Tract." *Viator* 33 (2002): 294–309.

Haigh, Christopher. *English Reformations: Religion, Politics, and Society under the Tudors.* Oxford University Press, 1993.

Hanna, Ralph. "Miscellaneity and Vernacularity: Conditions of Literary Production in Late Medieval England." In *The Whole Book: Cultural Perspectives on the Medieval Miscellany,* edited by Stephen G. Nichols and Siegfried Wenzel, 37–51. Ann Arbor, MI: University of Michigan Press, 1996.

Pursuing History: Middle English Manuscripts and Their Texts. Stanford University Press, 1996.

Hanrahan, Michael. "'A straunge succesour sholde take youre heritage': The *Clerk's Tale* and the Crisis of Ricardian Rule." *Chaucer Review* 35 (2001): 335–50.

Harvey, John. *English Mediaeval Architects: A Biographical Dictionary Down to 1550.* Gloucester: Sutton, 1984.

Harvey, Margaret. "Adam Easton and the Condemnation of John Wyclif, 1377." *English Historical Review* 113 (1998): 321–34.

"The Diffusion of the *Doctrinale* of Thomas Netter in the Fifteenth and Sixteenth Centuries." In *Intellectual Life in the Middle Ages: Essays Presented to Margaret Gibson,* edited by Lesley Smith and Benedicta Ward, 281–94. London: Hambledon, 1992.

The English in Rome 1362–1420: Portrait of an Expatriate Community. Cambridge University Press, 1999.

"John Whethamstede, The Pope and the General Council." In *The Church in Pre-Reformation Society*, edited by Caroline M. Barron and Christopher Harper-Bill, 108–22. Woodbridge: Boydell, 1985.

Hendrix, Scott H. "'We Are All Hussites'? Hus and Luther Revisited." *Archiv für Reformationsgeschichte* 65 (1974): 134–61.

Herold, Vilém. *Pražská univerzita a Wyclif.* Prague: Univerzita Karlova, 1985.

"Vojtěch Raňkův of Ježov (Adalbertus Rankonis de Ericinio) and the Bohemian Reformation." Trans. Zdeněk V. David. In *The Bohemian Reformation and Religious Practice*. Vol. vii, edited by Zdeněk V. David and David R. Holeton, 72–9. Prague: Filosofický časopis, 2009.

Hiatt, Alfred. *The Making of Medieval Forgeries: False Documents in Fifteenth-Century England.* University of Toronto Press, 2004.

Hobbins, Daniel. *Authorship and Publicity before Print: Jean Gerson and the Transformation of Late Medieval Learning.* Philadelphia: University of Pennsylvania Press, 2009.

Hornbeck, J. Patrick. *What is a Lollard? Dissent and Belief in Late Medieval England.* Oxford University Press, 2010.

Hudson, Anne. "The Debate on Bible Translation, Oxford 1401." In *Lollards and Their Books*, 67–84.

"From Oxford to Prague: The Writings of John Wyclif and his English Followers in Bohemia." *Slavonic and East European Review* 75 (1997): 642–57.

"*Laicus litteratus*: The Paradox of Lollardy." In *Heresy and Literacy, 1000–1530*, edited by Peter Biller and Anne Hudson, 222–36. Cambridge University Press, 1994.

"A Lollard Compilation in England and Bohemia." In *Lollards and Their Books*, 31–42.

"A Lollard Sect Vocabulary?" In *Lollards and Their Books*, 165–80.

Lollards and Their Books. London: Hambledon, 1985.

"Notes of an Early Fifteenth-Century Research Assistant, and the Emergence of the 267 Articles against Wyclif." *English Historical Review* 118 (2003): 685–97.

"Peter Pateshull: One-Time Friar and Poet?" In *Interstices: Studies in Middle English and Anglo-Latin Texts in Honour of A. G. Rigg*, edited by Richard Firth Green and Linne R. Mooney, 167–83. University of Toronto Press, 2004.

The Premature Reformation: Wycliffite Texts and Lollard History. Oxford University Press, 1988.

Studies in the Transmission of Wyclif's Writings. Aldershot: Ashgate, 2008.

"The Survival of Wyclif's Works in England and Bohemia." In *Studies in the Transmission of Wyclif's Writings*, ch. 16.

"Which Wyche? The Framing of the Lollard Heretic and/or Saint." In *Texts and the Repression of Medieval Heresy*, edited by Caterina Bruschi and Peter Biller, 221–37. Woodbridge: York Medieval Press, 2003.

"William Taylor's 1406 Sermon: A Postscript." *Medium Aevum* 64 (1995): 100–6.

"Wyclif Texts in Fifteenth-Century London." In *Studies in the Transmission of Wyclif's Writings*, ch. 15.

Hughes, Jonathan. *Pastors and Visionaries: Religion and Secular Life in Late Medieval Yorkshire.* Woodbridge: Boydell, 1988.

An Inventory of the Historical Monuments in London. 5 vols. London: H. M. Stationery Office, 1924–30.

Jurkowski, Maureen. "Lawyers and Lollardy in the Early Fifteenth Century." In Aston and Richmond, *Lollardy and the Gentry*, 155–82.

Kaminsky, Howard. *A History of the Hussite Revolution.* Berkeley: University of California Press, 1967.

Ker, N. R. *Books, Collectors and Libraries: Studies in the Medieval Heritage.* Edited by Andrew G. Watson. London: Hambledon, 1985.

Kerby-Fulton, Kathryn. *Books under Suspicion: Censorship and Tolerance of Revelatory Writing in Late Medieval England.* University of Notre Dame Press, 2006.

Knowles, David. *The English Mystical Tradition.* London: Burns and Oates, 1961.

Kuczynski, Michael. "Rolle among the Reformers: Orthodoxy and Heterodoxy in Wycliffite Copies of Rolle's Psalter." In *Mysticism and Spirituality in Medieval England*, edited by William F. Pollard and Robert Boenig, 177–202. Rochester, NY: D. S. Brewer, 1997.

Latinitatis medii aevi lexicon Bohemorum. Edited by Československá akademie věd. Prague: Academia, 1977–.

Lechler, Gotthard. *Johann von Wiclif.* 2 vols. Leipzig, 1873.

Lindley, Phillip. "Absolutism and Regal Image in Ricardian Sculpture." In *The Regal Image of Richard II and the Wilton Diptych*, edited by Dillian Gordon, Lisa Monnas and Caroline Elam, 60–83 (notes pp. 288–96). London: Harvey Miller, 1997.

Loserth, Johann. "Über die Beziehungen zwischen den englischen und bömischen Wiclifiten in den beiden ersten Jahrzehnten des 15. Jahrhunderts." *Mittheilungen des Instituts für österreichische Geschichtsforschung* 12 (1891): 254–69.

McFarlane, K. B. *Lancastrian Kings and Lollard Knights.* Oxford: Clarendon, 1972.

Marzac, Nicole. *Richard Rolle de Hampole (1300–1349): vie et oeuvres.* Paris: Librairie Philosophique J. Vrin, 1968.

Menache, Sophia. *The Vox Dei: Communication in the Middle Ages.* Oxford University Press, 1990.

Minnis, Alastair. *Fallible Authors: Chaucer's Pardoner and Wife of Bath.* Philadelphia: University of Pennsylvania Press, 2008.

Translations of Authority in Medieval English Literature. Cambridge University Press, 2009.

Mirot, Léon and Eugène Deprez. *Les Ambassades anglaises pendant la Guerre de Cent Ans: catalogue chronologique (1327–1450).* Paris: Alphonse Picard et Fils, 1900.

Mittellateinisches Wörterbuch bis zum ausgehenden 13. Jahrhundert. Edited by Otto Prinz and Johannes Schneider. Munich: Beck, 1959–.

Molnar, Amedeo. "L'Internationale des Taborites et des Vaudois." *Bolletino della Società di Studi Valdesi* 122 (1967): 3–13.

Moretti, Franco. *Graphs, Maps, Trees: Abstract Models for Literary History.* New York: Verso, 2007.

Mudroch, Vaclav. *The Wyclyf Tradition.* Edited by Albert Compton Reeves. Athens, OH: Ohio University Press, 1979.

Mugnai, Massimo. "La *Expositio reduplicativarum* chez Walter Burleigh et Paulus Venetus." In *English Logic in Italy in the 14th and 15th Centuries*, edited by Alfonso Maierù, 305–20. Naples: Bibliopolis, 1982.

Muir, Laurence. "The Influence of the Rolle and Wyclifite Psalters upon the Psalter of the Authorised Version." *Modern Language Review* 30 (1935): 302–10.

Neddermeyer, Uwe. *Von der Handschrift zum gedruckten Buch: Schriftlichkeit und Leseinteresse im Mittelalter und in der frühen Neuzeit.* 2 vols. Wiesbaden: Harrassowitz, 1998.

Niermeyer, Jan Frederik. *Mediae Latinitatis lexicon minus.* 2 vols. Darmstadt: Wissenschaftliche Buchgesellschaft, 2002.

Novotný, Václav. *M. Jan Hus. Život a učení.* vol. 1, pts. 1 and 2. Prague: Jan Laichter, 1919–21.

Odložilík, O. "Z počátků husitství na Moravě. Šimon z Tišnova a Jan Vavřincův z Račic." *Časopis Matice Moravské* 49 (1925): 1–170.

Oxford Dictionary of National Biography. Edited by H. C. G. Matthew and Brian Harrison. 60 vols. Oxford University Press, 2004.

Parsons, John Carmi. "'Never was a body buried in England with such solemnity and honour': The Burials and Posthumous Commemorations of English Queens to 1500." In *Queens and Queenship in Medieval Europe: Proceedings of a Conference Held at King's College London, April 1995*, edited by Anne J. Duggan, 317–37. Woodbridge: Boydell, 1997.

Pfaff, R. W. *New Liturgical Feasts in Later Medieval England.* Oxford: Clarendon, 1970.

Pletzer, Karel. "Českobudějovická rodina Faulfišů." *Jihočeský Sborník Historický* 39 (1970): 51–7.

Polc, Jaroslav. *De origine Festi Visitationis B. V. M.* Rome: Pontificia Università Lateranense, 1967.

"La Festa della Visitazione e il Giubileo del 1390." *Rivista di Storia della Chiesa in Italia* 29 (1975): 149–72.

Poole, Reginald L. "On the Intercourse between English and Bohemian Wycliffites in the Early Years of the Fifteenth Century." *English Historical Review* 7 (1892): 306–11.

Pyper, Rachel. "An Abridgment of Wyclif's *De mandatis divinis.*" *Medium Aevum* 52 (1983): 306–10.

Rennhofer, Friedrich. *Die Augustiner-Eremiten in Wien.* Würzburg: Augustinus, 1956.

Rigg, A. G. *A History of Anglo-Latin Literature 1066–1422.* Cambridge University Press, 1992.

Riley, H. T., ed. *Memorials of London and London Life in the XIIIth, XIVth, and XVth Centuries*. London, 1868.

Robbins, Rossell Hope. "An Epitaph for Duke Humphrey." *Neuphilologische Mitteilungen* 56 (1955): 241–9.

Röhrkasten, Jens. "Thomas Netter: Carmelite and Diplomat." In *Thomas Netter of Walden: Carmelite, Diplomat and Theologian*, edited by Johan Bergström-Allen and Richard Copsey, 113–35. Rome: Edizioni Carmelitane, 2009.

Sanderson, M. H. B. *Ayrshire and the Reformation: People and Change 1400–1600*. East Linton: Tuckwell, 1997.

Sargent, Michael G. "A Source of the *Poor Caitiff* Tract 'Of Man's Will'." *Mediaeval Studies* 41 (1979): 535–9.

"The Transmission by the English Carthusians of Some Late Medieval Spiritual Writings." *Journal of Ecclesiastical History* 27 (1976): 225–40.

Saul, Nigel. *Richard II*. New Haven: Yale University Press, 1997.

Scase, Wendy. "'Heu! quanta desolatio Angliae praestatur': A Wycliffite Libel and the Naming of Heretics, Oxford 1382." In *Lollards and Their Influence in Late Medieval England*, edited by Fiona Somerset, Jill C. Havens and Derrick Pitard, 19–36. Woodbridge: Boydell, 2003.

Literature and Complaint in England, 1272–1553. Oxford University Press, 2007.

Piers Plowman and the New Anticlericalism. Cambridge University Press, 1989.

"St. Anne and the Education of the Virgin: Literary and Artistic Traditions and Their Implications." In *England in the Fourteenth Century: Proceedings of the 1991 Harlaxton Symposium*, edited by Nicholas Rogers, 81–96. Stamford, CT: Paul Watkins, 1993.

Scattergood, John. "Fashion and Morality in the Late Middle Ages." In *England in the Fifteenth Century: Proceedings of the 1986 Harlaxton Symposium*, edited by Daniel Williams, 255–72. Woodbridge: Boydell and Brewer, 1987.

Scattergood, V. J. "The Authorship of 'The Boke of Cupide'." *Anglia* 82 (1964): 137–49.

Schofield, A. N. E. D. "The First English Delegation to the Council of Basel." *Journal of Ecclesiastical History* 12 (1961): 167–96.

Sebald, W. G. *Austerlitz*. New York: Modern Library, 2001.

Sedlák, Jan. "Pálčův spis proti Husovu traktátu 'De ecclesia'." *Hlídka* 29 (1912): 508–12.

Sharpe, Richard. *A Handlist of the Latin Writers of Great Britain and Ireland before 1540*. Turnhout: Brepols, 1997.

Šmahel, František. *Husitská revoluce*. 4 vols. Prague: Univerzita Karlova, 1993.

Die hussitische Revolution. 3 vols. Monumenta Germaniae Historica, Schriften 43. Hannover: Hahnsche Buchhandlung, 2002.

Idea národa v husitských Čechách. Prague: Argo, 2000.

"The Idea of the 'Nation' in Hussite Bohemia." *Historica* 16 (1969): 143–247; and 17 (1969): 93–197.

"The Kuttenberg Decree and the Withdrawal of the German Students from Prague in 1409: A Discussion." In *Die Prager Universität im Mittelalter*, 159–71.

"Leben und Werk des Magisters Hieronymus von Prag: Forschung ohne Probleme und Perspektiven?" *Historica* 13 (1966): 81–111.

"Magister Peter Payne: Curriculum vitae eines englischen Nonkonformisten." In *Friedrich Reiser und die "waldensisch-hussitische Internationale" im 15. Jahrhundert*, edited by Albert de Lange and Kathrin Utz Tremp, 241–60. Heidelberg: Regionalkultur, 2006.

Die Prager Universität im Mittelalter. Leiden: Brill, 2007.

"Wyclif's Fortune in Hussite Bohemia." In *Die Prager Universität im Mittelalter*, 467–89.

Somerset, Fiona. "Wycliffite Spirituality." In *Text and Controversy from Wyclif to Bale: Essays in Honour of Anne Hudson*, edited by Helen Barr and Ann M. Hutchison, 375–86. Turnhout: Brepols, 2005.

Spěváček, Jiří. *Václav IV. 1361–1419*. Prague: Nakladatelství Svoboda, 1986.

Spunar, Pavel. *Repertorium auctorum Bohemorum provectum idearum post Universitatem Pragensem conditam illustrans*. Vol. 1. Wrocław: Institutum Ossolinianum, 1985; vol. 2. Prague: Academia scientiarum Bohemica, 1995.

Steiner, Emily. *Documentary Culture and the Making of Medieval English Literature*. Cambridge University Press, 2003.

Stotz, Peter. *Handbuch zur lateinischen Sprache des Mittelalters*. 5 vols. Munich: Beck, 1996.

Stow, George B. "Richard II in Thomas Walsingham's Chronicles." *Speculum* 59 (1984): 68–102.

Strohm, Paul. *England's Empty Throne*. New Haven: Yale University Press, 1998.

Hochon's Arrow: The Social Imagination of Fourteenth-Century Texts. Princeton University Press, 1992.

Swanson, Robert N. *Universities, Academics and the Great Schism*. Cambridge University Press, 1979.

Taylor, Andrew. "Anne of Bohemia and the Making of Chaucer." *Studies in the Age of Chaucer* 19 (1997): 95–119.

Thomas, Alfred. *Anne's Bohemia: Czech Literature and Society, 1310–1420*. Minneapolis: University of Minnesota Press, 1998.

A Blessed Shore: England, and Bohemia from Chaucer to Shakespeare. Ithaca, NY: Cornell University Press, 2007.

Thompson, E. M. *The Carthusian Order in England*. London: Society for Promoting Christian Knowledge, 1930.

Thomson, John A. F. *The Later Lollards, 1414–1520*. Oxford University Press, 1965.

Thomson, Williell R. *The Latin Writings of John Wyclyf: An Annotated Catalog*. Toronto: Pontifical Institute of Mediaeval Studies, 1983.

Trapp, Damasus. "Clm 27034: Unchristened Nominalism and Wycliffite Realism at Prague in 1381." *Recherches de Théologie Ancienne et Médiévale* 24 (1957): 320–60.

Tříška, Josef. *Životopisný slovník předhusitské pražské univerzity, 1348–1409*. Prague: Univerzita Karlova, 1981.

Tuck, J. Anthony. "Carthusian Monks and Lollard Knights: Religious Attitude at the Court of Richard II." *Studies in the Age of Chaucer: Proceedings* 1 (1984): 149–61.

Vidmanová, Anežka. "Husův přívrženec Mikuláš Mníšek." *Husitský Tábor* 3 (1980): 51–66.

Von Nolcken, Christina. "Another Kind of Saint: A Lollard Perception of John Wyclif." In *From Ockham to Wyclif*, edited by Anne Hudson and Michael Wilks, 429–43. Oxford: Blackwell, 1987.

"Richard Wyche, a Certain Knight, and the Beginning of the End." In Aston and Richmond, *Lollardy and the Gentry*, 127–54.

Vyšný, Paul. "A Hussite in Scotland: The Mission of Pavel Kravař to St. Andrews in 1433." *The Scottish Historical Review* 82 (2003): 1–19.

Wallace, David. "Anne of Bohemia, Queen of England, and Chaucer's Emperice." *Litteraria Pragensia* 5 (1995): 1–16.

Chaucerian Polity: Absolutist Lineages and Associational Forms in England and Italy. Stanford University Press, 1997.

Walsh, Katherine. "Die Rezeption der Schriften des Richard FitzRalph (Armachanus) im lollardisch-hussitischen Milieu." In *Das Publikum politischer Theorie im 14. Jahrhundert*, edited by Jürgen Miethke, 237–53. Munich: Oldenbourg, 1992.

Walther, Hans. *Initia carminum ac versuum medii aevi posterioris Latinorum.* Göttingen: Vandenhoeck und Ruprecht, 1959.

Watson, Nicholas. "Censorship and Cultural Change in Late-Medieval England: Vernacular Theology, the Oxford Translation Debate, and Arundel's Constitutions of 1409." *Speculum* 70 (1995): 822–64.

Richard Rolle and the Invention of Authority. Cambridge University Press, 1991.

Waugh, W. T. "Sir John Oldcastle." *English Historical Review* 20 (1905): 434–56.

Weltsch, Ruben E. *Archbishop John of Jenstein 1348–1400: Papalism, Humanism, and Reform in Pre-Hussite Prague.* The Hague: Mouton, 1968.

Wright, Elizabeth Cox. "Continuity in XV Century English Humanism." *Publications of the Modern Language Association* 51 (1936): 370–6.

Wylie, J. H. *History of England under Henry the Fourth.* 4 vols. London, 1884–98.

Index of manuscripts

Note: Abbreviations for libraries which are commonly cited are listed in parentheses below.

General index

Acton, Roger, 109, 149
Aeneas Silvius Piccolomini, 17, 68, 70, 71, 110
  See also Pius II
Ancrene Riwle, 42, 54
"Anglica regina", 22, 23, 26, 30, 32–4, 52, 59, 129, 130, 134–5, 137–8
Anne, St, 28–31, 135
Anne of Bohemia, 9, 12–36, 62, 113, 129–41, 166 n. 41
  and *Canticum canticorum*, 27
  death, 16, 18–19, 24, 26, 27
  and devotion, 26, 31–2, 35
  eulogies for, 9, 16, 21–5, 26–31, 32–5, 36, 52, 59, 129–41
  and footwear, 19, 160 n. 28
  funeral, 17, 18–19, 23, 25, 29–30, 31, 32
  marriage, 15, 22, 24, 27, 32, 69, 88
  narratives about, 13–16, 19, 31–2, 126–7
  and *Pearl*, 19
  and pregnant women, 30–1
  and St. Anne, 28–31
  tomb, 21, 22, 26, 30–1, 36, 59–60, 162 n. 52
  and vernacular Bible, 14, 17–18, 159 n. 21
  and Virgin Mary, 27–8
  and Wycliffism, 13–17, 32, 35–6, 126
Arundel, Thomas, 12, 17, 19, 31, 56, 88–90, 92, 93–4, 95, 96–9, 102, 107, 108–9
  Constitutions, 54, 80, 84
  See also Oxford testimonial letter of Wyclif, Arundel's response

Bale, John, 27, 84, 181 n. 109
Barlow, William, 123
Beauchamp, William, 56, 60, 61
Beaufort, Henry, 110, 175 n. 39, 191 n. 18
  See also Hussites, Hussitism, crusades against the Hussites
Becket, Thomas, 21
Bekeryng, Thomas, 105
Bernard of Clairvaux, 42, 43
Bernardino of Siena, 42

Beverly, John, 109, 149, 151, 152, 154, 155
Biceps, Mikuláš, 68
Blackfriars Council, 34, 96
Bohemian Revolution, 119
Bohemian traveler (Václav?), 19–21, 24, 25, 26, 32, 37, 162 n. 52
  itinerary, 24, 37
  "Liber Wenceslai militis", 19
Boniface IX, 41, 44, 47, 48, 166 n. 41, 167 n. 53
Book of John Mandeville, 21
Bourdieu, Pierre, 4
Bramfield, Edmund, 47
Bridget of Sweden, St., 48, 51, 52, 167 n. 53
Broker, Nicholas, 23
Brut, Walter, 80
Burley, John, 136–7
Burton, Robert, 97

Castiglione, Zano, 110
Cavendish, George, 124
Caxton, William, 24
Charles IV, 21, 134, 135, 136, 138
Chaucer, Geoffrey, 12, 19, 24, 28, 62
  Legend of Good Women, 12, 19, 28, 62
  Parliament of Fowls, 62
Christopher, St., 19–20, 160 n. 32
Clanvowe, John, 55–6, 60, 61, 62
  Boke of Cupide, 62
  The Two Ways, 55–6, 60
Clerk, John, 122–3
Clifford, Lewis, 60
Cochlaeus, Johannes, 17
Cosmato de' Migliorati, 38, 40–2, 45, 46–7, 166 n. 41
  See also Innocent VII
Council of Basle, 97, 110, 111, 112, 114, 119, 192 n. 20
Council of Constance, 2, 6, 7–9, 10, 11, 34, 61, 66, 70, 71, 80–1, 85, 87, 88, 90, 91, 95, 97, 100, 103–5, 106, 109, 110, 111, 112, 113, 114, 127, 192 n. 20
Council of Pisa, 97

CAMBRIDGE STUDIES IN MEDIEVAL LITERATURE

1   Robin Kirkpatrick *Dante's Inferno: Difficulty and Dead Poetry*

2   Jeremy Tambling *Dante and Difference: Writing in the "Commedia"*

3   Simon Gaunt *Troubadours and Irony*

4   Wendy Scase *"Piers Plowman" and the New Anticlericalism*

5   Joseph Duggan *The "Cantar De Mio Cid": Poetic Creation in Its Economic and Social Contexts*

6   Roderick Beaton *The Medieval Greek Romance*

7   Kathryn Kerby-Fulton *Reformist Apocalypticism and "Piers Plowman"*

8   Alison Morgan *Dante and the Medieval Other World*

9   Eckehard Simon (ed.) *The Theatre of Medieval Europe: New Research in Early Drama*

10   Mary Carruthers *The Book of Memory: A Study of Memory in Medieval Culture*

11   Rita Copeland *Rhetoric, Hermeneutics and Translation in the Middle Ages: Academic Traditions and Vernacular Texts*

12   Donald Maddox *The Arthurian Romances of Chrétien de Troyes: Once and Future Fictions*

13   Nicholas Watson *Richard Rolle and the Invention of Authority*

14   Steven F. Kruger *Dreaming in the Middle Ages*

15   Barbara Nolan *Chaucer and the Tradition of the "Roman antique"*

16   Sylvia Huot *The "Romance of the Rose" and Its Medieval Readers: Interpretations, Reception, Manuscript Transmission*

17   Carol M. Meale (ed.) *Women and Literature in Britain, 1150–1500*

18   Henry Ansgar Kelly *Ideas and Forms of Tragedy from Aristotle to the Middle Ages*

19   Martin Irvine *The Making of Textual Culture: Grammatica and Literary Theory, 350–1100*

20   Larry Scanlon *Narrative, Authority and Power: The Medieval Exemplum and the Chaucerian Tradition*

21   Erik Kooper *Medieval Dutch Literature in Its European Context*

22   Steven Botterill *Dante and the Mystical Tradition: Bernard of Clairvaux in the "Commedia"*

23   Peter Biller and Anne Hudson (eds) *Heresy and Literacy, 1000–1530*